The Illustrated Encyclopedia of
PLANTS

NEW YORK

Academic Advisors:
Professor John Taylor, M.A., Ph.D.,
Professor of Mathematics,
King's College,
University of London.

Editors:
Michael Bisacre
Richard Carlisle
Deborah Robertson
John Ruck

Contents

The World of Plants

The Plant Kingdom

DIVISION 1

Thallophyta

simple plants with no roots, stems or leaves

DIVISION 2

Bryophyta

plants with leaves and stems but no true roots

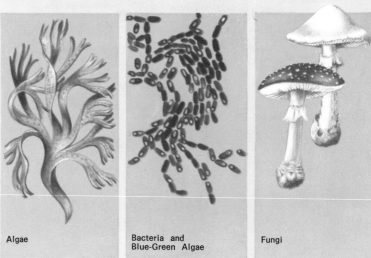

Algae

Bacteria and Blue-Green Algae

Fungi

Mosses

To help understand the living world it is convenient to divide it into distinct groups of similar organisms; each group having certain combinations of features which are common to it alone and which separate it from all other groups. These groups can then be divided into sub-groups or combined to make super-groups—a process which highlights both the similarities and differences between different organisms. The science of classifying living organisms is known as *taxonomy*. Once an organism has been correctly classified it is possible to succinctly summarize a great deal of knowledge about it simply in its name.

The fundamental unit of classification is the *species*. A species is a group of plants or animals which reproduce among themselves to give the same type of plant or animal. Generally the common names used to describe animals and plants refer to particular species such as tomato,

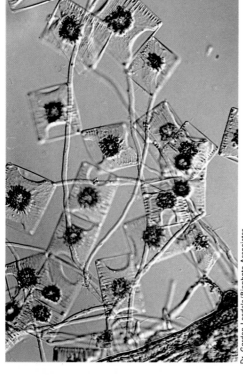

Left: A group of pennate diatoms, *Striatella*, clustered on the red alga, *Polysiphonia*. Algae are the predominant group of marine plants and vary from simple single-celled species to large complex seaweeds.

Below: *Mycena inclinata*, a fungus, growing on a fallen oak tree. Fungi do not have chlorophyll and are not related to any other plant groups. Some botanists claim they should be classified in a separate kingdom from plants or animals.

Above: The plant kingdom. All life developed originally in the seas and the earliest life forms were probably similar to the *prokaryotic* bacteria and blue-green algae.When the first *eukaryotic* cell (with

specialized organelles) developed is not known, but it is probable that it was much like the simple single-celled algae of today. From the algae all higher plant forms have evolved by improved adaption to life on land.

Lycopersicum esculentum, and man, *Homo sapiens*. Each species is then grouped in larger groups which in ascending order are: *genus* (the first name in the two-part Latin name), *tribe*, *family*, *order*, *class*, *phylum*, and finally *kingdom*. Just two kingdoms are generally accepted—the plant kingdom and the animal kingdom.

Bacteria, blue-green algae and fungi

Although classification is an indispensable aid to study, all divisions above species are entirely artificial. (This explains why whether one group is called, say, a class or a phylum is often in dispute). Many animals and plants are extremely difficult to classify satisfactorily. In particular there are a large number of organisms which cannot be

2

Dr. Gordon Leedale/Biophoto Associates

Heather Angel

Pteridophyta

plants with roots, stems leaves and water conducting tissue

Spermàtophyta

seed - bearing plants with roots, stems, leaves and water conducting tissue

erworts

Ferns

Horsetails

Clubmosses

Gymnosperms
(coniferous trees)

Angiosperms
(flowering plants)

Below: The Royal fern, *Osmunda regalis.* In many ways ferns resemble higher plants. They have a dominant sporophyte—the gametophyte being an inconspicuous filament many times smaller than the sporophyte.

Right: A species of silver fir, *Abies,* clearly showing the red mature cones. Firs are coniferous trees—the most distinctive group of the *Gymnospermae,* which also includes yews and the tropical cycads and ginkgos.

Giuseppe Mazza

Heather Angel

Right: Plants are classified into groups each of which has a set of characteristic features which distinguishes it from other groups. The family, *Rosaceae,* illustrated here, includes the *genera,*

Malus (apples), *Pyrus* (pears) and *Rubus* (raspberries and blackberries) as well as *Rosa* (roses). *Rosa* are further divided into species such as *Rosa canina,* the dog rose, and *Rosa odorata,* the tea rose.

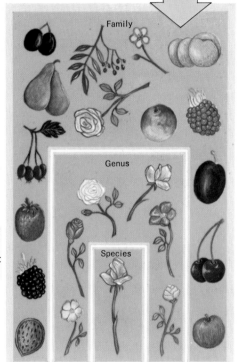

Family

Genus

Species

conveniently accommodated in either the plant or animal kingdoms. A vast group of such organisms are the *prokaryotes* which includes bacteria and blue-green algae. Their distinctive characteristic— they do not have cells with specialized structures or *organelles*—divides them so completely from all other organisms that many authorities consider them as a kingdom in their own right.

Another group, the *Fungi,* are normally considered to be plants but differ from the majority of plants by one factor—the absence of chlorophyll. Hence, all fungi lack the ability to make their own food. They obtain their nourishment in the same way as animals do by feeding on other living organisms (*parasitism*) or on their dead remains (*saprophytism*).

The three main classes of fungi are the *Phycomycetes,* the *Ascomycetes* and the *Basidiomycetes.* They differ in the way they produce their spores. Some species of phycomycetes have free-swimming *zoospores* though not all do so. The others such as pin-mould, *Mucor,* reproduce by non-mobile spores which are either enclosed inside a spore case (*sporangium*) or are unenclosed so that they can be blown away by the wind. Another characteristic of phycomycetes is that the young cells do not possess crosswalls.

In the *Ascomycetes* the cells have cross-walls and characteristically they also produce eight spores in special sporangia, called *asci,* which are often grouped within cup- or flask-shaped fruiting bodies. Ascomycetes also form

Right: Flowers in their many forms are the distinguishing feature of the phylum *Angiospermae*, the flowering plants, which are by far the largest group, in both numbers and species, of plant forms today. These flowers belong to the beech, *Fagus sylvatica*.

Below: *Chionochloa flavescens*, an alpine grass growing in New Zealand. Grasses are a most important family of the sub-phylum *Monocotyledonae*. Monocots have only one seed leaf (*cotyledon*) which develops inside the seed. The cotyledon of grasses absorbs food from another part of the seed (the *endosperm*) and passes it on to the developing plant. In other plants it is a food storage organ itself (as in legumes) or develops with the young plant to become the first green photosynthesizing leaf.

Above: *Quercus*, the oak. There are 450 species of oak—two of which, *Quercus robur* and *Quercus petraea*, are native to Britain and 60 to North America. Before extensive cultivation, oak forest was the dominant vegetation of Europe. The success of oak and other genera of trees relies upon their ability to lay down wood in thickened growths—a process known as *secondary thickening*. Secondary growth allows the tree to produce a tall, dense leaf canopy which suppresses other plants by overshadowing them.

the fungal part of the fungus-alga association which comprises a lichen. Two examples of an ascomycete are yeast (*Saccharomyces*) and *Penicillium notatum* from which penicillin is produced.

The third group of fungi, the *Basidomycetes*, includes the mushrooms and toadstools. All these have a spore-bearing structure, called a *basidium*, which swells at the end to form a spore, rather as a glass bulb is blown at the end of a piece of glass tubing.

Algae

The majority of plants, however, differ from animals primarily in their ability to manufacture their own food by photosynthesis. The simplest form of plants which do this are the *Algae*. Algae have no roots, stems, leaves or water-conducting tissue and are all totally dependent on water. Almost all are aquatic.

Colour is the most distinguishing characteristic of algae and the group is divided up into classes according to the predominance of one pigment or another in their cells. In the diatoms (*Chrysophyta*), which constitute the major element of marine plankton upon which all marine life ultimately depends for food, the predominant colour is brown. In the green algae, *Chlorophyta*, however, the green pigment, chlorophyll, is not disguised by the presence of other colouring matter. This class includes the majority of the simple fresh water algae such as *Chlamydomonas* as well as filamentous forms such as *Spirogyra*.

The brown algae, *Phaeophyta*, are almost all seaweeds and are probably the best known algae, owing to the size and complexity which many of them attain

and the extraordinary abundance in which they occur along the coasts. The brown/green colour of their body structure (*thallus*) results from the fact that they contain a brown pigment, *fucoxanthin*, as well as chlorophyll. Treatment with hot water, which dissolves the fucoxanthin, has the effect of turning brown seaweeds green.

Land plants

The simplest land plants are the *Bryophyta* which possesses many features which must have been common to the first land plants. They have an outer layer of cells, the *epidermis*, which surrounds the plants and to some extent prevents drying out. Nevertheless they are highly dependent on water for their reproduction and hence are limited in the habitats they can colonize. Nor do they have a well-developed conducting system for transporting food or water and thus their maximum size is also restricted.

The bryophytes are divided into two classes, the liverworts (*Hepaticae*) and the mosses (*Musci*). In both classes the gamete-producing generation (the *gametophyte*) is dominant over the spore-producing generation (the *sporophyte*). In the liverworts the gametophyte is a flat, green, ribbon-like thallus which grows horizontally with root-like *rhizoids*, while the sporophyte, which develops from a fertilized egg in the gametophyte, remains as a small simple structure dependent on the gametophyte for its nutrition.

The moss gametophyte is not unlike a higher plant. It has a vertical stem with simple leaves, but rhizoids, not roots, anchor it to the ground. Again the

sporophyte is simple, and at least partly dependent on the gametophyte for its food, but it is generally more complex than the sporophyte of the liverworts. Despite this, the structure of the moss gametophyte is quite different from that of the corresponding generation of higher plants, and so mosses and liverworts may be regarded as an isolated group, highly developed in their own way, but with no near affinities to other groups of plants.

This is not true of the ferns (*Filicinae*), the largest class of the phylum *Pteridophyta*. In ferns the situation is reversed with respect to the two generations. The sporophyte is dominant while the gametophyte is small and little more than a structure for producing sex organs and gametes. (Nevertheless it leads an independent life unlike the gametophyte of more advanced plants.) The ferns and their relations, the clubmosses and the horsetails, further resemble higher plants in possessing a sporophyte with roots, leaves and stems and also woody conducting tissue (*vascular tissue*) for transporting water and food. Unlike advanced plants, however, fern male gametes are mobile *spermatozoids*, similar to those of the bryophytes, which must swim to the female sex organs in a water film on the plant surface. Ferns, therefore, are still very dependent on water.

Though they have vascular tissue none of the existing pteridophytes possess the ability to lay down wood in annual rings (*secondary growth*) as do the flowering plants. Secondary growth, however, did occur in pteridophytes of the past and these were possibly related to the early ancestors of the flowering plants.

The *Gymnospermae* are further

advanced. In these plants secondary growth is usual, allowing the formation of trees like pine (*Pinus*), fir (*Pseudotsuga*) and spruce (*Picea*). Gymnosperms are also the oldest group of living plants which produce true seeds and in which the male gametophyte is reduced to a nucleus in small wind-borne spores (pollen). Unlike the flowering plants, however, the egg cells of gymnosperms are naked and not enclosed in *ovaries* and gymnosperms do not have flowers. The sporophyte gymnosperms of today are woody trees mostly with evergreen foliage and are particularly abundant as individuals, if not species, in the mountains and cool temperate regions of the world.

Flowering plants

A more recently evolved phylum than the *Gymnospermae* is the *Angiospermae* or flowering plants. This phylum contains the bulk of the present world flora. Like the gymnosperms, angiosperms do not have mobile gametes and hence they are not so dependent on water as the ferns and lower plants. This factor is responsible for their success in a great number of habitats including near deserts.

The characteristic feature of flowering plants is that the egg-bearing ovules are enclosed in an ovary which is usually crowned by a pollen-receiving surface, the *stigma*, borne on a stalk, the *style*. The pollen is produced on nearby reproductive structures called *anthers*. Both the ovary and anthers are then enclosed by special modified leaves, *petals*, and the whole constitutes a flower.

Flowering plants are divided into two sub-phyla: the *Dicotyledonae* which possess two seed leaves (*cotyledons*) and are mainly broad-leaved plants with branching leaf veins, and the *Monocotyledonae* which possess one seed leaf, and have long narrow leaves with parallel veins. Monocotyledons do not undergo secondary growth so all flowering trees are dicotyledons. A major class of the *Monocotyledonae* are the *Graminae*, which include all grasses and cereals.

Classification of the angiosperms is on the basis of the structure of the flowers, fruits and seeds, and a large array of families have been distinguished. Their diversity and adaptability are indicated by the many varied habitats they have invaded. Forms such as cacti and other succulent plants have colonized deserts and the salt sand of sea shores. Water storage tissue and thick wax layers around these plants help to conserve water. Others, such as mistletoe, *Viscum album*, have lost the ability to photosynthesize and have become parasitic.

Finally, a very few angiosperms have returned to the sea from which all plants originated. For example, *Poseidonia* grows on the bed of the sea in warm parts of the world. Thus the group of plants which have become the dominant vegetation of the world because of their success as land plants are now recolonizing the sea and may become a dominant group of marine plants as well. Nevertheless, the dominance of angiosperms cannot be expected to be unending. It is probable that another group of plants, possibly developing from some obscure and unimposing species, will in the future supersede the angiosperms just as they have superseded the ferns and gymnosperms of 300 million years ago.

Above: An example of a monocot flower—the lily, Royal Gold. Monocots are easily distinguished from dicots by their leaves which have parallel veins. Lilies and irises are monocots. Most other flowers are dicots with branched veins on their leaves.

Below: *Papaver rhoeas*, the common field poppy. Poppies are a family of simple dicot flowers with petals which are separated from each other. Some complex flowers, like those of daisies, *Compositae*, consist of many simple flowers fused to form a tube.

The Evolution of Plants

Throughout much of geological time, plants have been preserved as fossils in sedimentary rocks. Today this fossil record provides evidence of some of the major steps in the evolution and astonishing diversification of the plant kingdom. But the usefulness of this record goes far beyond the palaeobotanist's interest in the ancient history of plant life. Buried in this fossil record, there are clues to the origin of life itself.

Indeed, research into the Pre-Cambrian fossil record has been encouraged by the advances in space exploration. For, in anticipation of finding some primitive form of life on other planets, earth scientists are examining the oldest and most primitive remains of life on earth.

The first evidence of life

At present the oldest known remains of cellular organisms are found in the Fig Tree chert (black, glassy rocks made of silica) in Swaziland, which is some 3,100 million years old. The simple morphological structures are presumed to be bacteria because of their size and shape. From the same rocks scientists have also extracted many different kinds of complex organic substances which are the essential biochemical constituents of living matter. These include, for example, certain familiar amino acids and carbohydrates.

The search has been extended to other slightly younger rocks. This has shown that as the age decreases so cellular structure and chemical complexity increase. For instance, 2,800 million year old rocks in the Bulawayan Group from Rhodesia contain fossils of multi-cellular organisms, thought to be the remains of colonial algae which form reef-like calcareous banks called *stromatolites*. These are easily preserved as fossils because of the hard calcareous dome-shaped mats which the algal cells secrete.

Very similar organisms still survive today and grow in profusion in the quiet intertidal zones of western Australia. These *procaryotes* (lacking a true nucleus) are among the simplest known organisms. Their occurrence 2,800 million years ago marks the beginning of plant life as we know it, and the start of the development of greater complexity by living things.

The next major stage in the increasing sophistication of the fossil plant record is found in Canada. Certain blue-green algae have been identified in the 1,900 million year old Gun Flint chert. These still have simple procaryotic organization, but they are more complex than the algae which produced the stromatolites because their cells are ordered into filamentous chains. Once again, the specimens that have been found in these old rocks are very similar to types of blue-green algae that grow in ponds and lakes today.

More and more of these very old fossils are being discovered every year, particularly in Australia, where suitably preserved sediments a little younger than 1,000 million years old are quite common. The best known are from Bitter Springs where large numbers of multi-cellular photosynthetic organisms have been discovered. These fossils are among the oldest records of *eucaryotes*, organisms with highly organized cytoplasm, the earliest of which gave rise through evolution to all other types of plants. These more sophisticated organisms become widespread in younger fossil-bearing deposits and, though they often occur alongside the simpler procaryotes, they begin to dominate the vegetation from about that time.

Until about 400 million years ago, single-celled, colonial and filamentous algae formed the basis of plant life on this planet. Much of today's land surface was covered with water.

An environmental change enabling plants to adapt to new forms came over 400 million years ago. During the Silurian period, the seas retreated from earlier continental coastal regions. Palaeobotanists believe that multi-cellular algae began to colonize the new intertidal areas and to have differentiated into forms of plants that could best survive away from the seas. The new land environments had many advantages: they offered a stable base, a source of food in the newly developing soil and a warm humid atmosphere, with some concentration of oxygen for more efficient respiration.

Dr Michael Boulter

Left: About 400 million years ago, plants first made the transfer from sea to land. The oldest known vascular plant (with fluid-conducting cells) is *Cooksonia* (shown beside tall fern) which grew up to 10 cm high at the edge of the water. The fossil (above) shows the simple branching of the stem and the spore capsules. Many other very simple fern-like plants also colonized the land and some grew to over 1 m high. Intertidal zones continued to support the dome-shaped mats of secretions from various blue-green algae, which form the easily fossilized stromatolites. These vary from a few centimetres to several metres across. (Below) Section of a stromatolite dome. Stromatolites date back to 2,800 M.Y. ago.

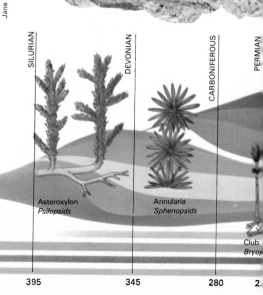

Jane Burton/Bruce Coleman

SILURIAN

DEVONIAN

CARBONIFEROUS

PERMIAN

PRE-CAMBRIAN

CAMBRIAN

ORDOVICIAN

Asteroxylon
Psilopsids

Annularia
Sphenopsids

Club
Bryo

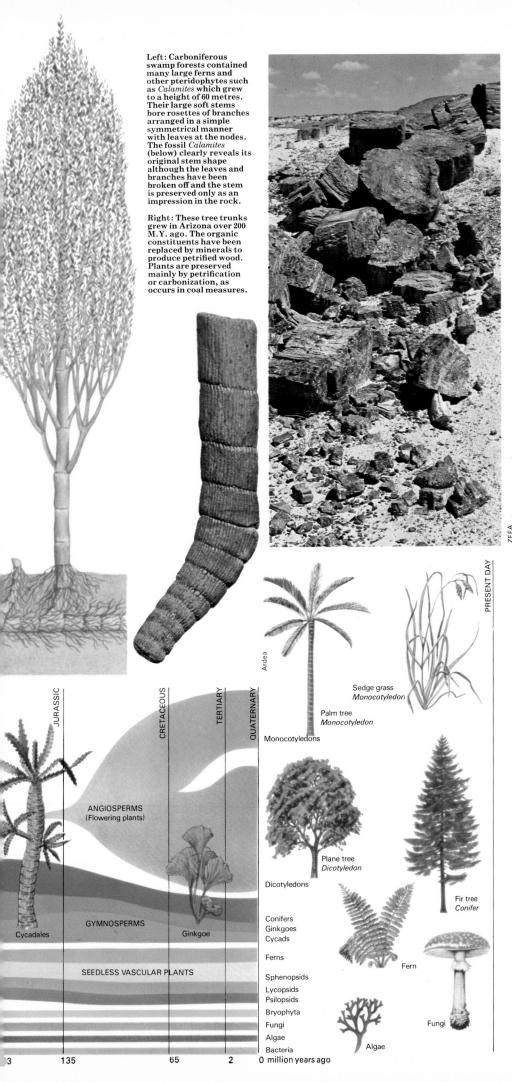

Left: Carboniferous swamp forests contained many large ferns and other pteridophytes such as *Calamites* which grew to a height of 60 metres. Their large soft stems bore rosettes of branches arranged in a simple symmetrical manner with leaves at the nodes. The fossil *Calamites* (below) clearly reveals its original stem shape although the leaves and branches have been broken off and the stem is preserved only as an impression in the rock.

Right: These tree trunks grew in Arizona over 200 M.Y. ago. The organic constituents have been replaced by minerals to produce petrified wood. Plants are preserved mainly by petrification or carbonization, as occurs in coal measures.

Ardea

ZEFA

PRESENT DAY

Sedge grass
Monocotyledon

Palm tree
Monocotyledon

Monocotyledons

Plane tree
Dicotyledon

Dicotyledons

Fir tree
Conifer

Conifers
Ginkgoes
Cycads

Ferns

Fern

Sphenopsids

Lycopsids

Psilopsids

Bryophyta

Fungi

Fungi

Algae

Bacteria

Algae

JURASSIC

CRETACEOUS

TERTIARY

QUATERNARY

ANGIOSPERMS
(Flowering plants)

GYMNOSPERMS

Cycadales

Ginkgoe

SEEDLESS VASCULAR PLANTS

3   135   65   2   0 million years ago

At the end of the Silurian, there began a rapid burst of evolution within the plant kingdom. Within just 25 million years—a very short length of geological time—land plants evolved complex vascular systems to transport food all over the plant body, leaves which specialized in photosynthesis, roots and stems for support, and, most dramatically of all, *sporangia* (in which spores were produced) and even seeds for reproduction. Moreover, the biochemical, physiological and genetical processes needed to support such complex organisms developed too.

Plants of the past

These events occurred during the Devonian—a period when much land surface was exposed—and now recognized as being one of the two intervals of greatest expansion in plant evolution. Consequently, at the end of the Devonian, 345 million years ago, not only were there diverse types of marine and freshwater algae, but also a huge variety of spore-bearing plants such as ferns, tree-ferns, horse-tails, club-mosses and many now unfamiliar little plants with simple stems and small sporangia.

All these plants are now extinct, though modern ferns, club-mosses and horse-tails do survive as rare representatives of the ancient lineages. Particularly unfamiliar to us would be the Devonian pro-gymnosperms which are thought to have grown up to 25 metres (88 feet) in height with woody trunks, conifer-like leaves and simple seeds which were fertilized by wind-blown pollen.

A similarly unfamiliar, completely extinct group of plants was particularly common during the Carboniferous period that followed. These were the *pterido-sperms*, with fern-like leaves, underground stems and very simple large seeds hanging loosely from the leaves. They relied on the wind blowing large pollen grains over the mouth of the seed for pollination to take place. Because this was a very inefficient process which encouraged inbreeding, they quickly became extinct. For a time, however, they achieved some success and are commonly found as fossils in the Carboniferous coal measure deposits.

The equatorial swamps of North America and Europe, then joined as a single land mass, also supported forests of very large *pteridophytes*. These plants reproduced by spores, like modern ferns, and were formed of very soft parts with a high water content. The best known of these is *Lepidodendron* which grew up to 35 metres (115 feet) in height and had a stem over 1 metre (39 in) in diameter. Just as common were giant horse-tails such as *Calamites* and ferns similar to, but larger than, those of modern times. These very warm, wet and humid swamps were environments in which plant life flourished, and where the rate of growth has been shown to have been considerable.

The relatively sudden and major changes in world environment that took place at the end of the Carboniferous period marks the end of this botanical paradise. Climatic and other changes forced an end to the profusion of the luxurious forest swamps, and large numbers of once abundant plants became extinct very quickly. The environmental changes enabled those plants with the more sophisticated seed reproduction systems, the *gymnosperms* (which include   7 the conifers and their relatives), to win over those with the simpler sporangia. Their woody nature also proved to be most suitable for the drier environments that were to follow.

The periods of the Mesozoic era saw a great diversification of these plants. Gymnosperms with short hard trunks and crowns of hard waxy leaves up to four metres (13 feet) long were commonplace. For 150 million years, until some 100 million years ago, the plant kingdom diversified more than it had done before. Trees with naked seeds relying on wind for pollination, ferns, and relatively few smaller pteridophytes formed the basis of the floras of the world. As in the Carboniferous, plants were able to consolidate on this type of structure once they had become established within a reasonably stable environment.

World vegetation during the Mesozoic was based on four separate floras, whose origins can be traced back to Carboniferous times. The Euramerican flora occupied most of Europe and North America, the *Glossopteris* flora most of what was Gondwanaland in the south, the Angaran flora most of northern Asia, whilst the Cathaysian flora occupied what is now central Asia, China and S.E. Asia.

The Glossopteris flora was the most distinctive. Alone, it has representatives of another quite extinct group of plants, which had veined spear-shaped leaves and complex seeds. Moreover, plants from this flora have been recognized for many years from South America, southern Africa, India, Australasia and Antarctica. They provided one of the major proofs that these land masses formed a single continent 280 million years ago.

Many recent studies of these Mesozoic floras have involved not only examination of the fossilized leaves, stems and seeds, but also of their pollen grains. Since these are well preserved (they are formed of *sporopollenin* which is one of the most stable and resistant chemical substances known) they are easily observed with a microscope. And since they are more readily obtained in narrow bore-hole samples than large fossils, the recognition of pollen is particularly important in the exploration for oil and other minerals. Most of the oil deposits in the North Sea, for example, are of Mesozoic age, and have been discovered with the help of fossil pollen studies to identify the age of the sediments.

The success of flowering plants

The Cretaceous period some 100 million years ago saw the second really large explosion of evolutionary activity in the plant kingdom. The environmental circumstances that were responsible for this event are more controversial than those for the Devonian expansion as many more factors were operating to cause the changes. But the effect of this second revolution was that the dominating gymposperms of the Mesozoic were replaced by the much more successful *angiosperms*, or flowering plants, with their widely varied morphology and specialized seeds enclosed in a protective carpel.

One current explanation for this dramatic evolutionary growth is that during the relative stability of the Mesozoic plants had been able to build up a large reserve of genetic facility, needing only the opportunity to use it. Whether this oppor-

tunity was afforded by the sudden expansion of insects during the Cretaceous (most angiosperms are pollinated by insects) or whether the particular climate and environmental circumstances of the Cretaceous were suddenly favourable is not fully understood.

The effect of this evolutionary explosion of plant life was far reaching. The first groups of flowering plants succeeded so well that they caused the greater number of Mesozoic gymnosperms to become extinct quite quickly. The disappearance of others has been more gradual, and even today there is one surviving species of the *Ginkgoales*, a few species of *Cycads* in isolated parts of the world and many conifers, though the last are restricted to extreme environments such as deserts and cool temperate regions. These are the only survivors. Today most areas of the world are more or less dominated by angiosperms.

The continuing debate on the evolutionary origin of the angiosperms remains the one most substantial unanswered question in palaeobotany. One difficulty is that there are very few fossil remains of early angiosperm plants, possibly because they first appeared on mountain tops where erosion has destroyed all evidence. Another is that so many advanced gymnosperm groups, such as the members of the Glossopteris flora, have leaves and other organs that are very similar to what the earliest angiosperms may have resembled. Also, many of the parts of simple angiosperms are likely to have been very soft and so unlikely to survive as fossils. But fossil pollen grains may hold important clues since they are distinctive and easily preserved. Current research suggests that discoveries of very primitive angiosperm pollen from Cretaceous rocks from southeast Asia and Africa may represent some of the first appearances of the flowering plants.

Once they had developed, angiosperms became established very quickly. The fossil record of 90 million years ago shows few traces. Yet at the end of the Cretaceous 25 million years later they form

the dominant group of plants in most fossil floras. So rapid was the rate of change that, by the beginning of the Tertiary 65 million years ago, the characters of primitive angiosperms were giving way to the relatively advanced features recognizable in modern plants.

The last 60 million years

The last 60 million years of history of the plant kingdom have been dominated by climatic fluctuations in most parts of the world. These have helped create a wider range of ecological niches and thus an increase in the potential for plant evolution to produce more species. The climax occurred just two million years ago with the beginning of the extensive ice ages, when ice at the poles produced a maximum range of climate from north to south.

The climate of the whole planet had been fluctuating from the beginning of the Tertiary. Successive waves of cooling were directed from the poles towards the equator. These changes in temperature had themselves caused a pattern of plant migration away from the poles for most of the temperate plants living in what are now polar regions, 50 and 60 million years ago. At the same time, substantial climatic changes were being caused by the effects of sea floor spreading and continental drift.

Scientists are in the process of trying to piece together the fossil evidence to explain the details of these effects of plant migration. Not only were subsequent generations of the same species of plants migrating as the climate changed, but new forms were also evolving and others were becoming extinct. One difficulty is that we know little enough of modern plants, particularly those that grow in the unexplored tropical parts of the world, to make adequate comparisons with the fossils that we might luckily find. From the huge variety of environmental and genetical factors influencing their development, it seems as though the last 50 million years in the history of plants are the hardest to understand.

Dr Michael Boulter

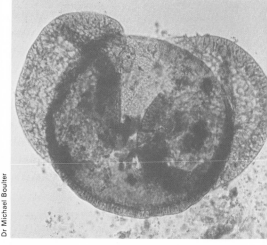

Dr Michael Boulter

Left: This fossil moss grew in Derbyshire in the English midlands, then enjoying a warm climate, about 8 M.Y. ago. Its perfect preservation shows many botanical features though no living moss is quite the same. It is one of the few fossils that record the warm climate of the time and like them it is extinct.

Below: A fossil pollen grain from an extinct species of silver fir. The grain is only 0.1 mm long but its delicate features are revealed under a microscope to aid in identifying the plant. *Palynology*, the study of pollen grains, is widely used in oil exploration to determine the age of sediments found in boreholes.

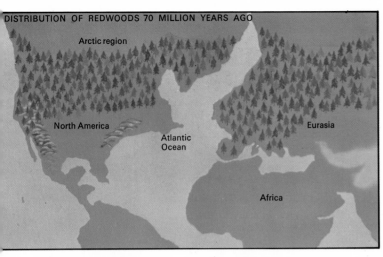

DISTRIBUTION OF REDWOODS 70 MILLION YEARS AGO

Arctic region

North America

Atlantic Ocean

Eurasia

Africa

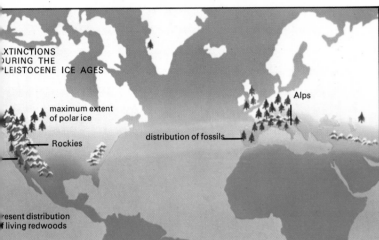

XTINCTIONS
URING THE
LEISTOCENE ICE AGES

maximum extent
of polar ice

Rockies

distribution of fossils

Alps

resent distribution
f living redwoods

Left: At the end of the Cretaceous, 70 M.Y. ago, when the Arctic was in a different position on the globe, the world's major mountain chains were not fully formed. Arctic regions supported temperate vegetation, of which many fossils remain. During the Tertiary period the east-west mountain chains of Europe and Asia were uplifted as the drifting continents collided. These formed a barrier to the plants trying to migrate south to escape the colder climates produced by advancing polar glaciations (below left). Many plant species became extinct. But in North America, where the mountain chains lie north-south, no such barrier existed and fewer species became extinct. Thus the modern flora of western North America represents a more ancient lineage than that of Europe. The redwoods of California, like these giants from Yosemite (below), survive today but their European and Asian counterparts from the Tertiary have long been extinct.

Dr Michael Boulter

Below: Fossil plants closely related to the present-day Californian redwood have been found in Tertiary rocks from many parts of the northern hemisphere. These portions of 8 M.Y. old trunks were found particularly well preserved in Miocene clays in Derbyshire. They have been identified as an extinct species of the *Sequoia* family by looking at thin sections of wood under a light microscope (left). The leafy shoots from the deposits (below) have similar botanical characters to the modern Californian forms, such as two types of leaves and a cone. Other fossil material from similar plants is found in many parts of the world.

Dr Michael Boulter

Dr Michael Boulter

10

Plant Species

Coconut palm (*cocos nucifera*) and young fruit. The sole member of a genus, it has been widely distributed throughout the tropics by ocean currents.

Algae

Algae are simple aquatic or semi-aquatic plants widely distributed in large numbers in most ponds, lakes, streams and the surface waters of oceans. They are perhaps the most numerous of all plants, forming, with small animals, the plankton of the seas which is the primary food source of fish.

They do not possess roots, stems or leaves, yet vary greatly in size from single cells one micron (0.001 mm) in diameter, through colonies and filaments, to large fronded seaweeds which may be up to 100 m (300 ft) in length. In evolutionary terms this variation is thought to indicate the course of the development of the higher plants which are generally supposed to have originated from the green algae.

Colour

Algae are among the simplest plants in which the different functions carried out by the cell occur in specialized structures called organelles—that is they are *eukaryotic*. (Blue-green algae are an exception: they are more closely related to bacteria than to other algae and their cells do not contain discrete organelles.) In particular, algal cells have structures called *chromatophores*, containing various pigments. Most important of these is the green pigment *chlorophyll*, which occurs in chromatophores called *chloroplasts*. Chlorophyll, together with the other pigments, is able to trap the energy of

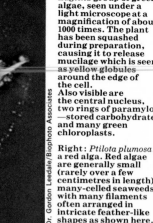

Dr. Gordon Leedale/Biophoto Associates

Left: A species of the *Euglena* group of green algae, seen under a light microscope at a magnification of about 1000 times. The plant has been squashed during preparation, causing it to release mucilage which is seen as yellow globules around the edge of the cell. Also visible are the central nucleus, two rings of paramylon —stored carbohydrate— and many green chloroplasts.

Right: *Ptilota plumosa*, a red alga. Red algae are generally small (rarely over a few centimetres in length), many-celled seaweeds with many filaments often arranged in intricate feather-like shapes as shown here.

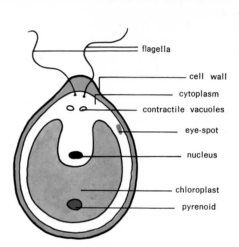

Right: The single-celled green alga *Chlamydomonas*, found in both freshwater and seawater, showing the organelles within the cell, each with a different function. The centre of the cell is the nucleus containing the genetic material DNA. Around this is the cup-shaped *chloroplast* containing a structure known as a *pyrenoid* in which starch is stored. The *contractile vacuole* is used to force out water which continuously enters the alga from the outside.

flagella
cell wall
cytoplasm
contractile vacuoles
eye-spot
nucleus
chloroplast
pyrenoid

Below: Green algae blooming round a soda spring in the Rift Valley of East Africa. The colour is produced by the photosynthetic pigment, chlorophyll.

Right: Two different algae taken from the Mediterranean. The long reddish-brown strands are part of a filamentous red alga, *Rhodophyta*, while the circular structure in the centre of the picture is a centric diatom—one of the *Bacillariophyta*. Most oceans, lakes and ponds contain diatoms.

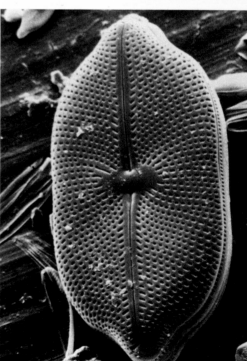

Lee Lyon/Bruce Coleman

Dr. Gordon Leedale/Biophoto Associates

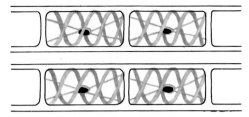

1. Two adjacent filaments come together

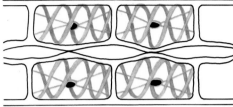

2. The cell-walls of each filament grow outwards towards the opposite filament

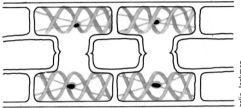

3. Where they meet the cell-walls break down forming narrow tubes connecting the two filaments

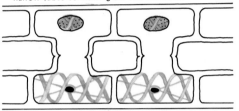

4. The contents of the cells in one filament condense to form a green mass—the male gamete

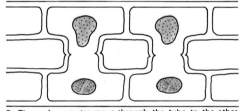

5. The male gametes move through the tube to the other filament where the cells have formed female gametes

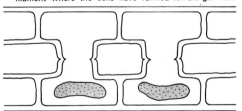

6. The gametes fuse to form a zygote

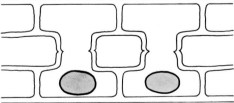

7. The zygote develops a resistant coat to become a zygospore

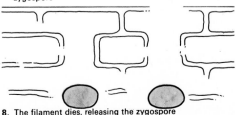

8. The filament dies, releasing the zygospore

Left: Two adjacent filaments of *Spirogyra* undergoing sexual reproduction by the process of *conjugation*. The zygospores are covered in a resistant case which can withstand drought, cold and heat until conditions are favourable. Then they germinate, each producing one new plant.

Right: The brown seaweed *Fucus vesiculosus*. It consists of flat blades (*laminae*) attached by a *stipe* to the holdfast which anchors the plant to the sea-bed.

Below: An example of a brown seaweed, 'tangle' (*Laminaria digitata*). The photograph, taken at low-tide, reveals the anchoring holdfasts.

air bladders (to give buoyancy)

reproductive swellings

midrib (to give support and to transport nutrients)

holdfast

Below: One of the uses of algae is the purification of sewage. The sewage is sprayed over beds of clinker on which the algae grow. While the sewage percolates through the clinker it dissolves oxygen produced during photosynthesis by the algae and so allows further purification by bacteria.

Leslie Jackman

P. Morris

latter type of life cycle, as in the higher plants, and the process is called *alternation of generations*.

This occurs in all brown and red algae and a few green algae. In some algae, such as the many celled red algae, these two plant generations are similar in appearance but in others they show marked differences. In the more complex algae, as in higher plants, the sporophyte is dominant and the gametophyte generation is greatly reduced. In the common large seaweed *Laminaria*, for example, the gametophyte generation is reduced to microscopic filaments of a few cells which produce either sperm or eggs. Fertilized eggs develop into the sporophyte.

Algae and man
Despite the great importance of algae as the primary food source of the oceans, their direct use by man is limited. Nevertheless, they can be eaten, for example, *Porphyra*, the lava bread of Wales, or fed to animals. In particular the mucilage from the large seaweeds, such as *Macrocystis*, is processed to make animal foodstuffs. The reproduction of algal cells has been studied to give a guide to the cause of cancer and algae are also used for oxidizing sewage and for pro-

ducing oxygen during space flights.

A jelly, known as *agar-agar*, is produced from some red algae such as *Gelidium*. It is widely used in bacterial and fungal culture, in confectionary, dentistry, in cosmetics and in baked foods. *Carageenin* extracted from the red alga *Chondrus crispus* is used in toothpaste. Other substances, *alginates*, produced from brown algae, are used as emulsifying agents in the treatment of latex for rubber tyres, and in ice-cream, coal briquettes, and paints. The alginates are extracted by disintegrating the plants in acid and then adding calcium carbonate (lime) to settle out the alginate.

Algae are used as food and in the preparation of processed foods. But they can also be harmful. Some are poisonous to animals; more importantly they may produce toxins which can spoil water supplies wanted for domestic use. Alternatively the death and decay of large numbers of algae following an algal bloom can use up all the available oxygen in water turning it fetid and causing fish to die. Despite this, the photosynthesis of the billions of algae in the sea is responsible in no small part for the production of the life-giving oxygen in the atmosphere.

Bacteria and Blue-Green Algae

Bacteria are minute organisms present everywhere, in vast numbers, on the Earth's surface. They live in countless millions in the soil, in the depths of the sea and in the air, in hot springs and in the Arctic. They multiply inside our bodies and on our skins, sometimes causing diseases but often acting beneficially. Some bacteria (*Bdellovibrio*) even prey upon other, larger, bacteria, boring through the cell wall and digesting the contents. Because of their large numbers and the variety of their activities bacteria must be regarded as among the most important of all living organisms.

Bacteria, blue-green algae and a few other similar creatures belong to a group of organisms called *prokaryotes*. The cells of all prokaryotes have an entirely different organization from the cells of the rest of living things (called *eukaryotes*). The most important difference is that the prokaryote cell does not contain the specialized structural components (*organelles*) which are present in the eukaryote cell: there is, for example, no definite nucleus. Specialized functions such as respiration, photosynthesis, secretion and excretion have to be carried on throughout the cell rather than in specially equipped parts of it.

Bacteria

The bacterial cell wall is made of protein; it forms a protective layer and determines the shape of the cell. Bacteria of different groups have characteristic shapes, so *bacilli* are rod-shaped, *cocci* are spherical, *spirilla* are spirally coiled and so on.

As already mentioned, the nucleus of a bacterial cell is not a well defined structure surrounded by its own membrane—the nucleic acid molecules are simply loosely bound together in a network. When the cell is about to divide, the nucleic acids are formed into a single ring called the *genophore* which then splits into two. Once this has happened, the cell itself divides. Given favourable conditions, a typical bacterial cell is capable of dividing once every hour, and if this continues it results in some 17 million cells in 24 hours. That bacteria are capable of very rapid multiplication is obvious to anyone who has suddenly been struck down by blood poisoning from an infected wound or wakened one morning to find that the milk which was reasonably fresh the night before is now undrinkable. One feature of bacteria which certainly contributes to their rapid metabolism and reproduction is their small size, which gives them a large surface area per unit mass. Over this large area a vast number of enzyme molecules can be liberated into the surrounding environment.

Bacteria are capable of using almost any type of animal or plant debris for food; they are rivalled only by fungi in this respect. With a variety of enzymes from a succession of different bacteria, the corpse of a rat or the product of the town sewers is broken down and used, either by the bacteria themselves or by any other organisms which happen to be

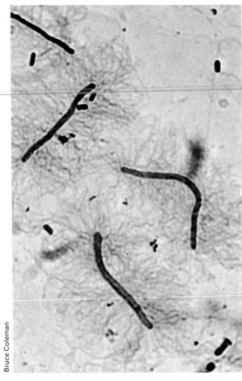

Above: Bacteria are among the smallest of living organisms. These examples of *Bacillus proteus* have been stained with silver and magnified about 2,500 times to make them visible. They are well equipped with flagella.

Below: Tiny helical bacteria seen through a microscope.

Right: A section of a bacterial DNA molecule showing the double helix structure.

Far right: The same as above but with a unit of the antibiotic *actinomycin* incorporated into the structure. The antibiotic is a 'spanner' in the genetic 'works', preventing the bacterium from replicating.

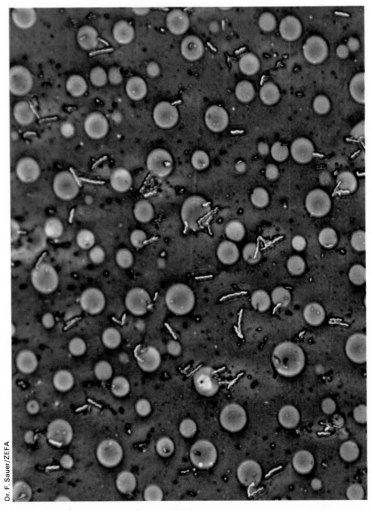

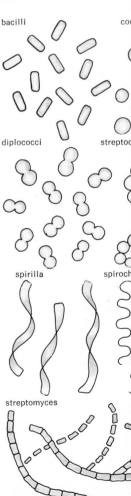

bacilli

coc

diplococci

streptoc

spirilla

spiroch

streptomyces

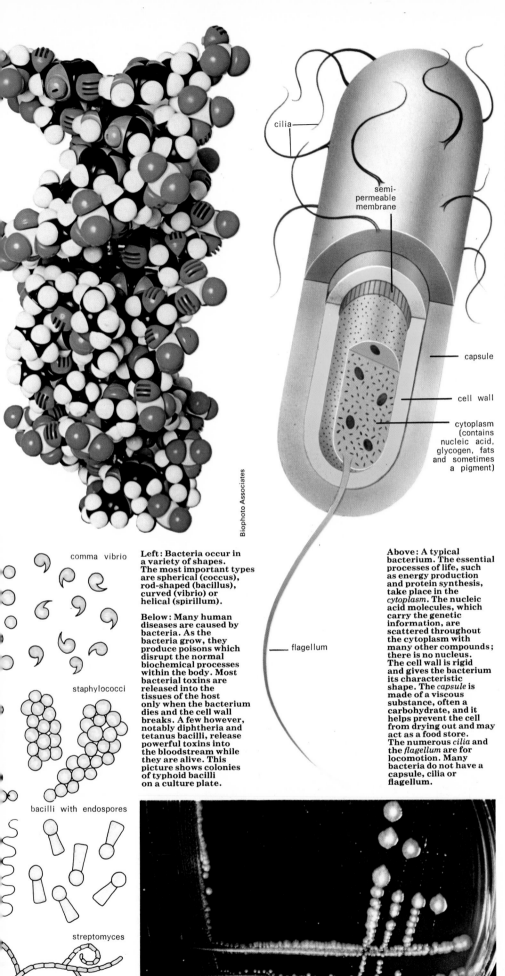

cilia

semi-
permeable
membrane

capsule

cell wall

cytoplasm
(contains
nucleic acid,
glycogen, fats
and sometimes
a pigment)

Biophoto Associates

flagellum

comma vibrio

staphylococci

bacilli with endospores

streptomyces

Left: Bacteria occur in a variety of shapes. The most important types are spherical (coccus), rod-shaped (bacillus), curved (vibrio) or helical (spirillum).

Below: Many human diseases are caused by bacteria. As the bacteria grow, they produce poisons which disrupt the normal biochemical processes within the body. Most bacterial toxins are released into the tissues of the host only when the bacterium dies and the cell wall breaks. A few however, notably diphtheria and tetanus bacilli, release powerful toxins into the bloodstream while they are alive. This picture shows colonies of typhoid bacilli on a culture plate.

Above: A typical bacterium. The essential processes of life, such as energy production and protein synthesis, take place in the *cytoplasm*. The nucleic acid molecules, which carry the genetic information, are scattered throughout the cytoplasm with many other compounds; there is no nucleus. The cell wall is rigid and gives the bacterium its characteristic shape. The *capsule* is made of a viscous substance, often a carbohydrate, and it helps prevent the cell from drying out and may act as a food store. The numerous *cilia* and the *flagellum* are for locomotion. Many bacteria do not have a capsule, cilia or flagellum.

within reach. This type of existence, breaking down the products of other organisms, is known as *saprophytism*, and the great majority of bacteria are saprophytes.

But not all bacteria are saprophytes. Bacteria must have played an important part in the early evolution of life on Earth and they could not, at that time, have lived on existing organic products. Almost certainly, many early bacteria were *autotrophic*, capable of synthesis of vital organic materials from simple constituents, and many of them do this today, obtaining the necessary energy by oxidation of inorganic or simple organic materials. A good example is found among the colourless sulphur bacteria, such as *Beggiatoa*, found in stagnant fresh water and marine habitats where hydrogen sulphide is abundant. They are capable of *chemosynthesis* by oxidizing the sulphide to sulphur, which is deposited within the rather large cell.

Thus, by a great variety of processes and under a wide variety of conditions, bacteria are able to degrade and synthesize a range of organic and inorganic substances. In this they are essential to the survival of all other living things: they make available chemicals which would otherwise be locked up in forms which cannot be directly assimilated. A good example of this is seen in the nitrogen cycle. The most satisfactory source of nitrogen for plant growth, on which animal growth also ultimately depends, is nitrate. During the decomposition of nitrogen-containing animal and plant remains by bacterial and fungal saprophytes, large quantities of ammonia are produced. The ammonia is oxidized to nitrite and then to nitrate by the autotrophic *Nitrosomonas* and *Nitrobacter*, and can then be assimilated by the plants. A few prokaryotes, including some bacteria such as the root nodule bacterium *Rhizobium*, have the astonishing ability to oxidize atmospheric nitrogen to nitrate. This process is called 'nitrogen fixation' and is an important part of the nitrogen cycle.

Given the wide variety of forms of nutrition in bacteria it is hardly surprising that they produce a wide variety of chemical by-products, many of which are useful to man. The production of acetic acid (vinegar) from alcohol by *Acetobacter*, and of fermented milk products like yogurt and cottage cheeses by *Lactobacillus*, are well known. Many soil organisms, including bacteria, produce antibiotics. In nature, these highly poisonous substances serve to protect the organism from competitors and predators. Not surprisingly, most of them are as toxic to man as they are to other organisms and hence cannot be used in medicine. Among those produced by bacteria, *tyrothricin* is not toxic to man if applied in small doses and so can be used to kill disease-producing bacteria.

Actinomycetes, or 'star-fungi', so called because they radiate out as they grow, are not fungi at all but organisms closely related to bacteria. Most of them live saprophytically in the soil, among them *Streptomyces griseus*, which produces the antibiotic *streptomycin*. Some are parasitic: *Streptomyces scabies* causes the troublesome common scab disease of potatoes, and *Nocardia* species cause tuberculosis-like diseases and other conditions in man and domestic animals.

Bruce Coleman

17

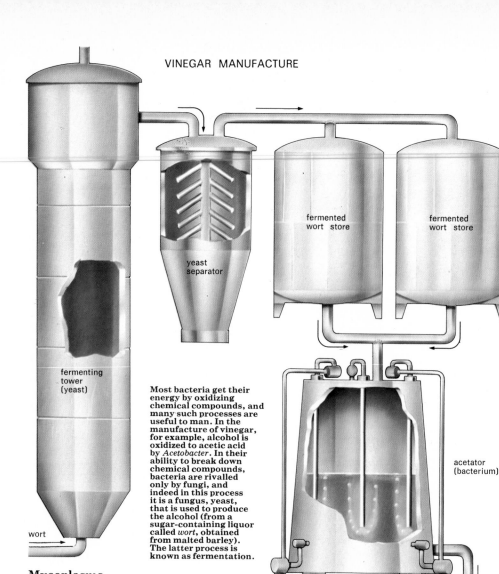

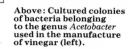

yeast
separator

fermenting
tower
(yeast)

wort

fermented
wort store

fermented
wort store

acetator
(bacterium)

vinegar
storage

vinegar
storage

filter

pasteurizer

pure vinegar

Most bacteria get their energy by oxidizing chemical compounds, and many such processes are useful to man. In the manufacture of vinegar, for example, alcohol is oxidized to acetic acid by *Acetobacter*. In their ability to break down chemical compounds, bacteria are rivalled only by fungi, and indeed in this process it is a fungus, yeast, that is used to produce the alcohol (from a sugar-containing liquor called *wort*, obtained from malted barley). The latter process is known as fermentation.

Mycoplasms

Other groups of organisms closely related to bacteria but generally even simpler are known. Among these the *mycoplasms* are specially interesting. They are basically like bacteria except that they are much smaller. It has been estimated that the genophore of an average mycoplasm, though it is structurally similar to that of a bacterium, may only have enough room to contain about 650 genes, one-fifth the number found in a typical bacterium. Because mycoplasms lack a cell wall they can change their shape and so are able to pass through a very fine filter which would retain bacteria.

Some mycoplasms are saprophytic and therefore particularly interesting: they represent the simplest forms of life capable of independent existence. Others are parasitic on man or other animals, causing pleuropneumonia-like diseases. Still others attack plants, including some important crop producers.

Blue-green algae

The chief difference between blue-green algae and bacteria is that the former use the same photosynthetic process as higher plants to extract energy from the Sun. By absorbing sunlight, molecules of the green pigment *chlorophyll* are raised to a higher energy state than usual. These high-energy molecules drive the synthetic process whereby carbon dioxide in the air and water are trapped and gradually built up into more complex molecules useful to the plant. After releasing their energy, the chlorophyll molecules are ready to absorb more sunlight, and so the process continues. Oxygen is a
18　by-product of the process and is released

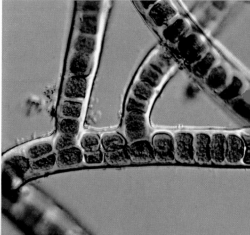

British Vinegars Ltd.

Above: Cultured colonies of bacteria belonging to the genus *Acetobacter* used in the manufacture of vinegar (left).

Below: Filaments of the blue-green alga *Stigonema* magnified 200 times. These organisms contain the green pigment chlorophyll and get their energy by photosynthesis.

Right: Grass fragments being digested in a cow's stomach (the spherical object is a gas bubble). It is the presence of bacteria in the animal's rumen (the first chamber of the stomach) that allows it to digest grass because grass consists largely of cellulose, which can be digested by bacterial enzymes.

Biophoto Associates

PROKARYOTE CELL
(BLUE-GREEN ALGA)

thylakoids

phyocyanin
granules

Right: Typical eukaryote and prokaryote cells in cross-section. There is much more organization in the former: it contains well defined structures (organelles) with specialized functions. The nucleic acid which carries the genetic information is confined to the *nucleus*, energy production is carried out in the *mitochondria*, protein production in the *endoplasmic reticulum* and photosynthesis in the *chloroplast*. The *dictyosomes* are concerned with breaking down waste products.

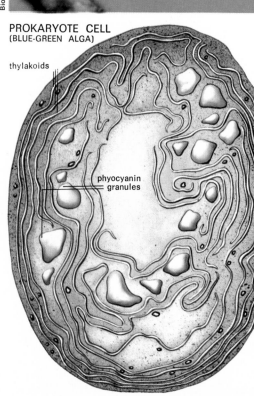

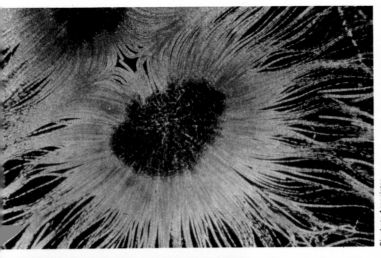

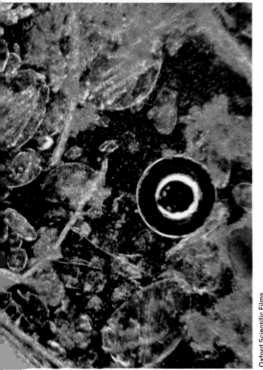

Above: A colony of the blue-green alga *Calothrix* magnified about 100 times. Filaments of algal cells radiate out from a tightly packed central region.

Right: Blue-green algae are found in all sorts of habitats. They occur as slimy masses in ponds, on soil and on the bark of trees, and they can often endure extremes of temperature which would kill higher plants. This picture shows blue-green algae growing on vegetation near a geyser at Whakarewarewa in New Zealand. In this case the designation 'blue-green' is not very apt, for the alga contains a pigment which makes it a conspicuous orange colour.

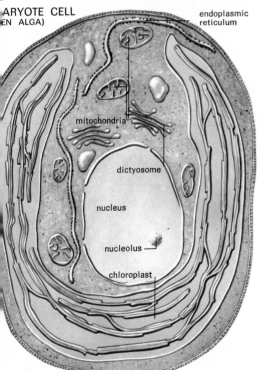

ARYOTE CELL
EN ALGA)

endoplasmic reticulum

mitochondria

dictyosome

nucleus

nucleolus

chloroplast

into the atmosphere. Some bacteria, such as *Chlorobium* and *Thiocarcina*, are capable of photosynthesis, but the process they use is somewhat different—in particular, no oxygen is released.

Blue-green algae are so called because a pigment, *phyocyanin*, partially masks the green of the chlorophyll in most species. Blue-green algal cells are usually larger and more complicated than bacterial cells, though they never have flagella of any sort. They often grow in long chains or filaments.

Blue-green algae are found in the same sort of habitats as bacteria. Being mainly photosynthetic, however, they are incapable of secreting the wide variety of enzymes necessary to break down complex organic materials. Nevertheless, many are able to grow under conditions where the light is too dim for photosynthesis, such as the top few millimetres of soil or at the bottom of turbid pools, by absorbing simple organic substances from their surroundings in a process known as *photoassimilation*. Some light is necessary for this process and so active blue-green algae are never found in totally dark environments.

The blue-green algal cell does not contain chloroplasts (the organelles where photosynthesis takes place) as in eukaryote algae, but the pigments are confined to membranous plates called *thylakoids*. The photosynthesis is carried out on these plates and the main storage product, not starch as in higher plants but a glycogen, related to those produced by red algae, fungi and animals, is deposited between the plates.

Soil fertility is known to be closely connected with the activities of nitrogen-fixing blue-green algae. For instance the world's rice production depends to a large extent on the presence of vast numbers of blue-green algae in the water and mud of paddy fields. In many multicellular species of blue-green algae nitrogen fixation is carried on in specialized cells called *heterocysts*. When heterocysts mature they lose most of their pigments, photosynthesis stops and the thylakoids are replaced by a more complicated membrane system where presumably the nitrogen fixation occurs.

Prokaryotic organisms afford a fascinating glimpse of the beginnings of life on this planet. Even among the present day mycoplasms there are forms capable of an independent existence which must resemble closely the first truly living things. The anaerobic bacteria may well resemble organisms which lived when free oxygen was not available. Blue-green algae are all aerobic, and so could not have achieved their present form until free oxygen began to diffuse into the air. Once it did become available, these small and perhaps, to our eyes, insignificant organisms would have nevertheless been responsible for increasing its concentration as a by-product of their new form of photosynthesis.

Today the prokaryotes are still a numerous and important group. The breaking down of organic materials by bacteria and Actinomycetes is essential to the recycling of elements, and the constant nitrogen fixation by a host of prokaryotic cells maintains the fertility of the soil. Its potential for rapid growth combined with physiological diversity, makes the simple prokaryote a useful friend and a formidable enemy.

19

Biophoto Associates

Heather Angel

Oxford Scientific Films

Viruses

Viruses are generally regarded as the smallest of all living things, although whether they are truly 'alive' is very much a matter of opinion. Certainly they are able to reproduce in the sense that they manufacture replicas of themselves from 'spare parts' borrowed from the cells they parasitize, rather as robots might be programmed to make more robots from stolen spares. On the other hand, like most chemical compounds, viruses can be crystallized, and this is certainly not a characteristic normally associated with life. Now that quite logical speculation about the origin of life on the Earth is possible, it has become difficult to draw the line between living organisms and complex aggregations of self-replicating molecules. Viruses plainly lie very close to this line.

Viruses are composed of nucleic acid and protein, and they are small enough to pass through a filter that would retain bacteria—hence their old name 'filterable viruses'. All known viruses are parasitic: they are incapable of an independent existence outside the cells of another living creature, whether animal, plant or bacterium. The diseases which they cause must be as old as man himself, and they include mumps and measles, chicken pox and rabies. Among plants, the striped tulip flowers beloved of Rembrandt, and the degeneration which makes it impractical to go on planting old stocks of potatoes year after year, are examples of virus diseases.

Tobacco mosaic virus

Strangely, perhaps, the virus about which most is known, and on which the first scientific experiments were done, is a plant virus, the agent of tobacco mosaic disease. At the end of the nineteenth century, Meyer and Ivanovski both showed that the disease could be transmitted by rubbing a healthy tobacco plant with sap from a diseased one. The sap could be rendered uninfective by heating it to 90°C (194°F). Ivanovski showed, however, that it was still infective after passing through a bacteriological filter, hence the infective principle could not be a bacterium, but was assumed to be a fluid. Comparable work on an animal virus, that causing foot and mouth disease, was done a few years later by Loeffler and Frosch.

By means of electron microscopy, X-ray crystallography and other methods, the structure of the tobacco mosaic virus (TMV) particle is now well-known. The virus is a narrow rigid rod about 3,000 Ångstrom units long (an Ångstrom unit is one ten millionth of a millimetre). The greater part of it is made up of a protective coat of interlocking protein molecules arranged in a dense left-handed spiral. This spiral fits neatly round a single, helical RNA molecule. It is the efficiency of the sheath which gives the particle its remarkable toughness, but the replicating mechanism, and hence the infectivity, are vested in the RNA molecule. *Ribonucleic* and *deoxyribonucleic acids* (RNA and DNA) are found in all living organisms. Viruses are unique in that they only possess one or the other. The nucleic acids are the

20

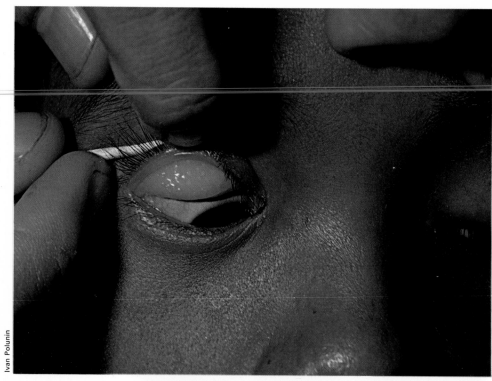

Ivan Polunin

Above: A great many animal and plant diseases are the result of infection by viruses. This picture shows a case of conjunctivitis caused by trachoma virus. The disease is recognized by small spots on the inner side of the eyelid, and it can lead to blindness.

Right: A model of an icosahedral (20-sided) virus. The outer shell is composed of protein molecules (represented here by table-tennis balls) and the core consists of a single molecule of RNA or DNA. Many viruses have this structure, including the polio virus, a very small DNA virus.

Below: Perhaps the strangest-looking viruses are the *bacteriophages*, which attack only bacteria. Shown here is a 'T-2' bacteriophage. Its 'head', shaped like a hexagonal prism, consists of a protein shell enclosing a molecule of DNA. From the base of the prism projects a narrow tube enclosed in a spiral sheath of protein molecules. Six protein 'legs' project from the lower end of the sheath.

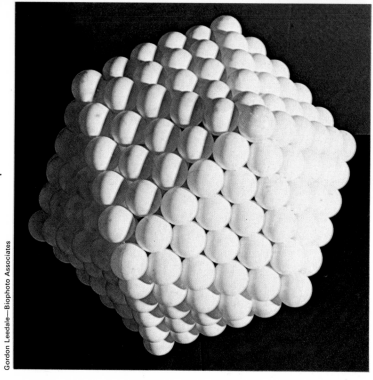

Gordon Leedale—Biophoto Associates

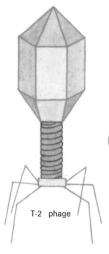

T-2 phage

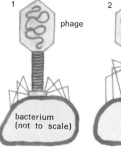

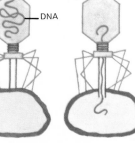

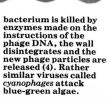

1 phage
2 DNA
3
4

bacterium (not to scale)

T-2 PHAGE ATTACKING A BACTERIUM

Above: A bacteriophage attacks a bacterial cell. The phage settles on the cell wall (1) using its legs to get a firm grip, and the spiral sheath contracts (2) to expose the inner tube. This then penetrates the cell wall, probably by secreting an enzyme, and the phage DNA enters the bacterial cell (3) where it begins to replicate. The empty and collapsed shell of the original phage remains outside the cell wall. Eventually the bacterium is killed by enzymes made on the instructions of the phage DNA, the wall disintegrates and the new phage particles are released (4). Rather similar viruses called *cyanophages* attack blue-green algae.

Greenfly aphids may
carry viruses from one
plant to another,
travelling on air
currents up to 2,000
feet high.

key to life: they carry the coded information and instructions which determine
the shape, the physiology and ultimately
the behaviour patterns of living things.

Reproduction

When material containing TMV particles
is rubbed on a leaf, the virus enters
through tiny wounds, such as broken
leaf-hairs, into the cells. (Only a few
viruses have a mechanism for boring
through an intact cell wall). However,
once in the cell the RNA strand quickly
sheds its protein coat. The 'bases',
which form part of the RNA molecule,
are arranged in such a way as to convey
an instruction or 'message' to the host
cell to produce a particular enzyme. The
enzyme in turn lays down a reversed
copy of the RNA molecule alongside the
original one, obtaining the nucleotide
'bricks' for the new molecule from the
host cell. The completed 'negative'
molecule then peels off from the original
'positive' and acts as a template for the
production of more positives. Finally,
the new positives lay down for themselves
the protective coating of protein molecules, making use of amino acids and
proteins in the host cell.

Though the method of multiplication is
apparently similar in all viruses, the
structure varies from one group of
viruses to another. In many viruses the
nucleic acid exists in the reduced form,
DNA. The molecule, whether of DNA or
RNA, may be either single- or double-
stranded. Also, there is considerable
variety in the way in which the molecules
of the protective coat are assembled. A
few viruses have the physical properties
of pure nucleic acid and apparently lack
a protein coat, but in the vast majority a
protein coat is present.

Perhaps the last word in parasitism is
a virus which parasitizes another virus.
At least one such exists. It is a very small
virus particle, known as satellite virus
(SV), which is sometimes found associated
with tobacco necrosis virus (TNV).
Because of their differences in weight,
mixtures of the two viruses can be
separated in a high speed centrifuge. On
its own TNV is capable of multiplication
in the tobacco plant, but SV cannot
multiply except in the presence of TNV.
It is probable that SV does not contain
enough RNA to carry the necessary
coded information to make all the proteins necessary for its own replication.
The protein coat of SV is chemically not
related to that of TNV, so it seems
possible that the SV makes its own coat.
Theoretical considerations suggest that
if SV contains the codes for its own coat,
it has only enough room on its RNA
strand to code for one more protein;
not enough to make a complete virus
particle. The other necessary protein
units appear to be manufactured under
'subcontract' by the TNV.

Pox viruses

Another interesting group are the pox
viruses responsible for smallpox, cowpox, fowlpox and so on. One of these,
thought to have originated from cowpox,
is the *vaccinia* virus. Pox viruses are
large as virus particles go, in fact vaccinia
virus can be seen in an optical microscope. The virus particle resembles an
egg with small tubules projecting inwards
from the shell to join up with a central
round body which contains the DNA.

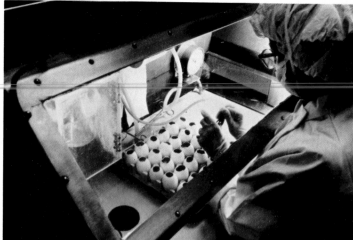

Glaxo

St. Bartholomew's Hospital

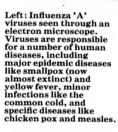

Left and below: Viruses
being harvested for the
production of an
influenza vaccine.
Influenza viruses are
first injected into
fertilized hens' eggs
where they develop on
the growing embryo and
its surrounding
membranes. They are
then harvested and
deactivated to form the
basis of the vaccine.

Left: Influenza 'A'
viruses seen through an
electron microscope.
Viruses are responsible
for a number of human
diseases, including
major epidemic diseases
like smallpox (now
almost extinct) and
yellow fever, minor
infections like the
common cold, and
specific diseases like
chicken pox and measles.

Below: Normal and
yellow-streaked
wallflower petals. The
streaking is caused by
a virus infection. Not
all virus infections
are regarded as a
nuisance: tulip bulbs
infected with a virus
that causes a particular
streaking effect in the
flowers can command
high prices as new
horticultural varieties.

The entire particle incorporates fats and
carbohydrates as well as protein in
relative proportions similar to those
found in bacteria, though it is important
to realize that these are not organized in
the same way as they would be in the
simplest bacterium.

At the end of the eighteenth century,
a country doctor called Jenner noticed
that patients who were used to handling
cattle were seldom infected with smallpox
and considered that this might be connected with their having previously
been infected with cowpox, which causes
only a relatively minor disease in humans.
He therefore obtained some serum from
cowpox spots and scratched it into the
skin of a boy, where it caused only a local
infection. After the lesions had healed
he subjected the boy to smallpox con-
tagion and was no doubt relieved to find
that the boy failed to contract the disease:
he had developed a resistance to smallpox.

The vaccinia virus is now propagated
only in laboratories and is not known in
the wild. It has some of the properties of
the original cowpox virus and some of
naturally occurring smallpox virus. It
can be grown on the membranes of
developing hens' eggs by making a small
hole in the eggshell, or by vaccinating

Dr. R. G. Milne

22

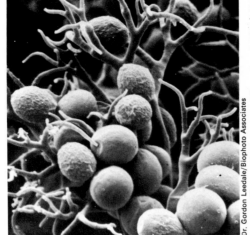

Left: Sporangia of the fungus *Peronospora parasitica* magnified about 400 times. This fungus is a 'downy mildew' which attacks such plants as turnips, cauliflowers, brussels sprouts and wallflowers. The sporangia appear as a white 'fur' on the swollen stems and under the leaves of the afflicted plant. The picture was taken with a scanning electron microscope (SEM) which has a much greater depth of field than other microscopes.

Below: On a forest floor in Thailand, the corpse of a fly is attacked by a fungus (seen as white patches on its thorax and abdomen). Like bacteria, fungi perform a useful function in breaking down dead organic matter.

C. B. Frith/Bruce Coleman

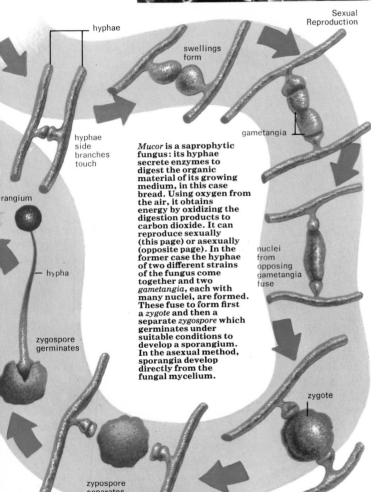

hyphae

Sexual
Reproduction

swellings
form

hyphae
side
branches
touch

gametangia

Mucor is a saprophytic fungus: its hyphae secrete enzymes to digest the organic material of its growing medium, in this case bread. Using oxygen from the air, it obtains energy by oxidizing the digestion products to carbon dioxide. It can reproduce sexually (this page) or asexually (opposite page). In the former case the hyphae of two different strains of the fungus come together and two *gametangia*, each with many nuclei, are formed. These fuse to form first a *zygote* and then a separate *zygospore* which germinates under suitable conditions to develop a sporangium. In the asexual method, sporangia develop directly from the fungal mycelium.

nuclei from opposing gametangia fuse

rangium

hypha

zygospore germinates

zygote

zypospore separates

Dr. Gordon Leedale/Biophoto Associates

Left: Fungi of the genus *Penicillium* are common on all kinds of decaying animal and plant remains. Seen here (stained blue) is *Penicillium notatum*, the species which is used commercially to produce the well known penicillin antibiotics. At the tips of the branching hyphae can be seen the *conidia*, which eventually split off and grow into new fungi. Reproduction is always asexual.

Right: Colonies of a bacterium which contains a red pigment when alive. *Penicillium* has been introduced at the centre of the dish: the penicillin it produces kills the bacteria in the central colonies. The outlying colonies are unaffected.

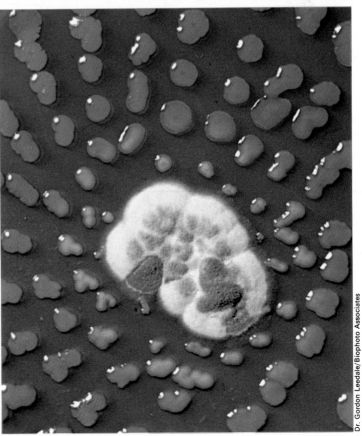

Dr. Gordon Leedale/Biophoto Associates

Dr. Gordon Leedale/Biophoto Associates

25

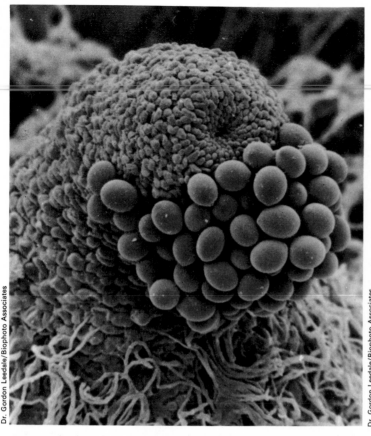

Above: A clump of ascospores on the fruiting body of *Sordaria macrospora*, an ascomycetous fungus. Fungi belonging to the genus *Sordaria* are often **found on the dung of plant-eating animals for their ascospores will only germinate readily after passing through the gut of an animal.**

Above right: The spore-bearing structure of *Aspergillus niger*, an ascomycetous fungus common in most soils. The spores (conidia) are carried at the ends **of the radiating branches. This picture and the one above left were taken with a SEM at magnifications of about 1,800 and 360 respectively.**

suitable soil conditions, it germinates to produce zoospores which infect new seedlings.

Among other common phycomycetous fungi are the pin-moulds, such as *Mucor*, the downy mildews, such as *Peronospora*, and the parasitic fungus *Phytophthora*, which is responsible for potato blight, perhaps the most notorious of all plant diseases.

Potato blight

Phytophthora is similar to *Pythium* but is less dependent on moisture. It was introduced into Europe in about 1840 from South America, the original home of the potato, and in the succeeding five or six years spread over the entire continent, including the British Isles.

Whereas the South American native potatoes were resistant to the disease, breeding of the potato in Europe, aimed at giving higher yields, had resulted in loss of resistance in the European varieties. From the appearance of the first few dark green blotches on the leaves of a single susceptible European potato to the time when whole fields were reduced to a blackened mass of rotting vegetation was only a matter of days.

As a direct result of the potato famine, the population of Ireland was reduced from eight million in 1845 to six million a decade later. Many people died and many more were forced to emigrate, mostly to the US. Apart from the direct human suffering, the reduction of the working population was on a scale that no country could afford, and it had long-term economic and political consequences. Fortunately, fungicides are now available to combat potato blight.

Ascomycetes

Ascomycetes and Basidiomycetes, the remaining two groups of the true fungi, are typical land creatures. They can grow and reproduce in the most exposed situations, like the tops of tall trees and the surfaces of rocks. In neither of these two groups is there any free-swimming stage in the life-cycle and the mycelium itself, perhaps from the unique construction of its cell walls, is much better able to resist dry conditions.

Ascomycetes are mostly saprophytic, but an interesting parasitic species is *Taphrina deformans*. This fungus causes the well-known leaf-curl disease of peaches, apricots and almonds. Leaves of peach trees permeated by the mycelium of *Taphrina* swell up and become discoloured and twisted in much the same way as the 'warts' on the potato caused by *Synchytrium*. If examined carefully, the leaves seem to be dusted with a white powder. This discolouration is caused by special spore-containing sacs which protrude through the skin of the leaf. Each of these sacs is a short cylindrical cell, the ascus, formed by the fusion of two cells of the mycelium in much the same way as the sexually produced spore of *Pythium*.

Within the young ascus the male and female nuclei first fuse and then immediately divide again to produce uninucleate spores. When the spores are ripe, pressure generated in the ascus causes it to burst, ejecting the spores. These are then carried by the wind and, if they happen to come to rest on the developing bud of a peach tree, they become trapped between the growing bud-scales where they remain until the spring. They

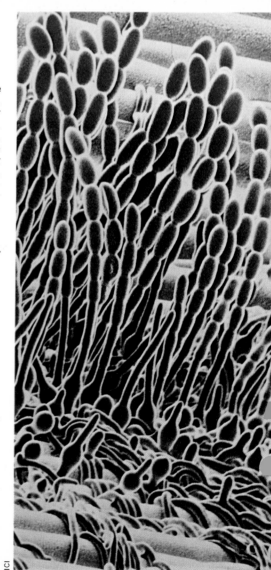

BUDDING OF YEAST

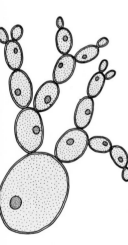

Above: Commonly called yeasts, the members of the genus *Saccharomyces* are among the most important fungi from a commercial point of view. They are used in both the baking and the brewing industries. By the process known as *alcoholic fermentation* yeast converts sugar into carbon dioxide and alcohol in the absence of oxygen. As shown here, yeasts reproduce by *budding*. A constriction forms in the parent cell, a nucleus moves into the bud and the constriction closes. Sometimes the buds do not separate from the parent cell, so large branching colonies develop.

Left: Powdery mildews can cause considerable damage to crops like wheat and barley. They get their name from their appearance on the surface of the host plant. This SEM picture shows a powdery mildew growing on barley— the hyphae and conidia are clearly visible.

Right: The toadstool-like fruiting body of the ascomycetous fungus *Helvella crispa*. The asci are formed in the 'head' of the fungus.

Above: Regarded as a great delicacy, the Périgord truffle, *Tuber melanosporum*, is found in parts of France. It is the fruiting body of an ascomycetous fungus which develops underground in association with the roots of oak trees. Having a strong and distinctive smell, truffles are often sniffed out by specially trained dogs or pigs. Another much sought after truffle is the white truffle, *Tuber magnatum*, from Piedmont in Italy.

germinate as soon as the peach bud begins to burst, and as the young leaves escape from the bud, the germ-tube of the spore enters the leaf and a new infection begins. This method of reproduction necessitates the production of thousands of spores since most of them fail to reach a developing peach and are wasted. Nevertheless it eliminates the need for free water.

Ascomycetes of the genus *Penicillium* are very common on all kinds of decaying animal and vegetable remains. *Penicillium glaucum* is a green mould frequently found growing in these situations. The green colour is not due to chlorophyll, which no fungus contains, but to a non-photosynthetic pigment. *Penicillium glaucum* produces millions of asexual spores, called *conidia*, on special upright hyphae. The tips of these hyphae are repeatedly forked, each final branch ending in a bottle-shaped, spore-bearing cell. The spores emerge in a long chain from the neck of each bottle, so that the whole conidium-producing structure looks like a minute paint brush. Conidia are detached by the wind or other agency and spread all over the Earth's surface and even up into the stratosphere.

On particularly nutritious substrates, *Penicillium glaucum* reproduces sexually as well. A special thin and flexible male hypha grows spirally round a thick female branch. Then a small hole develops in the cell walls at the point of contact of the two. The contents of the male hypha pass into the female, leaving the male as an empty shell. The male and female nuclei move towards each other, but do not immediately fuse. The fertilized female cell then begins to branch and divide and eventually a small knot of cells is formed. In the centre of this knot the asci develop, and at once the descendants of the paired nuclei fuse. The double nucleus immediately divides again to produce *ascospores*, which are spherical with thin flanges around them, reminiscent of the planet Saturn with its rings. If an ascospore encounters suitable conditions it germinates to produce a mycelium with slightly different properties from its parent, and so some variation is maintained within the species.

Many other species of Ascomycetes, however, including most of the penicillia, have lost their ability to reproduce sexually, or do so so rarely that it has never been observed. Some such fungi are used in industrial processes. One of them, *Fusarium graminiarum*, is grown for its high protein content and is used as an additive to human and animal foods —the fibrous texture of the mycelium makes it more acceptable as a human food than other vegetable proteins made from bacteria or soya meal. Another, *Saccharomyces cerevisiae*, is the well-known yeast used in the baking and brewing industries.

One interesting process is concerned with recycling. An enzyme produced by *Trichoderma viride*, another asexual fungus, breaks down cellulose into its constituent glucose molecules. It has been shown that in this way a very high yield of sugar can be obtained from old newspapers. The printing ink and other impurities are not acted upon by the enzyme and are left behind as a black sludge in the bottom of the tank, and the rich syrup can be used without further purification.

27

Giuseppe Mazza

Dr. Gordon Leedale/Biophoto Associates

Fungi—II

The mushrooms which are sold in markets belong to the group *Basidiomycetes*, generally regarded as the most complex and therefore the most advanced group of fungi. Many Basidiomycetes are large organisms, and cannot easily be called 'microbes' as are other fungi. Nevertheless, however large and complicated their fruiting structures may be, the majority of the fungus is hidden from view in the form of a *mycelium*, permeating the substance on which it lives and behaving in much the same way as other micro-organisms. The mycelium consists of a network of narrow, tubular branches called *hyphae*.

The common mushroom

The mycelium of the common edible mushroom is grown commercially under carefully controlled conditions in beds of horse manure covered with a top layer of soil. A freshly prepared bed of partially rotted manure is 'seeded' with tiny pieces of mycelium grown in the laboratory. If conditions are exactly right, the mycelium spreads rapidly and soon permeates the whole bed.

The mushrooms develop from tiny knots of mycelium under the soil. As the hyphae which make up the knot continue to grow and branch they begin to arrange themselves in a way which corresponds to the arrangement of the tissues in the mature mushroom—they grow vertically in the part which will become the stalk, radiate outwards and downwards in what is to become the cap, and so on.

Still nourished and supplied with water by the myriad hyphae in the bed, the stalk rapidly lengthens, pushing through the soil, and the cap expands. This causes the protective skin or 'veil', which in the 'button' mushroom joins the edge of the cap to the stem, to split and remain as a delicate ring around the middle of the stem. The splitting of the veil reveals the pink 'gills' of the fungus. These are closely packed, evenly spaced, radiating plates which hang down under the cap. They are called gills because they look rather like the gills of fishes. They do not, however, take any special part in respiration: they are the spore-producing organs of the fungus.

Although no longer protected by the veil, the gills are still sheltered from the worst of the elements by the cap. The flat surface of every gill is covered by a densely packed layer of cylindrical cells, the *basidia*, and from the free end of each basidium project two, small, pointed spore-stalks called *sterigmata*. The scientific name of the cultivated mushroom, *Agaricus bisporus*, records the fact that it is unusual in having only two sterigmata on each basidium: most Basidiomycetes have four.

A minute swelling on the tip of each sterigma rapidly enlarges to become a dark brown spore, and it is the presence of millions of spores which turns the gills of the fully grown mushroom from pink to brown. The mature spore is delicately and asymmetrically balanced on its sterigma, its rounded side turned away from the centre of the basidium and its flatter side facing inwards. On the flatter side, just above the point of

Heather Angel

J. Shaw/Bruce Coleman

Mary Evans

Above: One of the most colourful of all fungi is the fly agaric, *Amanita muscaria*. Although poisonous, it is not normally fatal and has been used as a hallucinogenic drug.

Left: In the folklore of many countries, toadstools are associated with fairies. This connection with the supernatural may have arisen from the toadstool's sudden overnight appearance in the fields and woods, or perhaps it stemmed from the effects of eating certain species.

Right: A drop of water sends a puff of dry, powdery spores shooting from a relative of the puffballs, the earth-star, *Gaestrum triplex*. It often grows in beech woods.

Below: Stages in the growth of the deadly death cap toadstool, *Amanita phalloides*. Like its cousin, the fly agaric, it is at first completely enclosed in a 'veil'. As the toadstool grows, the veil splits and the cap separates from the stalk, leaving behind a prominent ring. This toadstool's poison is highly toxic, causing a coma, paralysis and ultimately death. Although antidotes are known, they are virtually useless because the symptoms of poisoning do not appear until about 12 hours after the the fungus has been eaten. It is then too late for treatment.

GROWTH OF DEATH CAP TOADSTOOL

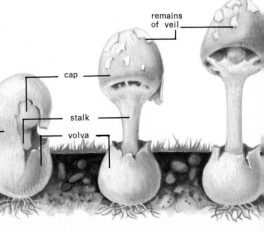

remains of veil

cap

stalk

veil

volva

28

Above left: A toadstool from North America belonging to the genus *Tricholoma*. Other species of this genus are common in Britain.

Above: This fungus, *Laccaria amethystea*, is fairly common in British woodlands—even its mycelium is lilac. The colour fades when the fungus dries.

Below: *Mutinus caninus*, the dog stinkhorn, is found among the dead leaves and treestumps of woodland habitats in the summer and autumn. The spores of the fungus are contained in a green mucus which covers the cap. As its name suggests, it has a distinct and unpleasant odour, though this is much less pronounced than that of its relative, the common stinkhorn, *Phallus impudicus*. The smell, reminiscent of rotting flesh, performs an important function for it attracts flies to the fungus. The insects feed on the spore-bearing mucus, and so the stinkhorn's spores are spread over the surrounding area.

Heather Angel

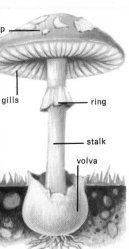

ap

gills

ring

stalk

volva

Yves Lanceau

Dr. Gordon Leedale/Biophoto Associates

attachment to the basidium, a swelling develops. This is actually a bubble formed between two layers of the wall of the spore. The bubble grows and finally bursts, propelling the spore a short distance away from the basidium. In the space between the gill on which it grew and the adjacent gill, it falls under the influence of gravity, until, emerging from between the gills, it is wafted away by air currents.

In order to achieve discharge by this method, the spore is precisely balanced on the sterigma so as to fly directly at right angles to the surface of the gill without hitting neighbouring spores. The quantity of energy released when the bubble bursts is exactly enough to carry the spore clear of the gill but not so much as to make it crash into the gill on the opposite side: if the spore touches any object it will stick to it instantly.

For the same reason the gills are absolutely vertical so the spores can fall freely down the narrow gap between them, and they are able to regain their vertical position when the cap moves slightly through growth or drying, or to compensate for movements of the soil. In spite of these remarkable abilities, the mushroom is by no means the most complex example of the kind of precision and elaboration that the Basidiomycetes can achieve.

Other Basidiomycetes

There are thousands of species of toadstools and they grow throughout the world wherever conditions are moist enough, for a few days, to allow their delicate fruit-bodies to grow and discharge their spores. Because of their numbers and their variety they must be regarded as biologically successful, but they suffer the disadvantage that water must always be abundant at the time when they operate their delicate spore-discharge mechanism. So, although successful, they are 'slaves' to the very delicacy of this mechanism.

The larger Basidiomycetes form quite a significant part of man's environment. In autumn, the woods smell of fungi and a glance around is usually sufficient to see how numerous they are in terms of both species and individuals. Each species plays its own role in the economy of nature. Many are saprophytes, playing a particularly important role in breaking down decaying leaf litter and wood. Many others form mutually beneficial associations with the roots of trees. Yet others are specialized parasites of trees.

Among these last, the 'bracket fungi' are specially interesting in that they have been able to conquer the problems of exposure attendant upon life in a tree-top. Their fruit-bodies are basically the same as in the mushroom, with the same spore discharge mechanism, but instead of having a stalk, bracket fungi grow directly out of the side of the branch of a tree like a wall-bracket. Instead of being borne on gills, the basidia line the insides of thousands of tiny pores on the underside of the fruit-body. Like their hosts, the trees, these fruit-bodies are woody, some of them being extremely hard. In addition to the usual thin, delicate hyphae, they contain specially toughened, thick-walled ones. They do not produce all their spores at once and then die as do the toadstools, but instead the bracket fungi discharge their spores a few at a time, in moist weather, and the

29

fruit-body lives for several months or even years.

One way of overcoming the need for constant supplies of water is seen in the puffballs and earth-stars. These fungi produce their spores on a basidium, but when they are ripe the basidia simply collapse leaving the dry outer sac full of loose spores like a pot of pepper. When a raindrop strikes the sac, it makes a small depression and a puff of spores is expelled through a small hole in the top of the fruit-body. The wall of the sac is non-absorbent and elastic so that the rain-drop simply bounces off and the sac regains its former shape, awaiting the next raindrop. The fruit-body persists on the ground for many months, releasing some of its spores every time there is a shower of rain.

The fungus with the largest fruit-body known also belongs to this group. The giant puffball, *Lycoperdon giganteum*, grows in gardens and pastures in northern temperate countries, including Britain, and may reach nearly 2 m (6.5 ft) in diameter: it is often mistaken, from a distance, for a recumbent sheep. Even a relatively small one will contain thousands of millions of spores which are dispersed by the wind through rents in the outer sac.

Fairy rings
Because of their method of growth, wild toadstools often produce the 'fairy rings' which are seen on lawns and playing fields. A young mycelium establishes itself from germinating spores and in season duly produces a crop of toadstools. These soon shed their spores and die, but the mycelium continues to grow until it has exhausted the nutrients in that patch of turf. It is then forced to spread outward while the original part of the mycelium dies.

As the dead mycelium is decomposed by other saprophytes, its accumulated supply of nutrients is released into the soil, stimulating the turf into lush, dark green growth. The following year, the crop of toadstools is produced in a ring,

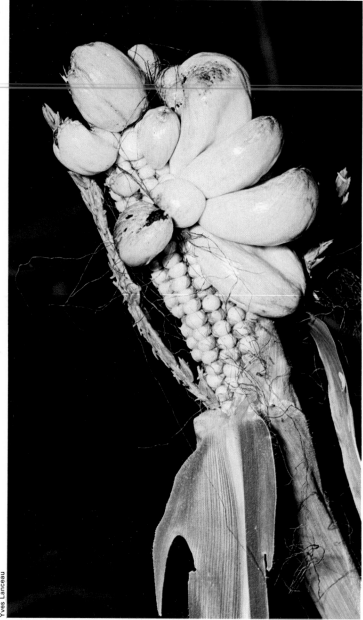

Yves Lanceau

Above: Spore cases (sporangia) of the slime mould *Trichia decipiens* magnified about 30 times. Slime moulds are strange creatures which combine characteristics of animals and plants. Although they produce spores, like a fungus, they spend much of their lives in amoeba-like form, creeping over plants and soil.

Heather Angel

Left: This photograph shows the broad, widely spaced gills of the fungus, *Oudemansiella mucida*, often called 'beech tuft'. It is a saprophytic fungus which grows from the trunk and branches of beech trees, and it is most often found in the autumn. It is pure white and covered with a sticky mucus.

Above: These pale blue galls growing on a cob of corn (maize) are caused by corn smut, *Ustilago maydis*, a parasitic fungus. Smut diseases are of considerable economic importance for they attack the cereal crops, such as wheat, barley and oats, which provide more than 50 per cent of all food eaten by man.

Below: A selection of British grassland and woodland fungi. One of the most distinctive is the shaggy ink cap, which is good to eat when young. Oak trees (far right) act as hosts to several species of parasitic bracket fungi. Perhaps the most striking, though only short-lived, is the 'beefsteak' fungus.

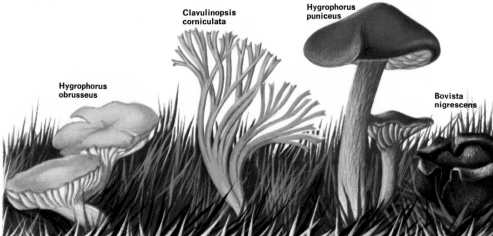

Hygrophorus obrusseus

Clavulinopsis corniculata

Hygrophorus puniceus

Bovista nigrescens

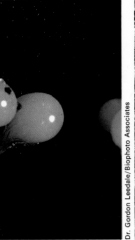

Below: This odd-looking fungus, *Anthurus archeri*, is common in Australia and New Zealand, and it has been introduced to several localities in Europe. At first the arms are joined at their tips, but they separate as the fungus grows. Clearly visible in this picture are the dark green patches of mucus which carry the spores.

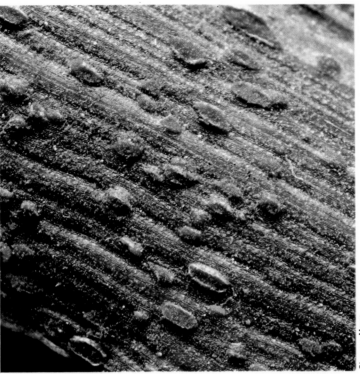

Above: Patches of rust, *Puccinia graminis*, on a wheat plant. This parasite can cause serious reductions in crop yields. In 1954, for example, about 70 per cent of the durum wheat crop in Minnesota and the Dakotas was lost as a direct result of rust infection. Fungi are responsible for more plant diseases than any other group of organisms. Among the most important of these are rust, smut, potato blight, ergot (a disease of cereal crops) and Dutch elm disease. In the 1970s thousands of British trees were infected and killed by the last of these. Its spores are spread by a beetle which bores under the bark of the trees.

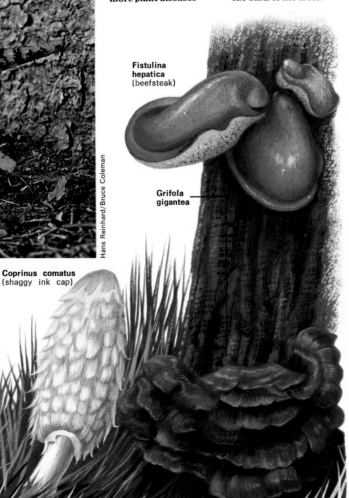

Fistulina hepatica (beefsteak)

Grifola gigantea

Coprinus comatus (shaggy ink cap)

Agaricus campestris (field mushroom)

where the hyphae are actually growing, around the original patch. The new hyphae compete with the turf for minerals and water and they compact the soil so that the grass roots cannot breathe. The grass in this zone dries up in the sun.

Rusts

Not all Basidiomycetes produce large fruit-bodies; an important group of them, the rusts, are highly specialized parasites of green plants. They are so called because of the little red-brown pustules of spores which they produce on the leaves of the plants they attack. Several kinds of rust attack wheat, and one of them, *Puccinia graminis*, has a particularly interesting life-cycle. The type of spore produced on the wheat plant just before harvest is called the *teliospore*. It is incapable of causing disease directly on another wheat plant; it can only infect the barberry plant.

On the barberry, the sexual stage of the fungus develops, eventually producing pustules of red-brown spores on the underside of the barberry leaf. These spores, the *aeciospores*, in their turn are unable to infect barberry. They can, however, grow upon wheat. Mycelium from these spores permeates the wheat tissues, boring into the cells with minute sucking organs. This of course deprives the grain of its nourishment, and the crop is reduced. The mycelium in the wheat produces two types of spore. The first, called *uredospores*, are round with a short stalk, and they burst in clusters through the skin of the leaf, like little flakes of rusty iron. The uredospores are capable of attacking other wheat plants and serve to spread the infection from one plant to its neighbours.

The second type of spore produced on the wheat plant is the teliospore, which of course, is capable of attacking only barberry. The teliospore is two-celled, with a short stalk and a thick wall. Because the wall is so thick, the spore is able to survive the winter and germinate in the spring, infecting a barberry plant and completing the life-cycle.

Slime moulds

The slime moulds, or *Myxomycetes*, form an entirely different group of fungi from the rest. They are probably not closely related to any of the others, and they have often been classified as animals, hence their alternative name *Mycetozoa* or 'fungus-animals'. Instead of possessing a mycelium they spend most of their lives as amoeba-like masses of protoplasm, creeping about the soil and over plants and ingesting other small creatures in just the same way as does an amoeba. At maturity, however, they become distinctly fungus-like, producing a fruit-body full of dry spores, like a small puff-ball.

In fact, the 'amoebae' which produce even a fairly small fruiting-body have to be quite large, and one species called 'flowers of tan' frequently causes some consternation to those who witness its fruiting, for its fruit-bodies are sometimes more than 10 cm (4 in) across.

Myxomycetes are easily grown in the laboratory and much of their interest lies in their use as 'laboratory animals' for they resemble the white blood corpuscles of animals, not only in their behaviour, but also in their reaction to various important chemicals.

Mosses and Liverworts

A major step in the evolutionary history of plants from aquatic green algae to the higher flowering plants was the colonization of the land. The exact stages by which this was achieved are not well understood, but a group of simple plants, the *Bryophyta*, which includes mosses, liverworts and hornworts, are probably representative of one stage in this development. In many respects the bryophytes are similar to many-celled algae (seaweeds), having a compact body many cells thick attached by a special structure, the *rhizoid*, (similar to the holdfast of seaweeds) to the underlying surface. Nevertheless, most bryophytes are true land plants. The body is surrounded by a layer of cells, the *epidermis*, which prevents the loss of water from the plant.

There are approximately 14,000 species of mosses and 9,000 species of liverworts. They are all small green plants, usually no more than a few centimetres long, with either a leafy stem, as in most mosses, or a flat, ribbon-like body, called a *thallus*, as in most liverworts. The body is anchored to the soil by the long, thread-like rhizoids.

Although to some extent the bryophytes have adapted to life on land they are still highly dependent on water. They generally have no specialized tissue for the transfer of water and nutrients and, because of this, must necessarily be small so that all parts of the plant are in close contact with water. Their reproduction is also highly dependent on water.

For these reasons the bryophytes are most abundant in, but not confined to, permanently moist places, such as bogs, damp woodlands and the edges of streams. They have their most luxuriant development in tropical climates. They may be found growing in soil, on the surface of other plants, on bare rock, in caves and on the roofs and sides of buildings. Only a few are aquatic and none are marine. One group, known as *copper mosses*, occur only on heavy metal deposits such as copper and antimony. Others occur only on dung.

Reproduction

Like most simple plants, bryophytes reproduce vegetatively by fragmentation —any severed part of the stem, leaf or rhizoid is capable of developing into a new plant. (One of the surest ways of spreading troublesome moss on a lawn is by trying to remove it by raking.) Alternatively they reproduce asexually by special structures, called *gemmae*, which appear on the upper surface of the body. Each gemma, about the size of a pinhead, grows on a small stalk and may be broken off by a small animal or by the wind. If it is carried to a suitably moist environment it will grow into a new plant.

More elaborately, the bryophytes reproduce sexually. As in the more advanced algae and in the higher plants there is a distinct alternation of generations, with two generations of plant, the *sporophyte* and the *gametophyte*. Unlike the higher plants, however, in the bryophytes the gametophyte generation (which develops

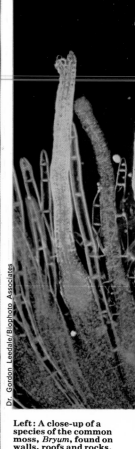

Dr. Gordon Leedale/Biophoto Associates

Jacana

Left: A close-up of a species of the common moss, *Bryum*, found on walls, roofs and rocks. The mosses are the major class of a group of primitive land plants, the *bryophytes*.

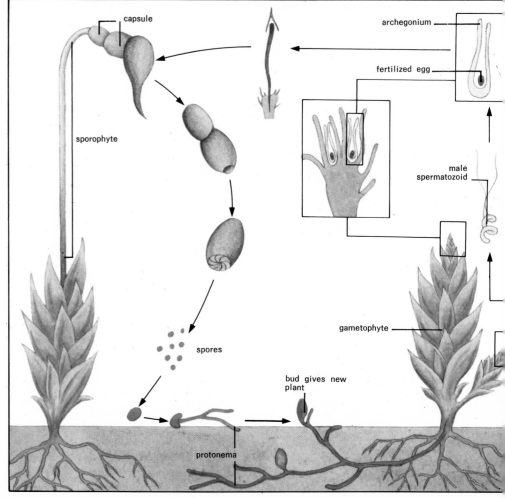

capsule

sporophyte

archegonium

fertilized egg

male spermatozoid

gametophyte

spores

bud gives new plant

protonema

Left: Female sex organs (*archegonia*) of a moss. The older archegonia are open at the top showing the channel down which the sperms swim to fertilize the eggs at the bottom. Among the archegonia are protective 'hairs', the *paraphyses*.

Right: Two kinds of bog moss, *Sphagnum rubellum* (red) and *Sphagnum recurvum* (green). Bog mosses are perhaps more important than all other bryophytes. Starting at the water line they spread by branching and vegetative reproduction to cover completely a stretch of water. In time the resulting bog fills in—gradually converting open water into rich soil composed of the decaying remains of the moss.

Right: Peat cutting in Donegal, Ireland. Mosses and liverworts are generally of little use to man. Peat, widely used as a fuel source, is a notable exception.

Below: Life history of a moss, showing the two different generations, the *gametophyte* and the *sporophyte*. The gametophyte produces green 'leaves' and both male (*antheridia*) and female (*archegonia*) sex organs. The male gametes swim to the archegonia to fertilize the eggs. The parasitic sporophyte which then develops eventually produces spores which each give a new moss plant from a simple vegetative plant, the *protonema*, which is a green filament when above the ground.

Right: A true Alaskan moss, *Splaknum leteum*. Another northern 'moss', reindeer moss (*Cladonia rangiferina*) is in fact not a moss at all but a lichen.

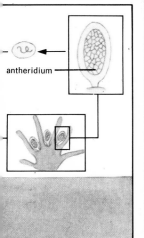

antheridium

from asexual spores) is dominant and the sporophyte generation (which develops from a *zygote* after the fusion of sex cells or gametes) is reduced. In this way the bryophytes resemble simple green algae, such as *Spirogyra* and *Chlamydomonas*.

Liverworts

The body (*thallus*) of some of the liverworts (*Hepaticae*) is short and looks like a lobed liver—hence the name for this class of plants. More often it is a regularly branching structure; the form and degree of branching varying as does the complexity of the thallus. In the more complex liverworts, such as *Marchantia*, there are air pores leading inside the body to air chambers where there are photosynthetic filaments and food storage tissue.

The sex organs are either on the upper surface of the thallus or, as in *Marchantia*, on special branches. When they are on the thallus surface, the male organs (*antheridia*) are spaced along the sides of a ridge, running the length of the thallus, while the female organs (*archegonia*) are on a slope facing the growing point at the tips of the thallus. Each antheridium is enclosed in a flask-like sheath with a narrow opening which, when mature, opens liberating the male gametes (*spermatozoids*) which are often spirally coiled cells with two long threads or flagella.

They are attracted by a chemical—the exact nature of which is unknown—which is secreted by the female archegonia and they use their flagella to swim towards this secretion. To reproduce successfully, therefore, the plant body must be covered in a water film; otherwise the spermatozoids are unable to swim to the archegonia.

Each archegonium is shaped like a long-necked jar. The lower part encloses the egg and is called the *venter*, the upper part is a long tube, filled with mucilage, and the spermatozoids swim into this, uniting with the egg. The fertilized egg, the *zygote*, is the first cell of the sporophyte generation. Of all the egg cells in each archegonium which may have been fertilized only one develops, probably because the first one fertilized monopolises all the available food.

The young sporophyte consists of three parts. First there is the foot, shaped like an arrowhead and pushed well into the archegonium for anchorage. Then there is a short stalk, the *seta*, and finally attached to this the *capsule* or *sporangium*. The capsule is normally spherical with a wall several layers thick enclosing the spores. When mature, the capsule bursts releasing the spores.

Mosses

Mosses (*Musci*), unlike the liverworts, all grow vertically. The slender stem may be branched or unbranched but is never more than 3 cm (1.2 in) tall and is anchored by rhizoids to the ground. The small thin leaves (often only one cell thick) are positioned spirally around the stem.

The sex organs are produced at the ends of the main stem or branches and are protected by small leaves and narrow filaments called *paraphyses*. The antheridia, unlike those of the liverworts, are not protected in flasks but stand on short stems while the archegonia, also borne on stalks, have a rather thicker venter than in the liverworts. When the spermatozoids are released the splash of raindrops helps

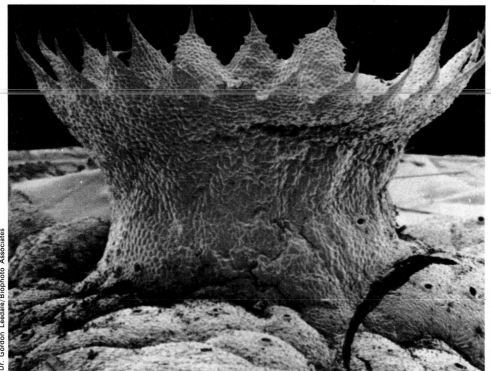

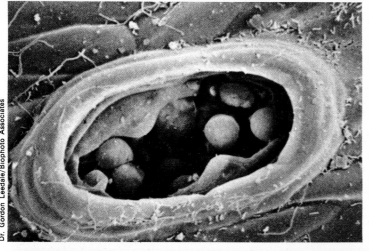

Above: An asexual reproductive structure, the *gemma cup*, seen on the surface of a liverwort (about 200 times life size).

Left: An air pore on the surface of the complex liverwort, *Marchantia polymorpha* (about 2000 times life size). Inside can be seen the tips of photosynthetic tissue. The white dots and lines on the surface are bacteria. The pores of liverworts cannot open and close, unlike the stomata of higher plants and hornworts which shut during times of water shortage.

Below: *Marchantia polymorpha*, common in marshy places. The parasol-like structures are the archegonia, the female sex organs.

to disperse them. Any deposited near the head of a female branch are lured to the neck of an archegonium by a chemical, in this case the sugar *sucrose*. As in the liverworts, the spermatozoids swim towards the secretion by means of thread-like flagella.

Fertilization once again results in a sporophyte with three parts, a capsule, seta and foot. The capsule, however, is a more complex structure than that of the liverworts. Only the upper part is fertile, the lower part is green and synthesizes some of its own food—the sporophyte of liverworts is completely parasitic on the gametophyte. The top half (containing the spores) is a large cavity through which extends a cylinder of tissue, the *columella*. Finally the top of the capsule is closed by a lid.

As soon as the spores are ripe, the capsule begins to dry up and the columella collapses, so the capsule consists finally of only the outside wall and a mass of dark green spores. The lid becomes detached and falls off but the spores cannot freely escape as a double row of 'teeth', the *peristome*, forms from strips of thickened cell-wall. These 'teeth' close over the opening when the air is wet but bend back when the air is dry, allowing the spores to be shaken out by the wind in dry weather when they are most likely to be widely dispersed.

If the spores land on a suitable damp place they germinate to produce a simple plant body called the *protonema*. This may form an extensive green felt, occasionally several square centimetres in size, before it buds to produce the normal leafy stem of mosses. The protonema, like the leafy stem, is the dominant gametophyte generation.

Hornworts

The hornworts (*Anthocerotae*) have a thalloid body similar to the liverworts but are distinguished from them by their capsules which are cylindrical, about 2.5 cm (1 in) long, rather than spherical. When ripe the capsules split from the tip downwards into two halves. Between the two halves is a supporting pillar, the *columella*, similar to that found in the capsule of mosses. In addition the capsules of hornworts have pores, *stomata*, which, unlike those in the liverworts, can open and close and are the same as those in flowering plants.

Economic importance

Mosses and liverworts are of little direct economic importance to man. The bog moss, *Sphagnum*, is used as a soil conditioner or as a lining for hanging baskets because of its water absorbent qualities. For the same reason, it was used as late as the First World War as a wound dressing. *Sphagnum* grows in bogs where acidic conditions and low oxygen availability decreases the rate with which bacteria and fungi can decompose the dead remains. As the remains accumulate they become compacted, forming *peat* which is used as a fuel in some countries.

Occasionally peat is used as a building material. Traditionally, poorer people in many parts of the world have also used some of the larger 'hair' mosses, *Polytrichum*, to make brushes, brooms and lamp wicks. The greatest importance of bryophytes, however, is their ability to grow on bare rock and begin the formation of soil in which all major plant types grow.

PHOTOSYNTHESIS

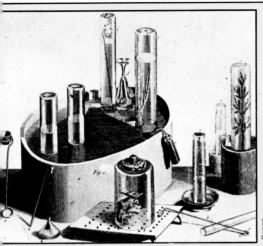

Above: Apparatus used by Joseph Priestley in his experiments on air.

Below: How light energy is trapped by chlorophyll. A bundle of light energy (a *quantum*) excites an electron of an atom in the chlorophyll molecule by pushing it into an outer orbit. Some of the energy given off as the electron returns to its normal state is used to produce the reactive chemicals which the plant uses to convert carbon dioxide into carbohydrate.

Right: Oxygen being given off by a water plant.

Just by being alive all living things continuously use up energy in the process known as *respiration*. The original source of this energy is sunlight. Green plants alone can trap sunlight and convert it into the complex organic compounds from which plant bodies are constructed and which, when eaten, form the food of animals.

The raw materials used by a plant to manufacture its body are carbon dioxide from the atmosphere and water and inorganic chemicals, such as nitrate, from the soil. These are converted into the plant body by a two stage process which is called *photosynthesis*. In the first stage carbon dioxide and water are converted by light energy into carbohydrates and oxygen; in the second stage the carbohydrates are combined with each other and with inorganic chemicals, such as nitrate and phosphate, to form the proteins, fats, oils and nucleic acids of which the plant body is formed.

Photosynthesis takes place mostly in the *mesophyll* cells of leaves. These cells, which are covered with a thin film of water, form the bulk of the leaf, but between them are numerous intercellular spaces which connect with the outside through pores, the *stomata*. Carbon dioxide diffuses through the stomata into the intercellular spaces, dissolves in the film of water, and diffuses in solution into the mesophyll cells. Oxygen leaves by the same route in reverse. Light is trapped by the green pigment, *chlorophyll*, which is contained within the cells in disc-shaped organelles called *chloroplasts*.

During the middle of the day, plants' consumption of oxygen and production of carbon dioxide by respiration is hidden by the much greater amounts of oxygen produced and carbon dioxide consumed by photosynthesis. As far as the individual plant is concerned oxygen is produced largely as a by-product. Nevertheless this oxygen replaces that removed from the atmosphere by animals. Without it all animal life would cease.

Different kinds of photosynthesis

Photosynthesis is often described in simple terms which make it appear that all plants photosynthesize in the same way. But it is now known that different plants have different kinds of photosynthesis which are adaptations to the environments in which they live. A large number of plants growing in dry tropical environments, including such important crops as maize, *Zea mays*, and sugar cane, *Saccharum officinarum*, have a special kind of photosynthesis using different chemical reactions which allows them to grow faster at higher temperatures.

Research into photosynthesis

Early experiments on photosynthesis were conducted by the English scientist Joseph Priestley (1733-1804). He took a closed jar, burnt a candle in it, and showed that a mouse would die if placed in the exhausted air. However a green plant could still live in this air, and after a few weeks the air was renewed by the plant so that a mouse could again breathe and a candle again burn in it. Priestley's experiments clearly showed the way in which respiration or combustion remove oxygen from air and photosynthesis replaces it. In the twentieth century, the American, Melvin Calvin, was awarded the 1961 Nobel Prize for Chemistry for working out the complex series of chemical reactions, often called the *Calvin cycle*, by which carbon dioxide is incorporated into glucose and other carbohydrates during photosynthesis.

quantum of light

heat energy

higher energy level

light energy

electrical energy

chemical energy

electron

lower energy level

nucleus of atom

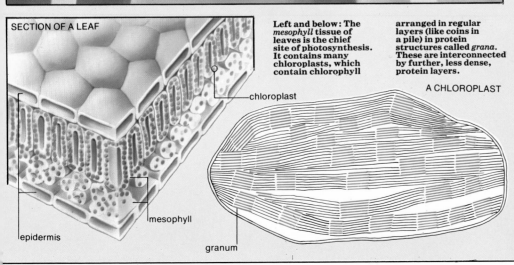

SECTION OF A LEAF

Left and below: The *mesophyll* tissue of leaves is the chief site of photosynthesis. It contains many chloroplasts, which contain chlorophyll arranged in regular layers (like coins in a pile) in protein structures called *grana*. These are interconnected by further, less dense, protein layers.

A CHLOROPLAST

chloroplast

mesophyll

epidermis

granum

Ferns, Horsetails and Clubmosses

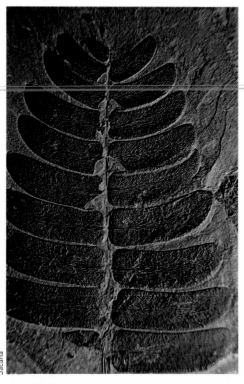

As early plants colonized the land, they evolved several features not found in mosses and algae. These features include an outer layer of cells impervious to water (the *cuticle*) and specialized tissue for conducting water and food between the water-absorbing organs, the roots, and the food-producing organs, the leaves.

The first group of plants to develop these features were the *Pteridophyta*: the ferns, clubmosses and horsetails. Though now of minor significance, as the first successful colonizers of the land they were a dominant group of plants for some 100 million years; from their appearance about 350 million years ago to the development of the advanced seed plants of the present day. Particularly in the Carboniferous period (280-345 million years ago) they were extremely abundant, and they grew luxuriantly into many forms in extensive forests. The carbonized remains of these tree ferns contributed to the formation of coal.

Structure

Ferns, *Filicinae*, have leaves, a stem and roots. Of these the leaves are generally the most conspicuous part of the fern. The basic plan of a mature leaf is a central axis, or *midrib*, with smaller side branches. This type of leaf form is called *pinnate* and is common to almost

Above: A fossil 'fern' leaf. The difficulty of correctly classifying a fossil leaf or stem meant that until 1903 fossil fern-like leaves were wrongly identified as ferns. A large number, however, like *Linopteris* shown here, are not ferns but seed-bearing plants of the extinct group, *Pteridospermae*.

Below: Tree ferns growing at 1,200 m (4,000 ft) in the mountains of Malaysia. Tree ferns have erect, unbranched stems with a crown of palm-like leaves growing from the top. The stems are unlike those of other trees —they have no bark and no secondary wood laid down in annual growth rings beneath the bark.

all ferns, though a few, such as *Ophio-glossum*, have simple or lobed leaves. A large pinnate leaf is called a frond. The fronds of some species, such as *Cyathea*, commonly grown in conservatories, may reach over 5 m (16 ft) long and 1 m (3 ft) wide.

Fern stems vary from the tall trunks of tree ferns that may be over 70 m (230 ft) tall, down to short, 5 cm (2 in) stems growing horizontally underground like the stems of an iris. Such stems are called *rhizomes*. Although the rhizome is the most common stem form, many ferns are vine-like, shrub-like or tree-like. In the tree ferns the leaves grow directly from the stem and die away leaving leaf bases which help protect the stem and give the surface of tree ferns such characteristic features. In addition to the leaf bases the stems are covered in hairs or scales. These are called *ramenta* and are generally tan or brown in colour.

Internally the stem contains specialized water-conducting tissue (*vascular tissue* or *xylem*) which forms *wood*—a characteristic of higher plants. The wood is arranged in strands like those in a young flowering plant, but in the ferns these interconnect to form a lattice pattern. No *secondary growth* (growth of wood mainly for structural support) occurs, so heavy, strong, wooded trunks are not found in fern trees. Instead fern trees are supported by the thick leaf bases and the high buttressing roots which grow out from the stem above ground level.

The roots of ferns all grow out directly from the stem—that is they are *adventitious*. Otherwise they are similar to the roots of flowering plants. They have

central wood for conducting water, and root hairs, when young, for absorbing water. They do not, however, grow in thickness as they grow older.

Life-cycle and ecology

As with the mosses and liverworts, ferns and their allies have a life-cycle with two generations—the *gametophyte*, which is a sexual phase producing gametes, and the *sporophyte*, which is an asexual phase producing spores. The spores germinate to give the gametophyte generation again. In mosses the dominant phase in the life-cycle is the gametophyte, for the sporophyte is parasitic upon the gametophyte throughout its life. But in the ferns the sporophyte is dominant, forming a fern plant with leaves, stem and roots. The gametophyte, by contrast, is tiny and almost never noticed.

In this respect ferns are similar to the flowering plants—in all advanced plants the sporophyte is dominant. Ferns differ from higher plants, however, in that they produce spores and not seeds and do not have flowers or flower-like structures.

In a typical fern, such as *Dryopteris intermedia*, the broad-leafed fern used in flower arrangements, the spore-producing organs, the *sporangia*, are positioned together in groups called *sori* on the underside of the leaf frond. Each sorus is sited on a swelling (the *placenta*) on a leaf vein, and out of the placenta grows a kidney-shaped structure, the *indusium*. The indusium covers the sporangia like an umbrella and protects them when young. Indusia are initially pale in colour but darken with age, conferring a rough brown appearance to the back of a frond.

Bruce Coleman

Left: A fern showing the *epiphytic* life style—using another plant (in this case a tree) for support. This fern, *Platycerium bisurcatum*, the staghorn fern of Australia, has large lobed leaves, in contrast to the leaves of most ferns which have a central midrib with side branches.

Above left: *Salvinia auriculata*, a water fern. Though most ferns are land plants, some, like *Salvinia*, have adapted to live in water. The leaves of *Salvinia* grow from an underwater rhizome and float on the water surface. On the undersurface (shown here) many small sporangia develop.

Below left and below: A young fern plant (sporophyte) developing from the gametophyte generation of the fern, the *prothallus*. The prothallus lies on the forest floor, anchored to the soil by root-like *rhizoids*. The sporophyte is at first parasitic upon the gametophyte and draws nourishment through its 'foot' which is deeply embedded into the prothallus. On producing leaves the sporophyte becomes independent of the prothallus which eventually dies.

Eric Crichton

Heather Angel

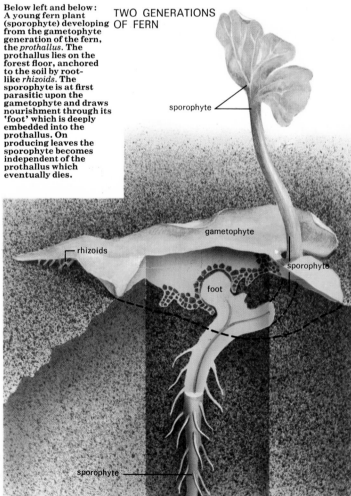

TWO GENERATIONS OF FERN

sporophyte

gametophyte

rhizoids

sporophyte

foot

sporophyte

Each sporangium consists of a long slender stalk ending in a spore case or *capsule* which is shaped rather like a watch case, and inside this the spores develop. Around the edge of the sporangium, starting from the stalk and extending over about three-quarters of the capsule, is a row of cells, the *annulus*, which have thickened inner walls. The rest of the capsule is formed of large thin-walled cells and is called the *stomium*.

This rather complex sporangium disperses its spores in an interesting way. By the time the sporangium is ripe the indusium covering it has withered so that it is freely exposed. The cells of the capsule now lose water by evaporation and the annulus begins to dry. As this continues the thin outer walls of the annulus cells are sucked inwards, becoming concave and trying to pull the sides of the cell in on itself. As all the cells of the annulus are trying to do this at the same time, but cannot since each is attached to its neighbour, a strain is set up in the capsule as a whole. The thin cells of the stomium are the weakest point and eventually they rupture. The capsule now curls back like an open watch. Finally, as even more water is lost, the inner walls of the annulus also rupture. Suddenly the bent, thick inner walls of the capsule are released from strain and the whole capsule springs back to its original position, catapulting spores into the air.

On germinating the spores produce the gametophyte generation, called the *prothallus*. In *Dryopteris*, this is a heart-shaped structure no more than 1 cm (0.4 in) long. It is very similar to the gametophyte of mosses. It has no true roots but is anchored to the soil by elongated single cells called *rhizoids*. There are also no woody cells in the gametophyte. Male sex organs, *antheridia*, are found on the underneath part of the prothallus and along its edges while the female organs, *archegonia*, are limited to the thicker end.

The antheridia are very simple, consisting of two ring-shaped cells, one above the other, and covered in at the top by a cell which forms a cap. Inside the antheridia are formed the male gametes (*spermatozoids*), small coiled cells possessing hair-like *flagella* used for swimming. When ripe the antheridia take up water and the increase in pressure bursts the cap, releasing the spermatozoids which swim towards the female archegonia, attracted by the secretion of a chemical, *malic acid*. When they reach the archegonia fertilization takes place, producing the first stage of the sporophyte.

The life-history of ferns, though more advanced than that of mosses—the sporophyte generation being dominant—still includes an independent gametophyte, whereas in the flowering plants the gametophyte is reduced to microscopic proportions and is completely dependent on the sporophyte. Moreover, fertilization in ferns relies on a free-swimming spermatozoid which must swim in a water film on the plant surface. Thus, though ferns were the first successful land plants and were once distributed over the majority of the land surface they are still dependent to a large extent on a moist environment.

This dependence on moisture explains both why they were superseded as the dominant vegetation by the higher plants and their present range of habitats. Their preferred environment in temperate

38

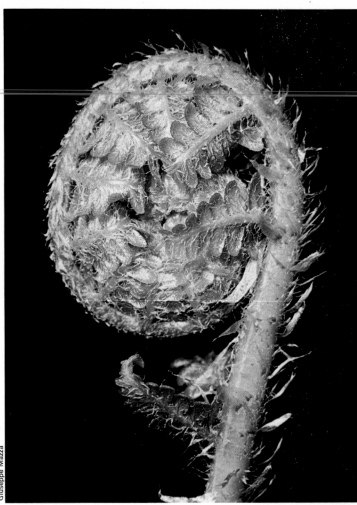

Giuseppe Mazza

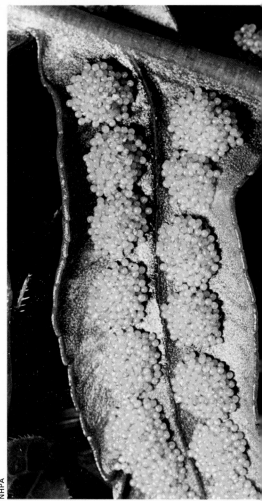

NHPA

Above: The lattice arrangement of the water-conducting tissue (*vascular tissue*) inside a fern stem. The leaf stalks grow out from the diamond-shaped spaces between the vascular tissue lattice. Vascular tissue is essential for successful land plants: it allows water to be transported from deep roots to the food-producing leaves.

Left: Young leaf of a fern unfurling. This way of folding the leaves is called *circinate vernation* and is common to all ferns except water ferns. When each leaf expands the inner side grows more rapidly than the outer, so that the curves straighten out as the leaf develops.

regions is a moist, cool, deeply shaded woodland with an abundance of leaf mould. Nevertheless, ferns may be found from Arctic regions to the hot, wet lowlands of equatorial jungles.

Clubmosses

The clubmosses (*Lycopsidae*) are a group of small herbaceous plants growing from rhizomes. In appearance they are small and moss-like, hence their name. They are relatively few in number—indeed only five genera exist today: *Lycopodium*, *Selaginella*, *Stylites*, *Isoetes* and *Phylloglossum*. In the past, however, tree forms were abundant in Carboniferous forests. *Lycopodium* is world-wide in distribution and occurs in almost all climates.

The life-history of clubmosses is very similar to that of the flowering plants, with two types of spores called *microspores* and *megaspores*. The microspores produce gametophytes bearing male sex organs and the megaspores produce gametophytes bearing female organs. The spermatozoids are produced from a few cells inside the microspore and are not released from the spore. They are thus analagous to the pollen of flowering plants. Unlike the flowering plants, however, the megaspores are shed on to the ground before they are fertilized. If the megaspore was not released but developed within the sporangia the lycopod life-history would resemble that of the flowering plants.

Horsetails

The final group of pteridophytes, the horsetails (*Sphenopsidae*), is a very ancient group but has now only one living genus, *Equisetum*, of 25 to 30 species. They are

Biophotos/Carolina Biological Supply Co

Below: The spore case (*capsule*) of a fern. It has been stained to show the spores inside (red), the cells of the *annulus* (left), with their thick inner and thinner outer walls, and the thinner-walled cells of the *stomium* (right).

Right: Catapult-like dispersal of fern spores. As the capsule dries it splits open and folds back. Further drying causes it to spring suddenly shut, throwing the spores into the air where they are caught by the wind.

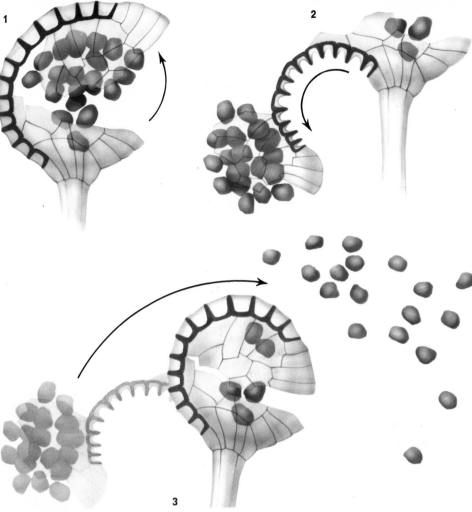

1

2

3

Bruce Coleman

Far left: Underside of the common fern, *Polypodium vulgare*, with its many sporangia clustered together in groups called *sori*.

Left: A species of horsetail (*Equisetum*). Often called a living fossil because of its relation to the giant horsetail, *Calamites*, of Carboniferous times,

the horsetail has its sporangia concentrated at the tip of the stem (the flower-like structure shown here) rather than on the underside of leaves as in ferns.

Below: *Equisetum telmateia*, widespread in Britain. The 'cones' at the end of the stems contain the sporangia.

strange-looking plants apparently with no leaves. In fact leaves are present but are scale-like and the manufacture of food that normally takes place in leaves occurs instead in the deeply ridged stem. Because of their scaly leaves the horsetails can be used as scouring pads—and are often referred to as 'scouring rushes'.

Ferns and man

Apart from their invaluable contribution to coal formation, ferns, past or present, are not of much use to man except for decoration. During the last century they were much in fashion and many species, native and exotic, were cultivated in gardens and conservatories. Among the best smaller houseplant ferns are the wood fern, *Nephrolepis*, with bushy rosettes of leaf fronds, the holly fern, *Cyrtomium*, which has rather glossy, leathery, dark leaves, and the leather fern, *Rumohra*, with its leathery, but lacy fronds. In additon to houseplants, most ferns are easy to grow in gardens, and have the advantage that they do well in shady areas where flowering plants would not thrive.

Other uses are few. The potting peat used in orchid potting is usually a mass of fibrous roots obtained from the cinnamon fern, while the trunks of the few remaining species of tree ferns are still used in the tropics for building purposes since they are resistant both to decay and to termite attack.

Nutritionally, ferns offer very little. In Hawaii the starchy pith of tree ferns is baked and eaten while in South America sugar is obtained from species of *Polypodium*. In some parts of the world young uncurled fern leaves are also eaten.

Biophotos/Carolina Biological Supply Co

Plant Partnerships

It is often accepted as the 'law of nature' that all living things live directly or indirectly by exploiting others. This is true of all life forms incapable of producing their own food from inorganic substances—that is, of everything except green plants. Nevertheless few plants live entirely independently; each forms part of a living community, the different organisms and species of which are interdependent on one another. The greatest degree of interdependence occurs when two plants of different species live attached to one another in an association known as *symbiosis* which is beneficial to both organisms. Symbiosis is the opposite of *parasitism* in which one partner benefits at the expense of the other.

Lichens

One very common group of plants has been used since the middle of the nineteenth century as an example of symbiosis. These are the *lichens*, the small grey, brown or sometimes brightly coloured plants which grow on walls, rocks and tree-trunks, often appearing as no more than a circular crust 1-2 cm across. Under the microscope a lichen can be seen to be two completely different types of plant—a fungus and an alga—living together in a close symbiotic relationship. The lichen consists of an interwoven network of fungal filaments (*hyphae*) packed together to form a *mycelium*. The mycelium has a number of distinct layers, in one of which, near the upper surface of the lichen, the hyphae are intermingled with cells of an alga which contain chlorophyll and can perform photosynthesis, in which the energy of sunlight is used to produce carbohydrate. Together the fungus and the alga form one unit, the *thallus* of the lichen.

The lichen fungus is usually a member of the group *Ascomycetes*, while the algal partner is most often a species of *Trebouxia*, a green alga, or *Nostoc*, a blue-green alga important because of its ability to *fix* nitrogen from the atmosphere—making it available to the fungus. A few lichens include both green and blue-green algae as well as the fungus, showing that symbiosis may include three types of plant living together.

The fungus and the alga can be seen to be living together in a lichen, but it is more difficult to show that both partners receive some benefit from the association. However, lichens grow on bare rock surfaces or walls where there is no decomposing organic matter, on which fungi normally live. The fungi of a lichen could survive in such conditions only if they obtained carbohydrate from the algae and experiments have verified that this is what happens—up to 70% of the carbohydrate produced by photosynthesis in the alga is released from the algal cells and enters the fungal mycelium. The carbohydrate is usually released as a chemical called a *polyhydric alcohol*, though some types of lichen algae release glucose. The alga benefit by receiving moisture, containing inorganic nutrients dissolved by the fungal mycelium.

Rod Borland/Bruce Coleman

Above: Lichens growing on rock at Cape Cross, South West Australia. Lichens are most commonly greyish in colour (bottom left of picture) but may be brightly coloured like the orange species here.

Right: *Cladonia sylvatica,* a very common lichen on moorland, on rocks and walls. *Cladonia* produces cup-shaped *podetia,* up to 1 cm in height, around the edge of which are borne small wind-dispersed spores or *soredia.*

Jacques Six

There are more than 18,000 species of lichen in the world; about 1,400 have been found in the British Isles alone. They can be divided according to thallus structure into three groups: *crustose* lichens, which form flat, scaly circular thalli, *foliose* lichens, in which the thallus has the form of a leaf, often with root-like structures growing out underneath, and *fruticose* lichens, in which the thallus is branched like a miniature tree. Wall lichens are commonly crustose, while foliose lichens are found on trees or (like reindeer moss, *Cladonia rangiferina*) covering the ground in tundra regions.

Little is known for certain about the reproduction of lichens. Some species of lichen fungi reproduce sexually, by means of *ascospores*, but these contain no algal cells. But an ascospore could grow into a new lichen thallus by combining with cells of the appropriate alga—which would be difficult, since neither fungus nor alga is likely to survive for long by itself. It is more likely that lichens normally reproduce either vegetatively, by *fragmentation*, when small pieces of the thallus break away and later begin to grow by themselves, or asexually by the dispersal of *soredia*, which are small groups of algal cells surrounded by fungal

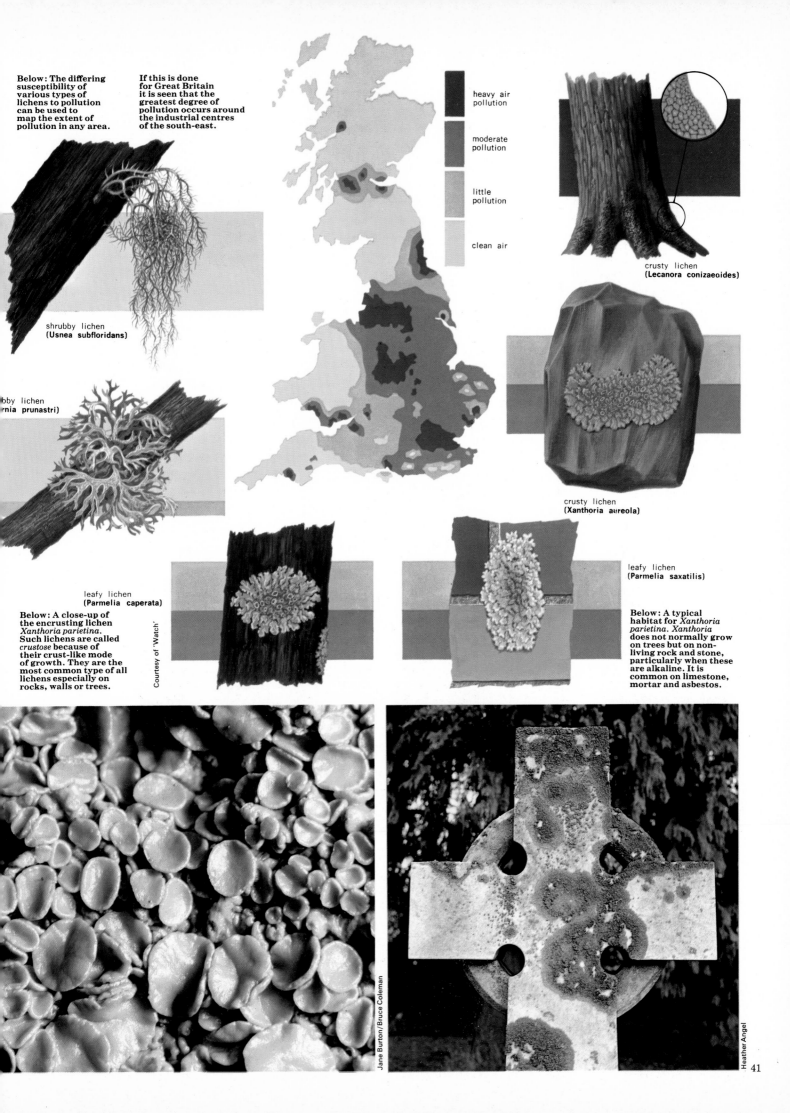

Below: The differing susceptibility of various types of lichens to pollution can be used to map the extent of pollution in any area.

If this is done for Great Britain it is seen that the greatest degree of pollution occurs around the industrial centres of the south-east.

heavy air pollution

moderate pollution

little pollution

clean air

shrubby lichen
(Usnea subfloridans)

bby lichen
rnia prunastri)

crusty lichen
(Lecanora conizaeoides)

crusty lichen
(Xanthoria aureola)

leafy lichen
(Parmelia caperata)

leafy lichen
(Parmelia saxatilis)

Courtesy of 'Watch'

Below: A close-up of the encrusting lichen *Xanthoria parietina*. Such lichens are called *crustose* because of their crust-like mode of growth. They are the most common type of all lichens especially on rocks, walls or trees.

Below: A typical habitat for *Xanthoria parietina*. *Xanthoria* does not normally grow on trees but on non-living rock and stone, particularly when these are alkaline. It is common on limestone, mortar and asbestos.

Jane Burton/Bruce Coleman

Heather Angel

41

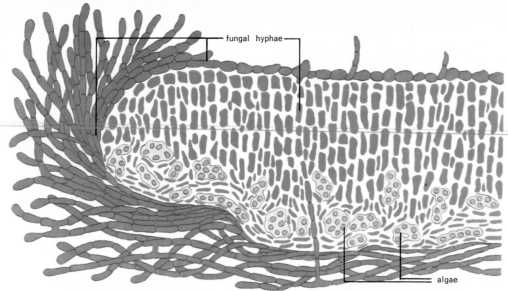

fungal hyphae

algae

Above: Stylized section through the body of a lichen (the *thallus*) showing the two types of plant—fungus and alga—which together combine to form a third type—the lichen. The alga and fungus do not intermingle randomly in the lichen, but the lichen is divided up into layers which are more or less distinct from one another. Three of these layers are composed of a network of intertwining fungal filaments, or *hyphae*, while the fourth layer contains the algae. The algae contain chlorophyll and can photosynthesize, and a few fungal hyphae grow into the alga layer and obtain carbohydrate produced by them.

Leslie Jackman

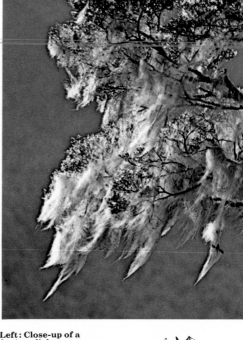

G. R. Roberts

Left: Close-up of a *fruticose* lichen. These lichens have a many branched body, producing a shrub-like or antler-like structure. Most are very small—no more than several centimetres in size—but some tropical forms may be up to a metre in length, hanging from trees.

hyphae. Soredia are often visible as a powdery deposit on the surface of a lichen thallus. They are light, and can be blown around by the wind.

In the laboratory, it is possible to grind up the lichen thallus, separate the fungus and alga, and grow them separately. The fungus grows into a simple colony quite unlike the complex structure of a lichen thallus, and the alga no longer releases carbohydrate. The obvious next experiment—taking the separate cultures of fungus and alga and trying to recombine them to form a lichen—has, however, proved to be almost impossible. This may be because it is difficult in a laboratory to simulate the harsh natural environment of a lichen, where growth is limited by low levels of nutrients and the frequent drying-out of the thallus.

Root nodules

Farmers have known for centuries that the fertility of their soils could be maintained by including in their crop rotations a planting of clover or beans. These plants, and others such as the widespread group of tropical trees, *Acacia*, are in a family called *Leguminosae* (legumes). During the nineteenth century it was discovered that the increase in soil fertility was the result of the ability of legumes to absorb nitrogen from the atmosphere and fix it—that is, convert it into the organic forms contained in plant and animal tissues. Later still it was found that this process, called *nitrogen fixation*, is carried out not by the plants alone, but with the help of bacteria present in *nodules* (swellings) on their roots. This is an example of symbiosis involving a higher plant and a bacterium.

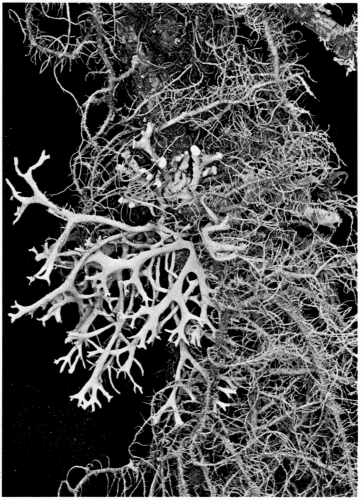

Giuseppe Mazza

Above: An early woodcut of the root of the broad bean, *Phaseolus vulgaris*, showing the nitrogen-fixing nodules on the root. Beans provide a very cheap source of protein because they do not need large dressings of expensive nitrogen fertilizer—nitrogen being provided by the root nodules. In contrast to the action of symbiotic bacteria in root nodules the industrial process used to manufacture nitrogen fertilizer requires a temperature of 450°C and a pressure of 200 atmospheres—and correspondingly consumes large amounts of energy and money.

Above right: Nodules on the root of alder, *Alnus glutinosa*. Unlike the legumes, the nitrogen-fixing organism in the nodules of alder is probably a fungus and not a bacterium.

Left: Two different fruticose lichens of the groups *Evernia* (left) and *Usnea*. *Usnea* lichens form long tangled masses—often up to 15 cm (6 in) long—and are commonly called 'old man's beard'.

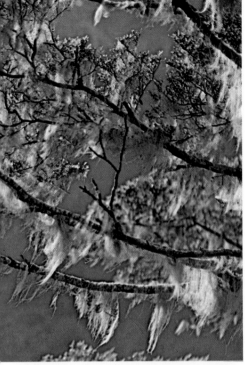

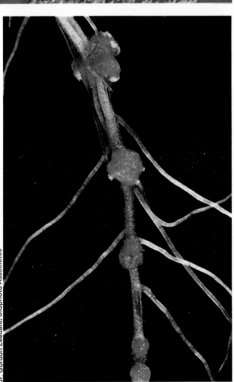

Dr. Gordon Leedale/Biophoto Associates

Above left: Large growth of lichen hanging from a tree in a beech forest in the Eglinton valley of New Zealand. A plant which uses another merely for support, as the lichen does here, is called an *epiphyte.* **Epiphytism benefits one partner alone, but only rarely harms the other plant.**

Above: The common woodland fungus, the fly agaric, *Amanita muscaria.* **Woodland fungi appear to be growing independently but are often in fact symbiotic with the roots of trees such as pine or birch. The fungus is connected to the tree by a mass of fungal filaments in the soil.**

That the bacteria are separate plants from the legumes in which they are growing is shown by the fact that legumes grown from seed in sterile soil do not have nodules and do not fix nitrogen. Instead, nodules develop only after the bacterium, *Rhizobium,* normally present in the soil, infects the roots of the young legume. Inside the nodule the bacteria enlarge to form modified bacterial cells called *bacteroids.*

The bacteroids fix nitrogen using an enzyme called *nitrogenase* which catalyzes the reaction by which nitrogen is converted to ammonia—free-living *Rhizobium* does not have nitrogenase and cannot fix nitrogen. This ammonia is then used by the legumes to synthesize amino acids and ultimately protein used in the construction of plant tissue. Root nodules are thus of great value to the legume as

nitrogen is an essential nutrient, often in short supply.

Numerous plants other than legumes are now also known to have nitrogen-fixing root nodules. Among these are alder, *Alnus,* sea buck thorn, *Hippophäe,* bog myrtle, *Myrica,* and a tropical tree called *Casuarina.* These plants, however, differ from legumes as the symbiotic organism is probably a fungus and not a bacterium.

Mycorrhizas

A further example of a symbiotic association occurring between the roots of higher plants and fungi is called a *mycorrhiza.* In these, common woodland fungi are connected, through extensive networks of hyphae in the soil, to the roots of trees. Mycorrhizal relationships are in fact extremely common; most common temperate trees including birch, beech, eucalyptus, spruce and larch are known to form mycorrhizas with several species of fungi. Scots pine, *Pinus sylvestris,* forms mycorrhizas with more than 100 species of fungi.

In one type of mycorrhiza, called *ecto-trophic,* the fungus forms a sheath of hyphae covering the fine absorbing roots of the tree. This gives the tree a greatly increased area of absorbing root and thus it is able to absorb greater amounts of mineral nutrients such as nitrogen, phosphorus and potassium. Experiments have shown that in its turn the fungus receives a supply of carbohydrate from the tree.

In nutrient-rich soils mycorrhizas are of little value to the tree and the fungus is virtually a parasite on the tree. However, in most soils at least one nutrient is

in short supply and a tree with ecto-trophic mycorrhizas will grow faster than an uninfected tree.

A completely different type of mycorrhiza is called *endotrophic.* In this, the fungal hyphae grow inside (instead of outside) the cells of the higher plant. Such mycorrhizas are found in all orchids and in many other plants—indeed possibly in *all* higher plants. In orchids, the mycorrhizal fungus, usually of the group *Basidiomycetes,* infects the roots as they begin to grow from the germinating seed. The hyphae grow into the cells of the root and form coils inside each cell. Later, some of the orchid cells digest the hyphae within them, releasing fungal nutrients for the benefit of the orchid. Because of this a young orchid can grow underground for several years, unable to perform photosynthesis, but obtaining a supply of carbohydrate from its fungal partner.

Eventually most orchids produce leaves and photosynthesize their own carbohydrate, some of which may be passed on to the fungus—a mutually beneficial association. A few orchids, however, never produce leaves and are therefore always dependent on their fungus; in such cases the orchid is a parasite on the fungus.

On plants other than orchids, endotrophic mycorrhizas are often formed with a fungus called *Endogone* from the same group, *Phycomycetes,* as the familiar pin mould, *Mucor.* The fungal hyphae grow into the root cells, branching within them to form structures called *arbuscules* (because of their tree-like appearance) and also thick-walled swellings called *vesicles.* Because of this, this type of mycorrhiza is sometimes called *vesicular-arbuscular.*

Experiments have compared the growth of plants, such as strawberries and tomatoes, with and without endotrophic mycorrhizas, and have shown that the fungus can help to supply the plant with mineral nutrients if these are in short supply in the soil. In most cases the fungus also benefits by receiving a supply of carbohydrate from its partner. This is obviously of vital importance to the most common mycorrhizal fungus, *Endogone,* as it will not grow except as a mycorrhizal partner.

Other kinds of symbiosis

Many other cases are known of associations between different kinds of plant which may be instances of symbiosis. In practice, it is often difficult to discover whether both plants benefit from the presence of their partners, so botanists tend to use the term symbiosis when neither plant is harmed by the other. Examples of possible symbiosis exist between the blue-green alga, *Nostoc,* and cycads (a group of primitive plants like giant ferns) and between green algae and the moss, *Sphagnum,* which forms peat bogs. Much research would be needed in every case to discover whether the association was or was not true symbiosis; whether nutrients are transferred between the two plants, and whether the association is necessary for the survival of either or both partners. Nevertheless, it is clear from an understanding of lichens, root nodules and mycorrhizas that symbiosis is an extremely widespread phenomenon, essential to the normal functioning of nearly all plant communities.

Parasitic and Climbing Plants

Higher plants are generally the *producers* of the world. All other life forms are *consumers*, dependent on the food which plants manufacture during photosynthesis. But in a few species and families of plants this normal pattern is upset. These plants are themselves dependent. They are *parasites* and *climbers*, dependent to a greater or lesser extent upon a host plant.

Parasitic and climbing plants, although different in many ways, have several features in common. Both groups use neighbouring plants to aid them to grow —either as a prop to enable a climber to reach the light, or as a source of food for the parasitic plant. Indeed, many species, like dodder, *Cuscuta*, are both climber and parasite.

Additionally, although particular species in both groups are confined to specific areas of the world, they are all largely non-specific in relation to their choice of host: the neighbouring plant used as a support or food source will simply be that which was nearest to the germinating seed of the climber or parasite. The only exception to this is the observation that parasitic plants, only rarely, and then usually unsuccessfully, parasitize monocot plants. The reasons for this selectivity, however, are not clearly understood.

Parasitic plants

Despite the fact that most plants are producers synthesizing their own food, it is wrong to think that parasitism among plants is rare. Two extremely large and important groups of plants, *fungi* and *bacteria*, are all either parasites or organisms that live on the dead remains of others (*saprophytes*). Even among the higher plants parasites are not all that uncommon, particularly in the tropics. Four families, the *Loranthaceae*, the *Balanophoraceae*, the *Orobanchaceae* and the *Rafflesiaceae* are composed entirely of parasitic plants. Other families, such as the *Convolvulaceae* and the *Lauraceae*, contain both parasitic and non-parasitic members.

Parasitic plants obtain water and food from the host plant through specially developed organs, called *haustoria*, which secure the parasite to the host and grow into the host's tissue, particularly its vascular tissue. Most parasites have a multiplicity of these connections with their host, but some have only a single primary connection. Indeed there are many levels of parasitism in the several families containing parasitic plants, and several forms of growth.

The extent to which a parasite is dependent on its host largely determines its vegetative form. True parasites, such as the dodders, *Cuscuta* and *Cassytha*, are entirely devoid of chlorophyll and rely entirely on the host as a food source. In this case the vegetative parts are very small—the leaves are present only as tiny scales on the thin, weak stem which itself possesses only poorly developed vascular tissue.

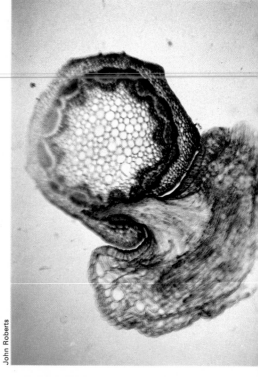

John Roberts

Above and below left: The common climbing parasite, dodder, *Cuscuta*. Dodder twines around the plant which it parasitizes—its *host*—and extracts nutrients and water from it through specialized organs called *haustoria*. These can be seen (below left) as small foot-like pads growing into the host stem; one is more clearly shown in the cross-section above. Here the dodder is located beneath the stem of the host plant. The projection from the dodder into the host is the haustorium.

Below: The red fruits of the tropical mistletoe *Viscum minimum.*

ZEFA

Dr. G. Leedale/Biophoto Assoc.

Nevertheless, dodders are quite conspicuous, varying in colour from bright yellow to red. After emerging from seed the seedling immediately begins to grow in a circular fashion, searching for another plant around which to twine. Once a suitable host is found, the thin stem of the dodder then twines round the host's stem in a manner similar to that of the related climber, bindweed, *Convolvulus*. Unlike bindweed, however, the dodder stem has haustorial pads which become attached to and grow into the host stem. These pads break through the epidermis of the host stem into its interior, where they branch and form connections with the xylem and phloem. In the mature dodder the initial connection with the ground then withers away. The dodder is then entirely dependent on its host.

Other parasites, such as the toothwort, *Lathrea*, and the broomrape, *Orobanche*, are parasitic on the roots of other plants, rather than their stems. Correspondingly these plants are generally less conspicuous than dodders for most of their vegetative parts are usually below ground. Normally, the only growths above ground are flowering parts. Some root parasites, however, such as *Gaiadendron*, appear as a substantial bush above ground. In such cases the plants are almost certainly not entirely parasitic, but also manufacture some of their own food.

A well known example of a partial parasite is mistletoe, *Viscum*, which grows as a cluster of branches hanging from trees, commonly apple or poplar in Britain. The mistletoe produces a haustorium which connects with the host's xylem and extracts water and mineral nutrients, but it also has green leaves capable of producing much of the food it requires in the same way as other green plants. The host plant is used chiefly as a support but also as a 'root', as the mistletoe has no roots of its own.

In contrast to mistletoe, the tropical *Rafflesiaceae* are completely dependent on their hosts. Although *Rafflesia* bear the largest flowers of all plants, there is virtually no visible trace of the vegetative parts, which are buried in the tissues of the host (normally a liana). These consist of slender filaments, resembling the mycelium of a fungus. Like a fungus, too, these filaments are frequently only single-celled strands. The only large masses of cells are the *floral cushions*, groups of cells which give rise to the massive flowers.

The *Rafflesiaceae* are perhaps the ultimate example of the parasitic tendency to minimize all but the reproductive parts. All that remains of the varied structure of a higher plant is the reproductive apparatus. Such parasitic plants, relieved of the need to produce an elaborate vegetative structure, are able to devote most of the energy extracted from their host to the production of seeds.

Climbing plants

Although climbing plants live on their hosts, and in many cases harm them, they are not, strictly speaking, parasites. They do not obtain nourishment from their host but use it merely as a means of support. Nevertheless, this is no mean benefit. It enables climbers to grow high up in a dense vegetation canopy so that

Above: The bird's nest orchid, *Neottia nidus-avis*, **is white because it lacks chlorophyll. It is normally regarded as a saprophyte but, though its food ultimately comes from dead remains in the forest litter, it obtains them parasitically through a mycorrhizal** *Basidiomycete* **fungus.**

Below: The largest flower of any plant belongs to a parasite, *Rafflesia arnoldii* **(shown here). The flowers can be up to 1m (3 ft) in diameter and weigh up to 6 kg (15 lb).**

Right: The common European mistletoe, *Viscum album*. **The white berries ripen in winter and are eaten** by birds, especially thrushes, but the sticky seeds cling to the birds' beaks. The birds wipe them off on to the boughs of trees, such as apple, so dispersing them. The germinating seedling then connects itself to the host's water conducting tissue (*xylem*) through a haustorium.

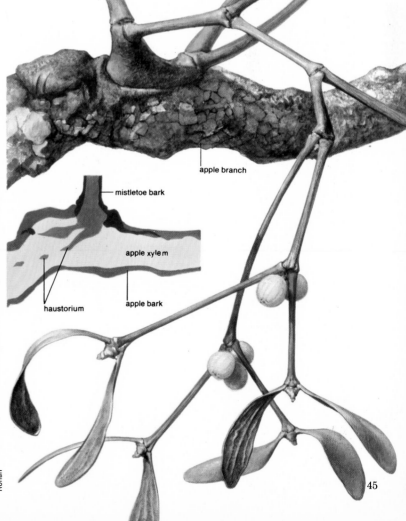

apple branch

mistletoe bark

apple xylem

haustorium

apple bark

Giuseppe Mazza

Heather Angel

Left and above: The climber, honeysuckle, *Lonicera periclymenum*. Because they do not need to expend energy producing supporting tissue climbers often overwhelm their hosts, in this case a young fir tree.

Below left: The sweet pea, *Lathyrus odoratus*, an ornamental climber.

Below: White bryony, *Bryonia dioica*, belongs to the same family, *Cucurbitaceae*, as cucumber and marrow. It produces long, tightly coiled and spring-like *branch-tendrils* which coil around any object with which they come into contact. The result is a very strong yet flexible support.

NHPA

Clematis *'Xerxes'*. The stalk of the leaf, rather than the blade, forms a tendril to cling to the wall, showing off the delicate bloom.

their leaves receive more light and their fruits can be more easily dispersed by the wind.

Climbers have these advantages without the need to produce the structural tissues that their hosts must produce. This enables them both to grow faster than their hosts and to devote more of their energy to the production of flowers and fruits. If a climber fails to find a host, however, it has little chance of survival.

The simplest climbers, such as bramble, *Rubus*, or goosegrass, *Galium aparine*, have stems which are provided with curved hairs, all with tips pointed downwards. These hairs hook the plant on to its support. Goosegrass has single-celled hook-hairs, which are very small and not easily seen, though they are quite effective in aiding the plant to cling to any available support. Brambles, on the other hand, have large multicellular hairs, or thorns.

The hairs of the runner bean *Phaseolus multiflorus* are especially interesting. They do not all grow downwards but are arrayed in all directions. The cells at the base of the hairs are flexible. They allow the hooked tips to twist in different directions around the base, so that purchase may be obtained in several directions at once.

A more specialized method of gaining support is the use of *tendrils*. There are several kinds of tendrils, though most are modified leaves or leaf parts. In the *Leguminosae*, well illustrated by the sweet pea, *Lathyrus odoratus*, leaflets of the compound (*pinnate*) leaf blade serve as tendrils, while leaf-like structures in the bud axils (the *stipules*) are enlarged to compensate for the loss of photosynthetic surface. In extreme cases, as in the meadow vetchling, *Lathyrus aphoca*, the whole of the leaf blade is transformed into a tendril—in which case the large stipules provide the major photosynthetic surface.

A less common form of tendril is produced by old man's beard, *Clematis*. Here the leaf stalk (*petiole*) rather than the leaf blade forms the tendril. In yet another group of climbers, including the virginia creeper, *Ampelopsis veitchi*, and the passion flower, *Passiflora*, the tendril, known as a *branch-tendril*, grows directly from the stem. In virginia creeper the tendrils grow from opposite each leaf, while in the passion flower they grow from the axils of the leaves.

The most tightly attached climbing plants, however, are those in which the plant itself behaves as a 'tendril' and twines about its support. Good examples are bindweed, *Convolvulus*, and honeysuckle, *Lonicera*. Initially the shoots of these plants grow up unsupported, but after some time the tip leans over and begins to revolve until it finds some support about which to twine. The climber then continues to twine up the stem of the support. In most species the direction of twining is always the same. For example, honeysuckle always twines clockwise while larger bindweed, *Calystegia sepium* twines anti-clockwise. A few species, however, like woody nightshade, *Solanum dulcamara*, have no fixed twining habits.

Entwining climbers have one particular adaptation to this life style. The growing point (*apex*) of most plants is surrounded by a cluster of expanding young leaves. These would tend to interfere with the encirclement of the supporting plant. The apex of entwiners, however, is surrounded by only very small leaves and the stem immediately below the apex grows particularly quickly so that there are large spaces (*internodes*) between the leaves.

Disadvantages

The advantage to a plant of the climbing life-style is that it enables it to grow high up in a plant canopy without producing a massive stem. Paradoxically, the lack of a large stem is also a major problem. It is difficult to transport enough water over the often long distances from ground to tip through the thin stem, and consequently small amounts of vascular tissue, of the climbing plant.

To overcome this problem climbing plants have adapted by increasing the efficiency of each individual xylem vessel. Resistance to the flow of water through the xylem is largely caused by the adhesion of water to the walls of the vessels and this is comparatively reduced if the cross-section of the vessels is larger. The vessels in the stems of climbers are very wide in comparison to those of other plants. Indeed they are occasionally visible to the naked eye.

Parasitic plants, dependent as they are on other plants, are of little value to man, but several species of climbers are of major economic importance. These include important pulses, such as peas, *Pisum sativum*, and beans, *Phaseolus*. Other climbers enhance man's enjoyment of life. For many life would not be so pleasant without the grape vine, *Vitis vinifera*, or the hop, *Humulus lupulus*.

Above: An unusual form of support. *Ampelopsis crampons* (shown here) uses *suckers* which grow on a short branch from the stem and hold the plant to its host. Also unusual, and superficially similar, are the *adventitious* roots which grow from the stem of ivy, *Hedera helix*, and hold it to its support.

Below: A more usual way of climbing is by means of downward growing hairs. This electron micrograph (about 50 times life size) is of the stem of goosegrass (or cleavers), *Galium aparine*. Poultry, and geese in particular, like to eat this plant which explains the origin of its name.

Jean-Pierre Bourret

Dr. G. Leedale/Biophoto Assoc.

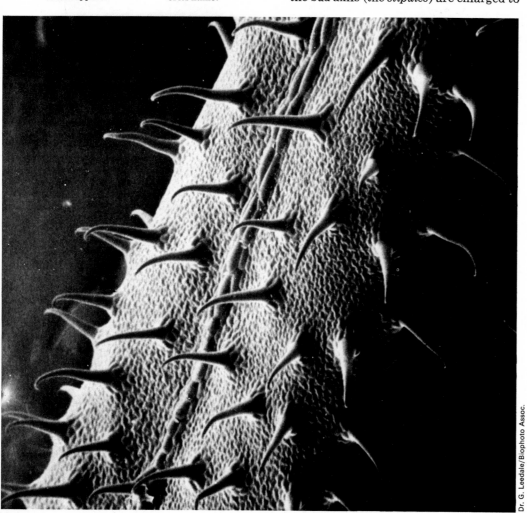

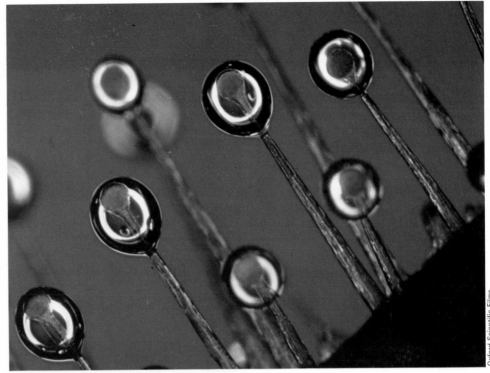

Oxford Scientific Films

Below: A bladderwort, *Utricularia*. An aquatic plant, it catches its prey, typically water fleas, by means of small bladders carried by the leaves. Each bladder, closed by a hinged 'trap door', is first emptied of most of its water by means of special glands. When trigger hairs near the entrance are touched, the door springs open and water floods in, carrying the prey with it. The door then closes to prevent escape, and digestion begins.

Natural Science Photos

Left: The pink butterwort, *Pinguicula lusitanica*, catches its prey by means of sticky tentacles carried by the upper leaf surfaces. The captured insects supply nitrogen, which is usually lacking in its boggy habitat.

Above: A close-up of the stalked glands of a sundew, *Drosera*. The globules of sticky fluid are plainly visible. Glands on the leaf surface secrete enzymes to digest the prey once it has been caught by these tentacles.

the threshold, thus ensuring a water-tight fit. Two long antennae curve down over the entrance and numerous stiff bristles surround the trap door.

Bifid and *globular* glands, which are located on the inner side of the threshold and on the outer surface of the trap respectively, pump water from the interior of the bladder in order to set the trap. Up to 90 per cent of the original water is expelled so that the door is pressed tightly against the threshold by external water pressure. Glands located on the outer surface of the door and threshold secrete a sugary mucilage which attracts prey and seals the door. The bristles guide prey towards the door until, by pushing against the trigger hairs, the lower part of the door levers open. Within 0.0015 sec the pressure forces the door inwards and both water and prey are sucked in. The door then springs shut, ensuring that the prey cannot escape, and water is pumped out so that digestion can begin.

Lobster-pot traps

Genlisea grows as a small free-floating rosette partially submerged in shallow water and is often found with bladderworts. The trap-leaves, only a few centimetres long, have a short stalk which divides into two tubes. These hang down into the water. A slit runs in a spiral all the way down the tubes, and along the inner edge of this is a row of inward-pointing hairs. The outer edge is covered in glands which secrete mucilage. Small aquatic animals can easily find their way past the hairs and get into the trap, but then cannot find the entrance and are caught. The inner surface has numerous glands similar in appearance to those of bladderworts.

bladder trap (cutaway)

digestive glands

trigger hairs

water flea

entrance

bladder trap (section)

Flowering Plants

Over the last 100 million years one group of plants has become dominant on the Earth, both in numbers and species. Called the *Angiospermae*, the flowering plants, the group includes well over 200,000 species, more than a hundred times as many as the next major group, the gymnosperms. It contains most of the trees grown by man for timber and almost all of the plants grown for food.

The dominance and variety of the flowering plants is closely linked with the three features used to distinguish them from other groups, such as the gymnosperms. These features are flowers, seeds enclosed in fruits, and a well-developed conducting system. Flowers encourage *cross-pollination* (fertilization with pollen from another plant rather than the same plant) by insects or other animals; seeds enclosed in fruits encourage widespread dispersal; and a fully developed system of conducting tissues means the efficient transport of water and nutrients within the plant.

Origin of the flowering plants

It is probable that the angiosperms evolved from the gymnosperms, though this can never be known for certain as most species of gymnosperms are known only as fossils. Plants have no skeleton and so plant fossils give only a limited picture of the appearance of the living plant. It is difficult, therefore, to deduce the important details of reproduction and development from a fossil. Nevertheless, it seems that the angiosperms are most like a group called the *pteridosperms*, the seed ferns. These plants, which have been extinct for at least 100 million years, were similar to the *cycads*, a few species of which still survive.

The earliest angiosperm fossils date from the Lower Cretaceous period (100-135 million years ago). Some of these are very similar to present day flowering plants; but the great explosion in the number of species of flowering plants probably took place more recently, during the early Tertiary period (about 80 million years ago). At that time, insects such as bees and butterflies, which are important pollinators, evolved to their present day forms. It is easy to relate the amazing diversity of flowering plants to the equally remarkable diversity of their insect pollinators.

Flowers

Flowers vary enormously in their size, colour and structure. When a flower is described, the first things normally mentioned are the *sepals* and *petals*. The petals are the brightly coloured structures that make flowers attractive to people, and, more important as far as the plant is concerned, to the insects or other animals that pollinate the flower. The sepals are a ring of smaller, leaf-like structures outside the petals. They enclose and protect the flower bud before it opens. All the sepals together are called the *calyx*, and all the petals together the *corolla*. In a few flowers, such as lilies (*Liliaceae*), the calyx is as large and

Above: The beautiful forms, colours and perfumes of flowers exist not to be aesthetically pleasing to man but as an attraction to bees and other insects. In their hunt for both pollen and *nectar* (a sugary substance produced by some flowers in glands, *nectaries*, on the petals) insects become covered by pollen produced by the male sex organs (*anthers*). This pollen is then transferred to the female sex organ(s) (*stigma*) of another plant. The pollen of one flower therefore fertilizes the eggs of a second flower—a process known as *cross-pollination*—which produces a plant with characteristics slightly different from either parent and a total population of plants each slightly different from the other. Such a variable population allows the gradual adoption of favourable characteristics by natural selection.

Right: The surface of a stigma (magnification about 500 times) showing *epidermal hairs* and pollen grains between them.

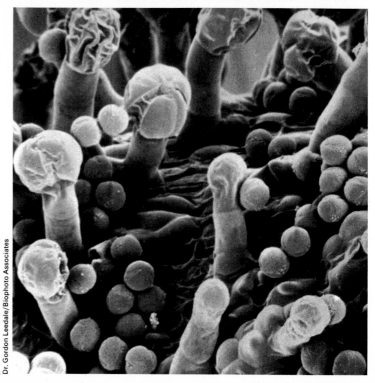

Dr. Gordon Leedale/Biophoto Associates

52

The fragile fuschia, seen in cross section. The pollen tube, stamen and stigma are exposed (see diagram, page 77).

Ronan

Heather Angel

Above: The Swedish botanist, Carl von Linné (1707-78) whose system of classification, based on flower structure, was a great help to early botanists.

Above right: Nodding (or musk) thistle, *Carduus nutans*. Thistles are members of the daisy family, *Compositae*. Each

'flower' is in fact an inflorescence of many small flowers and is called a *capitulum*.

Below right: Flower of the tulip tree, *Liriodendron tulipifera*. Tulip and tulip tree flowers look similar but the plants are not closely related. Tulip trees are dicots, tulips (*Tulipa*) are monocots.

brightly coloured as the corolla, and the term *perianth* is then used to describe both calyx and corolla.

It was realized in very early times that pollination is necessary for seed and fruit production; Assyrian kings performed a ceremonial pollination of date palms. However, the discovery that plants have two sexes is credited to Rudolph Jacob Camerarius (1665-1721). He realized that, less conspicuous than petals and sepals, there are male and female reproductive structures at the centre of a flower.

The male structures are called *stamens*. Each normally consists of a stalk supporting a bright yellow or orange head, the *anther*, which contains thousands of *pollen* grains, inside which are contained the male gametes. The female parts of the flower are more variable. The essential features, however, are the *ovules*, each of which contains one female gamete; the *ovary*, which contains the ovules; and the *style*, an elongated projection from the ovary. The style carries at its tip a flattened, often sticky, surface called the *stigma*.

A flower may have one or several styles and stigmas, and the ovary may be a single structure or be composed of a number of separate parts. When a pollen grain finds its way on to a stigma, it germinates to form a *pollen tube* which grows down through the style and into the ovary where fertilization—the fusion of male and female gametes—takes place. Each fertilized ovule develops into a seed.

The structure of flowers and the details of the reproductive organs in flowering plants are different from anything found in other plants. Flowering plants do, however, have a life-cycle with an alter-

Oxford Scientific Films

Right: Cross section of a typical flower. *Pollen grains*, deposited on the *stigma*, each produce a *pollen tube* which grows down through the style and into the *ovule* through a small pore, the *micropyle*. Inside the ovule is an *embryo sac* typically containing 8 nuclei—*antipodals, polar nuclei, synergids*, and the *female egg*. The pollen tube discharges two *sperms* which fertilize the ovule—one fuses with the egg, the other with the two polar nuclei. The other nuclei usually disintegrate.

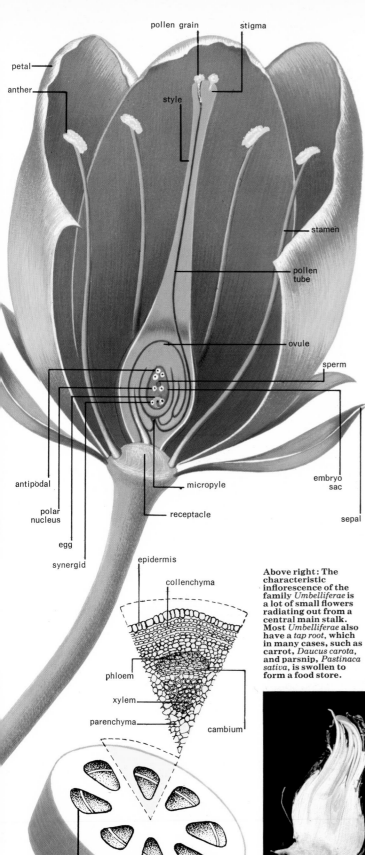

pollen grain · stigma
petal
anther
style
stamen
pollen tube
ovule
sperm
antipodal
micropyle
polar nucleus
receptacle
embryo sac
egg
sepal
synergid

epidermis
collenchyma
phloem
xylem
parenchyma
cambium

vascular bundles

Jean Pierre Bourret

Above: The inside of a stem of a herbaceous flowering plant contains *bundles* of conducting tissue each composed of three types of tissue—*xylem*, *phloem* and *cambium*. The rest of the stem is also composed of three tissues, the *parenchyma*, at the centre of the stem, the *collenchyma* and the *epidermis*.

Right: Roots differ from stems in having no leaves or buds and in possessing conducting tissue arranged in a central core rather than in vascular bundles. The absorbing area of roots is greatly increased by thousands of tiny root hairs which are in intimate contact with the soil particles.

Above right: The characteristic inflorescence of the family *Umbelliferae* is a lot of small flowers radiating out from a central main stalk. Most *Umbelliferae* also have a *tap root*, which in many cases, such as carrot, *Daucus carota*, and parsnip, *Pastinaca sativa*, is swollen to form a food store.

Below: Flowering plants also reproduce vegetatively. A *bulb* is a modified stem (the darker yellow portion at the base) from which grow fleshy *scale leaves* in which food is stored. An onion, *Alium cepa*, is an example of a bulb eaten for its food. This bulb, however, is the daffodil, *Narcissus*.

Leslie Jackman

G. R. Roberts

nation of generations, like mosses, ferns and gymnosperms, though one generation is hardly noticeable. The plant as we see it is the sporophyte. The gametophytes are so much reduced in size and complexity that only careful research shows that they are actually present. The male gametophyte, consisting of only three cells, develops inside the pollen grain. The female gametophyte remains buried within the ovule and is never released from inside the sporophyte.

The flower of an angiosperm is different in appearance from the cone of a gymnosperm, but the processes of pollination and fertilization are much the same. The most important difference is indicated by the word *angiosperm*, which means 'covered seed'. In gymnosperms the seed is exposed, whereas in flowering plants it is contained within the ovary. In some plants, as the seed forms, the ovary and other parts of the flower expand to form a *fruit*, surrounding the seed.

Another distinctive feature of many flowering plants is the way the flowers are arranged together in groups called *inflorescences*, giving a large patch of colour which may help to attract pollinating insects. Inflorescences are also useful to the botanist: the different types are often an easy way of recognizing the family to which a plant belongs.

Stems, roots and leaves

Flowers, being conspicuously colourful and varied in structure, are probably the most immediately interesting part of a flowering plant. Nevertheless, the growth and flowering of plants depends on intricate structures and complex processes which occur within stems, roots

55

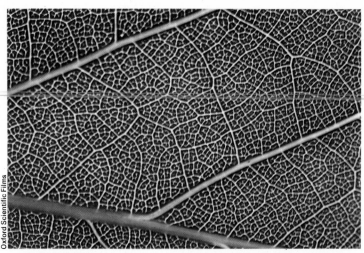

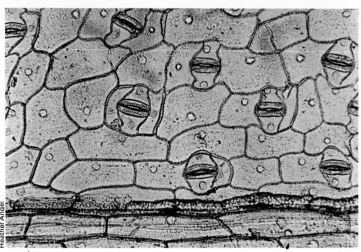

Oxford Scientific Films

Heather Angel

simple lobed
oak

compound
digitate

horse
chestnut

simple
lanceolate
willow

simple
cordate
ovate
lime

Above left: Intricate pattern of the leaf veins of a tulip tree, *Liriodendron tulipifera*, showing the elaborate branched network of dicotyledons. In monocotyledons the veins are unbranched and parallel.

Left: A close-up of a leaf of *Tradescantia* (x50) showing the small pores, *stomata*, through which water vapour is lost from the plant. The opening and closing of each stoma is controlled by two guard cells at its mouth. These cells respond to changes in the water pressure (*turgidity*) in the cell. As water is lost the pressure falls and the guard cells close the stomata so preventing any further loss of water.

and leaves. The non-flowering parts of plants are by no means always similar: they vary in an almost infinite number of ways.

The stem of a plant provides the framework to which are attached the leaves and flowers. Within it are contained two types of tissue, *xylem* and *phloem*, specially modified for conducting water and nutrients from one part of the plant to another. Xylem consists of long tubes, called *vessels*, formed from dead cells with missing end walls and thickened side walls. It provides the pathway along which water and inorganic nutrients pass upwards from the roots to the leaves. Phloem, on the other hand, consists of two kinds of living cells, *sieve tube cells* and *companion cells*, and is concerned with the transport of organic nutrients—particularly *sucrose* (sugar)—downwards from the leaves to the roots.

Sieve tube cells are elongated cells linked together but separated by perforated end walls to form a tube. The smaller companion cells are arranged alongside the sieve tube cells and apparently control their activity. Additionally, between the xylem and phloem, are a few layers of narrow cells called the *cambium*. Cambium cells continuously form new cells which replace aging xylem and phloem cells.

In the stems of herbaceous plants, xylem and phloem run alongside one another in *vascular bundles*, each of which forms a cylinder of conducting tissue running from the roots up into the leaves. The vascular bundles are either arranged regularly in a ring towards the outside of the stem (in *dicotyledons*), or they are scattered irregularly throughout the stem

(in *monocotyledons*). The number of bundles also varies—from about ten to more than a hundred in some species.

The vascular tissue of roots is not arranged like that of stems. In roots the xylem and phloem are gathered together into a single vascular cylinder running down the centre of the root. Externally, however, root systems vary quite considerably. For example, some plants have a *tap root*, a main root which grows downwards with smaller roots branching off it. A carrot, *Daucus carota*, is a swollen tap root containing a reserve supply of nutrients for the carrot plant. Other plants, such as grasses, have a relatively shallow network of small fibrous roots, which are efficient in extracting water and nutrients from the upper region of the soil.

Leaves are attached to the stem at places called *nodes*: if there is a single leaf at each node the leaves are called *alternate*; if there is a pair of leaves, they are called *opposite*. In either case, each leaf consists of a flat blade attached to the stem by a leaf-stalk, the *petiole*, through which runs a vascular bundle which begins in the stem. (New vascular bundles are created along the length of the stem by the branching of old bundles, thus keeping the total number of bundles in the stem roughly constant.) The vascular bundle of the leaf-stalk branches within the leaf to form *leaf veins*.

Internally, a leaf's structure is related to its function as the main site of photosynthesis. The surface layer of cells, the *epidermis*, is perforated by pores called *stomata*. Stomata allow air, containing carbon dioxide, to enter the intercellular spaces within the leaf, and so reach the

Ronan

Above: A great number of terms have been coined to describe the various shapes of leaves. Among other things, these terms may describe leaf blade composition, like *simple* (all parts of the blade in one piece) or *compound* (composed of separate leaflets); the general shape of the leaf, such as *linear* (several times longer than broad) or *reniform* (kidney-shaped); or the margin of the leaf, such as *entire* (no indentations) or *serrated* (saw-like indentations).

Dr Gordon Leedale/Biophoto Associates

simple ovate alder

simple
triangular
lombardy
poplar

compound
pinnate
rowan

simple
linear
grass

simple
palmate
sycamore

simple
oval beech

simple ovate-
assymetric
elm

Eric Crichton

Alphabet & Image

Left and below: The importance of flowering plants as food sources is inestimable. They are the basic food of virtually all life outside of the oceans. They are also of major economic importance in other ways. The most significant of these is timber production but other uses include textiles, drugs, dyes, resins, and perfumes. These women (left) are sorting roses for perfume manufacture (France 1891), while (below) vegetable dyes are exhibited for sale in India.

cells where photosynthesis takes place. Stomata may be found on the upper, lower or both surfaces of the leaf, although it is most usual to find them only on the lower surface.

Water is lost from the plant by diffusion from the intercellular spaces through the stomata—a process, called *transpiration*, which can be controlled by opening and closing the stomata. Water loss by evaporation from the epidermis is reduced by a layer of waxes, called the *cuticle*, which extends over the whole of the above-ground surface of the plant.

Monocotyledons and dicotyledons
The English botanist John Ray (1627-1705) was the first person to recognize the fundamental division of the flowering plants into two groups, the *Monocotyledonae* and the *Dicotyledonae*. They are divided by four obvious differences. Firstly, monocots, as their name implies, have only one seed leaf (*cotyledon*), while dicots have two. (Cotyledons are the simple leaves that appear first when a seed germinates, although in some plants they remain inside the seed.) Secondly, monocots have leaves with parallel, unbranched veins while in dicots the veins form a branched network. Thirdly, though the form of the flowers in both groups is very variable, as a general rule monocots have three or six of each flower component, for example three or six petals and three or six stamens, while dicots have their flower parts in fours or fives or in much larger numbers. Finally, although some monocots, such as palms and bamboos, appear woody, none show the *secondary thickening* by which woody dicots increase in girth each year.

As examples, buttercups (*Ranunculaceae*) and cabbages (*Cruciferae*) are familiar plants with obvious dicot features, while lilies (*Liliaceae*) and irises (*Iridaceae*) are monocots. The division into dicots and monocots reflects evolution; the dicots are probably more like the earliest angiosperms than the monocots.

Success of the flowering plants
Flowering plants are successful because of their flowers, their fruits and their efficient water-conducting systems. Many are also successful because they are *herbaceous* (not woody). Herbaceous plants can grow from seed to flower within a very short time—sometimes only a few weeks. This means that they can spread more rapidly than trees which may grow for decades before flowering and producing seed. One extreme example, the herbaceous desert plant, *Boerhaavia repens*, can produce seed eight days after germination. Such adaptation is of great advantage in harsh environments where to survive it is necessary to produce seed quickly before short-lived favourable conditions pass away.

In inhospitable environments the adaptability of the flowering plants has enabled them to grow where other plants would not be successful. In favourable conditions this same adaptability has resulted in a diversity of forms which together dominate the vegetation of the Earth—from tropical rain forest to the upland meadows of the Alps. The scenery of the Earth is largely the scenery of flowering plants. More importantly, they provide food, shelter and clothing for most of the world's population.

Lilies, Irises and Orchids

Few plants are as beautiful as the lilies, *Liliaceae*, irises, *Iridaceae*, and orchids, *Orchidaceae*. These three monocot families have evolved conspicuous flowers with fully developed petals and often other highly specialized structures to promote cross-pollination by insects and other animals. They are probably the most highly evolved of all plants.

Specialization within these families (particularly the orchids) to promote pollination by particular insects has resulted in a large number of species—about 25,000 in all. Also, because of their specialization, most species are confined to very limited habitats. These plants do not dominate large areas as grasses do.

The lily family

In one way the evolution of monocot flower structure parallels that found in the dicots. Lily and iris flowers are *actinomorphic* (symmetrical about more than one plane) while orchids are *zygomorphic* (irregular).

The actinomorphic flowers of lilies typically have petals and sepals that are similar and form a *perianth* with six segments. There are six stamens and the ovary is divided into three compartments —following the general monocot character of having flower parts in multiples of three.

A typical lily is the Madonna lily, *Lilium candidum*, which grows wild around the eastern Mediterranean, and has been cultivated since Roman times. Its large white flowers are often associated in paintings with the Virgin Mary. Other plants in the family include lily-of-the-valley, *Convallaria majalis*, the English bluebell, *Endymion non-scriptus*, and the snake's-head fritillary, *Fritillaria meleagris*. These plants, and most other members of the family, are perennial herbaceous plants which spend part of the year in a *dormant* state, thereby avoiding the need to maintain stems and leaves during seasons when growth is slowed down by low temperatures or lack of rain. They have evolved highly specialized storage organs to enable them to grow quickly once the dormant season ends.

In many genera, such as tulips, *Tulipa*, and lilies, *Lilium*, the dormant plant consists of a *bulb*, which is made up of a number of overlapping whorls of modified leaves. These leaves contain the plant's reserve of nutrients, and are thick and fleshy.

Similar in appearance and function, but structurally quite different, is the *corm*, which is the storage organ in a few

Jean-Pierre Bourret

Right: A wild lily, white asphodel, *Asphodelus albus*.

Below: Arum lilies are not *Liliaceae* but belong to another family, *Araceae*. Most are herbaceous perennials growing from rhizomes. This is an 1891 illustration of *Amorphophallus campanulatus*.

Below right: Some other plant families have lily-like flowers. One of these, the *Amaryllidaceae*, includes daffodils, *Narcissus*, and snowdrops, *Galanthus*, as well as onions and garlic, *Allium*. Another family, the *Agavaceae*, are mainly tropical woody plants like *Nolina*, shown here.

Heather Angel

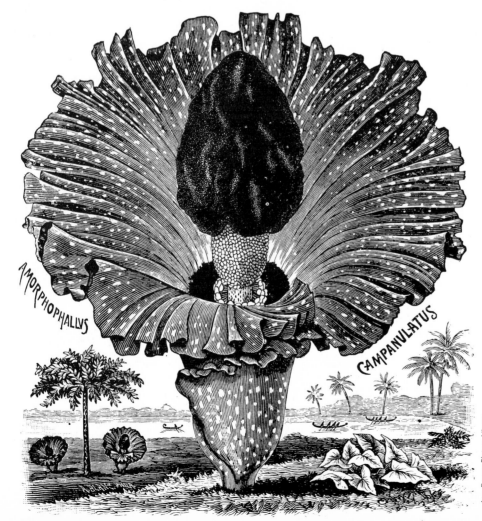

Ann Ronan Picture Library

Alphabet & Image

Above: The tiger lily, *Lilium lancifolium* (earlier *Lilium tigrinum*) has been cultivated for centuries in China, Korea and Japan because of its edible bulbs. Many garden lily varieties (the 'Mid Century' group) are derived from crosses of this with other species.

Right: The orchid family, *Orchidaceae*, is a family of remarkably beautiful and highly evolved flowers. Many tropical and sub-tropical species are also *epiphytic*—growing for support on other plants. The genus *Onchidium* (shown here is *Onchidium kramerianum*) are epiphytes from the West Indies and Central America. A few species also occur in Florida.

Giuseppe Mazza

The orchid family

The most highly specialized flowers are found in the orchid family. Estimates of the number of species of orchids vary from 10-20,000, so that this is either the largest family of flowering plants or the second largest after the *Compositae*, depending on which figure is taken. Whatever the exact number of species, however, all orchids are herbaceous plants, either of tropical or temperate regions. Temperate orchids generally grow in the ground but many tropical orchids are *epiphytes*, that is they grow on the trunks or branches of trees.

Epiphytes are likely to be found in wetter regions, because, as they cannot tap ground water, they must obtain water either from rainfall or from a humid atmosphere. Epiphytic orchids have three types of roots, some for attachment to the tree on which they are growing, others for the absorption of mineral nutrients, and a third kind, *aerial roots*, which absorb water from the atmosphere and, since they contain chlorophyll, act as additional photosynthetic tissue. Mineral nutrients are obtained either from rainwater flowing over the bark of the tree or from the small amount of soil which may accumulate around the plant. Many orchids, both epiphytes and ground orchids, also store nutrients or water in thickened sections of stem called *pseudobulbs*. Alternatively, in some species root storage organs, called *root tubers*, are formed.

The seeds of orchids are generally minute. They contain so little stored nutrient that the development of the seedling depends upon their forming *endotrophic mycorrhizas* in symbiotic association with a fungus, normally a *Basidiomycete*. At this stage the orchid seedling is a *saprophyte*, a plant obtaining its nutrient supply from decaying organic matter, in this case parasitically through the fungus. After a time the orchid produces leaves and photosynthesizes its own carbohydrate, some of which may be passed on to the fungus. Thus the orchid does not normally remain as a parasite but both the fungus and orchid benefit from their relationship. Such an association, which benefits both partners, is called *symbiosis*.

The time during which the orchid is dependent on the fungus may be as little as a few months, or as long as ten to fifteen years, as in the burnt orchid, *Orchis ustulata*. Indeed some orchids never leave this stage. The bird's nest orchid, *Neottia nidus-avis*, for example, never produces leaves and remains as a saprophyte.

In many orchids, flowering, too, is delayed for many years after the seed germinates—and even then may not occur every year. Vegetative reproduction (by spreading rhizomes or the production of several tubers or pseudo-bulbs at the end of the growing season) is therefore important because it allows an orchid to colonize a suitable habitat rapidly without the need for flowering and seedling establishment.

Flowering is more associated with dispersal. The very light seeds can be blown long distances by the wind to spread the species to new sites. Some species, such as the bee orchid, *Ophrys apifera*, normally die after flowering once, but the common twayblade, *Listera ovata*, has been found with as many as twenty-

members of the family, including the meadow saffron (autumn crocus), *Colchicum autumnale*. Instead of leaves a corm develops from a short section of stem which becomes swollen with nutrients and covered with a single layer of scale-like leaves.

Other plants in the family, such as the bog asphodel, *Narthecium ossifragum*, grow from a creeping underground stem, called a *rhizome*, or, as in *Aloe*, possess whorls of persistent succulent leaves crowded at the base of the plant. These leaves can themselves survive periods of particularly dry weather. Over 300 species of *Aloe* grow in the dry areas of Africa. The relationship of these plants to the temperate herbaceous members of the lily family is not immediately obvious but their flowers, red or yellow in colour and carried in upright spikes, have the characteristic structure of lily family flowers, with a six-segmented perianth and six stamens.

The iris family

The iris family, with only about a thousand species, is not a particularly large family, but it is notable for its spectacular flowers and specialized growth forms. As in the lily family, the flowers typically have an actinomorphic perianth. In irises, however, it is often elongated into a narrow tube with the ovary found well below the opening of the flower. In some genera, *Crocus*, for example, the ovary is below the soil surface.

The iris family are herbaceous plants, often found in areas with Mediterranean-type climates. The plants, like lilies, survive the lengthy dry period in the summer in a dormant state as a bulb, corm or rhizome. For example, the bearded iris, *Iris germanica*, forms a rhizome; *Crocus* species, which grow wild in Southern Europe, grow from corms; while the dwarf *Iris reticulata*, from the Caucasus, forms bulbs.

Many members of the iris family are native to South Africa or America. About a hundred species of *Sisyrinchium*, small grass-like plants with perianths subdivided into six blue, white or yellow petal-like segments, are found in North America. In South Africa, *Freesia* grow wild, as do less familiar plants, such as *Antholyza*, which are pollinated by sunbirds, *Nectarinidae*. In these plants, the inflorescence incorporates a 'bird-perch', a section of stem so placed that the bird can rest on it while probing into the flowers for nectar.

Oxford Scientific Films

four old flowering stalks. Since only one flowering stem is produced each year, and since the species is normally fifteen years old when it first flowers, such a plant must be some forty years old. Plants of some tropical epiphytic orchids have survived, in cultivation, even longer— for more than seventy years.

Pollination in orchids

Many flowers have evolved physiological or structural mechanisms to promote cross-pollination by insects. But it is the orchids which have the most complex adaptations, normally associated with cross-pollination by but one species, or group of species, of insect. The exact mechanism and the insect involved differ from one species of orchid to the next, but there are some features common to all orchids.

Orchid flowers consist of a perianth, one segment of which, the *labellum*, is enlarged and normally has a distinctive shape or colouring. In some species it is also extended as a tube-like *spur* containing nectar. At the centre of the flower, there is only one stamen, which is combined with the ovary to form a structure called the *column*, and two stigmas. The stigmas are separated from the stamen by a projection called the *rostellum*. Both the column and the rostellum vary greatly in shape from one species to another. Pollen grains produced by the stamen are clumped together into one or more bundles, called *pollinia*, and each pollinium has a short stalk, the *caudicle*. Each caudicle is then attached to the rostellum by a sticky disc.

The early purple orchid, *Orchis mascula*, shows a fairly typical version of the

The complex life-histories and the extravagant yet fragile flowers of orchids endear them to botanists. Some of the variation in their flower structure is shown here.

Above: The Australian spider orchid, *Caladenia huegelii*.

Right: The European lady orchid, *Orchis purpurea*, with its human-like flowers.

Below: The Central American epiphytic orchid *Brassia longissima*.

Eric Crichton

Eric Crichton

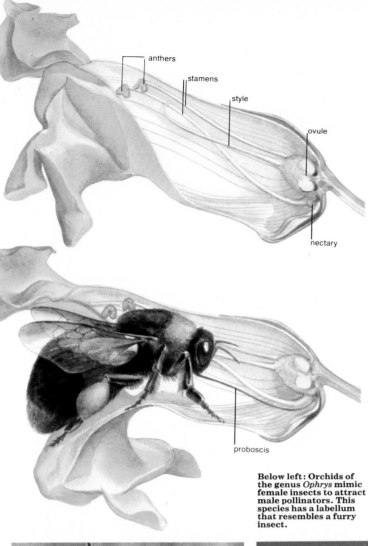

anthers
stamens
style
ovule
nectary
proboscis

Left and below: The purpose of brightly coloured flowers is to attract insects to carry out cross-pollination between different plants. *Antirrhinum* (left, a dicot) shows the general mechanism by which this is done. A bee feeding on nectar at the base of the ovary has pollen dusted on to its back by the anthers. This pollen is then transferred to the stigma of another plant. Below bees are pollinating an arum lily, *Anthurium.*

Bottom: Some flowers attract insects by mimicking the female so that the male attempts to mate with the flower. Here an *ichneumon* wasp 'mates' with the orchid *Cryptostylis leptochile.*

Below left: Orchids of the genus *Ophrys* mimic female insects to attract male pollinators. This species has a labellum that resembles a furry insect.

general mechanism of orchid pollination. The flowers are visited by humble bees, *Bombus,* seeking nectar secreted at the base of the spur. The bee alights on the labellum, which forms a sort of landing-pad, and then pushes its head into the centre of the flower, below the column, in order to insert its proboscis (tongue) into the spur. As it does so, it touches the rostellum and dislodges the sticky discs of the caudicles which immediately become attached to its head—the sticky substance sets like glue in a few minutes—like a pair of horns. Within thirty seconds the caudicles then bend downwards, so that the pollinia are properly positioned for pollinating the stigma of the next flower to be visited by the bee.

Other species of orchids have variations of this mechanism. For example in the

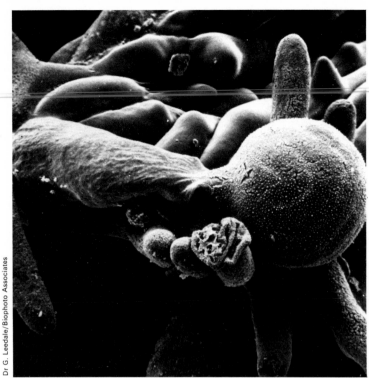

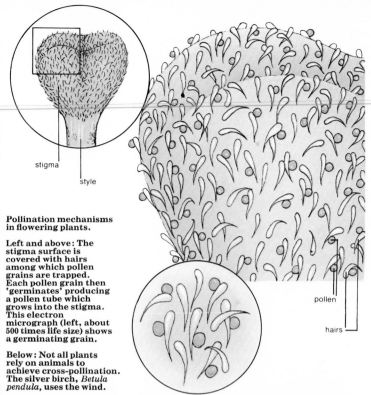

Pollination mechanisms in flowering plants.

Left and above: The stigma surface is covered with hairs among which pollen grains are trapped. Each pollen grain then 'germinates' producing a pollen tube which grows into the stigma. This electron micrograph (left, about 500 times life size) shows a germinating grain.

Below: Not all plants rely on animals to achieve cross-pollination. The silver birch, *Betula pendula*, uses the wind.

stigma

style

pollen

hairs

American epiphytic orchid, *Catasetum*, the rostellum is extended to form two *antennae*, and when these are touched by the bee the pollinia are released; but in this case with such force that they may travel up to 1 m (3 ft) if they are not intercepted by the body of the bee.

Catasetum is also interesting for another reason: the plants are unisexual, and originally, the female plants, whose flowers are very different in appearance, were placed in a different genus, *Monachanthus*. Only by careful observation of the plants in nature, and by experimental cross-pollination, was it possible to show that the male and female plants did in fact belong to the same species.

A particularly variable feature of the orchid flower is the length of the spur. Many orchids, such as the pyramidal orchid, *Anacamptis pyramidalis*, have extra long spurs, and are pollinated by insects such as moths and butterflies, which have longer proboscises than bees. In general, the length of the spur is related to the length of the proboscis of the pollinating insect. Orchids with long spurs and white or greenish flowers, such as the butterfly orchids, *Platanthera*, often emit a powerful smell at night, and are pollinated by night-flying moths.

But perhaps the most remarkable phenomenon in insect pollination, involving the closest adaptation of a plant species to one species of insect pollinator, is the attraction of male insects by orchids which mimic the female insect. This happens in a Mediterranean species, the mirror orchid, *Ophrys speculum*. It has a labellum with a dense fringe of hairs, and a metallic-blue reflective patch outlined with yellow. This apparently deceives the male insect—a *hymenopteran* wasp—into thinking that a female is resting on the flower. He attempts to mate with her; and in doing so at a number of flowers, brings about cross-pollination in the usual way. As well as imitating the female insect structurally, the mirror orchid also emits a *pheromone*, a volatile compound that attracts the male insect to the female.

Herbaceous Dicots—I

There are well over a quarter of a million species of flowering plants of which the majority (some 340 families) are *dicotyledons*—or more simply, *dicots*. Some of these are trees and shrubs but the majority are *herbaceous* plants. They do not produce lasting woody structures above ground, and in temperate regions the aerial parts generally 'die back' during the autumn. In *annual* plants the plants survive the winter as seeds, in *biennial* and *perennial* plants they survive as underground storage organs.

Among the herbaceous dicots there is a seemingly endless diversity. This is the result of millions of years of evolution during which different species of plants have adapted to differing environments. However, evolutionary trends in the flowering plants are extremely difficult to discover; there are very few useful fossils of herbaceous plants. Furthermore, the flowering plants appear not to have evolved in one straight evolutionary line but in a number of unconnected lines from an obscure common ancestor. This type of evolution can be likened to the spokes of a wheel radiating from a common hub and is called *radial evolution*.

One characteristic has been rather arbitrarily chosen by botanists as the basis by which to classify flowering plants. This is flower structure; and by concentrating on flower structure it is possible to list plant families in a rough evolutionary order. One way of doing this is to assume that the earliest flowering plants had simple regular flowers and that irregular flowers are a characteristic of more recently evolved families.

Regular flowers are called *actinomorphic*. They can be bisected vertically to give two identical or mirror-image halves along two or more planes. Less regular flowers are called *zygomorphic*. They are symmetrical about only one plane, as, for example, in the snapdragon, *Antirrhinum*. Some important regular-flowered families are the buttercup, water-lily, cabbage, hemp, dock, goosefoot, stonecrop, cactus, mesembryanthemum and parsley families.

Buttercups and water-lilies

The buttercup family, *Ranunculaceae*, is a good example of a regular-flowered family. Nevertheless it illustrates that even within families variations in flower structure can be marked. Typically, *Ranunculaceae* have five petals and many stamens but in *Anemone* and *Clematis* the sepals look like petals and the flowers appear to have anything from four to twenty petals. Leaf shape is also very variable, ranging from the large simple leaves of marsh marigold, *Caltha palustris*, to the feathery leaves of water crowfoot, *Ranunculus aquatilis*, which grows submerged in streams with its white flowers emerging above the water.

Another family, the water-lilies, *Nymphaeaceae*, are thought by many botanists to be most similar to the earliest dicots. They have a large indefinite number of petals, the inner of which are

structures developed from modified stamens.

The leaves of most water-lilies float on the water surface but the Egyptian lotus, *Nelumbo nucifera*, and its American counterpart, *Nelumbo pentapetala* have flowers which grow on stalks above the water. Buried seeds of *Nelumbo*, estimated to be a thousand years old, have been successfully germinated, illustrating the usefulness of seed dormancy for the survival of herbaceous plants in unpredictable environments. The parent plant may be killed, but so long as its seeds survive the species can re-establish itself when conditions improve—usually, when rain falls after a long interval.

Heather Angel

NHPA

Yves Lanceau

Left: A species of the common cactus, *Opuntia*, native to America, but now a weed in many parts of the world because of careless introduction.

Right: The Victoria water-lily, *Victoria amazonica*. Native to Brazil, it was first discovered by a European botanist in 1801. Its huge leaves, up to two metres (6 ft) across, are stiffened by a network of raised ribs along the underside. One Victoria lily, grown at Chatsworth House in Derbyshire by Joseph Paxton, gardener to the Duke of Devonshire, is said to have been the inspiration for the Crystal Palace in London. Paxton used the pattern of stiffening ribs as the basis of his unconventional design.

Below and below right: The stone (or window) plant, *Lithops rubra*, which mimics the stones among which it grows in its native southern Africa. The stone-like structures are leaves but do not contain chlorophyll. Instead they are translucent. Light enters the plants and passes down into its lower part, beneath the ground, where photosynthesis takes place. The plants may survive many years of drought, finally flowering soon after the first rainfall. The family to which *Lithops* belongs, the *Aizoaceae* also includes the genus *Mesembryanthemum* which are multi-coloured daisy-like succulents often grown in gardens

Commercially important families

Several families of regular-flowered dicots include commercially important species. Probably the most important of all is the cabbage family, *Crucifera*, most species of which have a distinctive four-petalled flower, in the form of a Maltese cross, which gives the family its name. The family includes water-cress, *Nasturtium officinale*, mustard, *Sinapis alba*, radish, *Raphanus sativus*, turnip, *Brassica rapa*, horse-radish, *Amoracia lapathifolia*, and cress, *Lepidum sativum*. But perhaps the most versatile species of all crucifers is the cabbage, *Brassica oleracea*. Brussels sprouts, cauliflower, broccoli, kohl-rabi and kale are all varieties of this one species.

Another particularly large family of regular-flowered dicots is the parsley family, *Umbelliferae*. Their characteristic features are their many lobed, often fern-like, leaves and an inflorescence, called an *umbel*, consisting of many small flowers whose stalks radiate from a central point. They are particularly important in north temperate regions, and include some familiar weeds such as cow parsley, *Anthriscus sylvestris* and hogweed, *Heracleum sphondylium*.

One interesting umbellifer weed, the giant hogweed, *Heracleum mantegazzianum*, presents an unusual hazard to humans. It produces sap containing a chemical, *furanocoumarin*, which can sensitize the skin to sunlight and lead to serious burns. It grows to four metres (13 ft) and its enormous creamy-white umbels are a conspicuous feature of stream and river banks in Europe and Britain. Other umbellifers, such as carrot, *Daucus carota*, celery, *Apium graveolens*,

tains only two genera, hops, *Humulus*, and hemps, *Cannabis*, but both are commercially important. Hops are climbing plants, grown extensively as a flavouring for beer. Cannabis, cultivated in Turkey and several parts of Asia, contains both strong fibres, which are used in rope and cloth making, and a resin, from which is produced the drug *marijuana*.

Not all flowering plants produce brightly coloured flowers. Wind-pollinated plants often have inconspicuous green flowers. Two important green, but regularly-flowered, families are the docks, *Polygonaceae*, and the goosefoots, *Chenopodiaceae*. Notable members of the goosefoot family are spinach, *Spinacea*

oleracea, and beet, *Beta vulgaris*, which has two commercial varieties, beetroot and sugar beet.

Sugar beet is a fine example of how, by crossing with wild plants, the yield of commercial varieties can be increased. In 200 years the average sugar content of sugar beet has been increased from 6% to nearly 20%. Sugar beet is biennial; the sugar is extracted from the swollen tap root which acts as a food storage organ during the winter.

Wild goosefoot species include many which are *halophytic*; that is they tolerate high levels of salt in the soil and are common on beaches and salt-marshes. Others, such as fat hen, *Chenopodium album*, are common weeds on waste and cultivated ground. One weed, Good King Henry, *Chenopodium bonus-henricus*, has

Left: Hemlock, *Conium maculatum,* is an umbellifer which contains a powerful respiratory poison, *coniine,* in its leaves. Hemlock is common in ditches, on stream banks and in damp meadowland in temperate regions throughout the world. It grows up to 2 m (6 ft) tall, flowering between May and August.

Above: The marsh marigold, *Caltha palustris,* a typical member of the buttercup family, *Ranunculaceae,* with five petals and numerous stamens— though it has no green sepals. The name 'marigold' is misleading; true marigolds, *Calendula officinalis,* are members of the daisy family, *Compositae.*

Below: The wild pansy, *Viola tricolor,* has regular flowers which appear extremely simple. However, the flowers have a specialized structure to prevent self-pollination. The stigma is protected by a valve which can be opened by a pollinating insect but closes again as soon as the insect leaves.

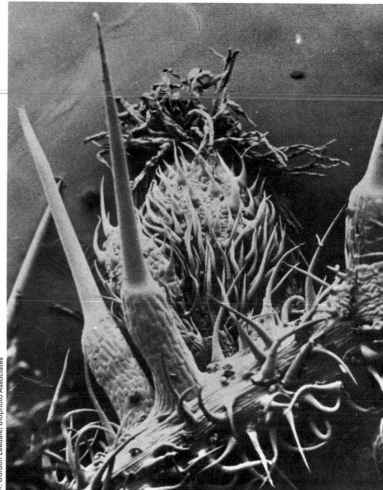

been grown and eaten as a vegetable since prehistoric times, though it is rarely cultivated today.

As well as docks, *Rumex*, the dock family includes rhubarb, *Rheum rhaponticum*. Even edible plants may accumulate toxic compounds in their leaves, and rhubarb leaves contain large amounts of poisonous oxalic acid. Plants store poisons in their leaves either to stop animals eating them or as a way of excreting unwanted substances which are lost when the leaves are shed in the autumn.

Xerophytic families

Another group of regular-flowered dicot families has adapted to a dry desert environment. Plants which can survive in a dry habitat are called *xerophytes* and usually possess succulent stems and leaves containing large quantities of water. More extreme adaptations include the absence of leaves to reduce transpiration, and a wide network of shallow fibrous roots to absorb water from the surface layers of soil immediately following rainfall before the rain can evaporate or run away. They often also have a dense covering of hairs or spines (sometimes both). Spines are to protect the plant from animals; in dry areas where vegetation is sparse, a plant without some means of defence against animals is very likely to be eaten. As further protection, desert and savannah plants often also contain toxic compounds in their leaves.

The stonecrop family, *Crassulacea*, contains many plants that are typical xerophytes. Some, like *Sedum*, are mainly northern hemisphere species, others, such as *Kalanchöe* and *Bryophyllum*, are confined to the drier parts of southern Africa. *Bryophyllum* shows an unusual kind of vegetative reproduction in which small plantlets develop, complete with roots, along the edges of the leaves. Eventually the plantlets drop off and take root in the ground, perhaps some distance off if they are blown by the wind.

The best known family of xerophytes, however, is the cactus family, *Cactaceae*. Cactuses are native to dry areas of North and South America, except for one

Above and right: Nettles, *Urticaceae*, are a green-flowered, wind-pollinated family, many members of which possess stinging hairs upon their stems and leaves. When touched by an animal the hairs break off releasing an acid which causes the sting. In the tree nettle, *Urtica ferox*, (above) which is native to New Zealand, the stings can be fatal. They are less serious in the common stinging nettle, *Urtica dioica*, (right). *Urtica* has single sexed flowers, normally with flowers of only one sex on each plant. This electron micrograph (magnification about fifty times) shows a female flower and several large stinging hairs. There are no brightly coloured petals—these are of no use to a wind-pollinated plant. Male flowers have four stamens which bend inwards towards the centre of the flower. When dried by the sun they suddenly contract catapulting the pollen into the air so that it can be more readily blown away by the wind.

Right: The cabbage—just one variety of species *Brassica oleraceae*.

species, *Rhipsalis baccifera*, which is found in Africa, although nobody knows how it arrived there. Another species, the prickly pear, *Opuntia vulgaris*, though native to the western states of the US, has become a weed in various parts of the world as a result of careless introduction. *Opuntia* was introduced into Australia as a hedge plant in 1839 but by the beginning of the twentieth century it covered four million hectares (ten million acres) making them useless for sheep grazing. By 1925 the infested area had increased to 24 million hectares (60 million acres). However in that year the moth *Cactoblastis cactorum* was released in the infested areas, and its caterpillars, by eating the *Opuntia*, cleared the grazing land so that the cactus now survives in Australia only as scattered colonies. The

use of an animal to control a pest or weed is called *biological control*.

A third family of xerophytes, the mesembryanthemum family, *Aizoaceae*, includes two genera, *Lithops* and *Conophytum*, which are notable for the way that they mimic the stones among which they grow. The chlorophyll bearing part of these plants is below ground level; the plants consist of a few swollen leaves the upper surfaces of which are translucent allowing light to pass down into the lower part of the leaf where the chlorophyll is found. *Lithops* and *Conophytum* can survive years of drought and produce large colourful flowers when rain eventually comes. Mesembryanthemum flowers appear at first glance to be similar to daisies, but are in fact far less complex.

Herbaceous Dicots—II

In adapting to different environments the flowering plants have developed in a bewildering variety of ways, both in growth habit and in structure. Flower structure, in particular, appears to be an extremely adaptable feature. From the earliest flowering plants, with simple regular flowers, evolution has generally been in the direction of increased complexity. Complex flowers tend to be irregular (*zygomorphic*), rather than regular (*actinomorphic*); to be grouped in *inflorescences*, rather than single; and to have flower parts joined together (such as the anthers fused together to form a tube, as in the *Compositae*) rather than separated.

The evolutionary pressure towards flower complexity is associated with the advantages to be gained by *cross-pollination*. Cross-pollination is one way in which plants can produce offspring which show variation in minor details of structure or physiology. Occasionally some of these offspring are better adapted to the environment than their parents. If these adaptations are advantageous enough, and particularly if the offspring are separated from their parents geographically, for example on islands, these adaptations may be incorporated in future generations and a new species may evolve.

Complex regular flowers

The most complex, and therefore the most highly evolved, flowers are zygomorphic, but many plant families have flowers which, though actinomorphic, are highly evolved in other ways in order to promote cross-pollination.

The primrose family, *Primulaceae*, has regular flowers which nevertheless have a complex structure related to their pollination by long-tongued insects, such as bees, and to a condition, called *heterostyly*, which increases the likelihood of cross-pollination. In a typical member of the family, the common primrose, *Primula vulgaris*, there are two slightly different types of flower. In both types the petals are used to make a *corolla* in the form of a tube. However, *pin* flowers have a long, slightly protruding, style with the anthers attached halfway down the corolla tube, while *thrum* flowers have a short style and the anthers are visible at the mouth of the tube. Pollen which is deposited on the back of an insect by the anthers of thrum flowers is liable to be deposited on the long style of pin flowers, while pollen deposited around the head of the insect by the anthers of pin flowers is liable to be deposited on the short style of thrum flowers.

As well as primroses, the primrose family includes a diverse range of flower and plant types, many of which, such as *Cyclamen* and *Dodecatheon*, are well known garden plants. Others are specialized to a particular habitat and are more rarely seen, for example the Alpine plants *Androsace* and *Soldanella*, and *Dionysia* from the mountains of the Middle East.

Another regular-flowered family, with an interesting structure adapted to one particular type of pollinating insect, is the milkweed family, *Asclepiadaceae*, whose common name derives from the milky sap which oozes out of the stems if they are damaged. The special feature of these plants is the pollen grains which are united into waxy bundles called *pollinia*. The arrangement of the stamens and nectaries is such that pairs of pollinia become attached to the legs of visiting insects, particularly flies, which are attracted to the flowers by their smell of rotting flesh.

Perhaps the most important complex-flowered dicot family from an economic viewpoint is the nightshade family, *Solanaceae*. It is a regular-flowered family and includes food plants, such as potato,

Giuseppe Mazza

NHPA

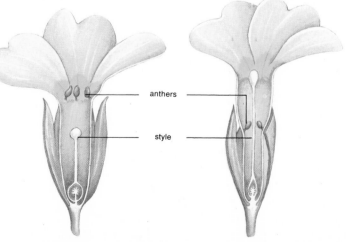

Left: The milkweed family, *Asclepiadaceae*, **contains many members which attract pollinating insects (particularly bluebottle flies,** *Calliphora*) **by emitting a fetid odour. This is especially true of carrion flowers (shown here). This species,** *Caraluma lutea*, **is common throughout southern Africa.**

Above: Cross-pollination is promoted in the begonia family, *Begoniaceae*, **by having single-sex flowers which are either male or female. In tuberous-rooted garden begonias (shown here) male flowers are large and conspicuous while female flowers are smaller and are partly hidden by the foliage.**

Below: *Thrum* **(left) and** *pin* **(right) flowers of the primrose,** *Primula*. **Bees, feeding on nectar secreted at the bottom of the corolla tubes, transfer pollen from the long anthers of the thrum plants to the long styles of the pin plants, and from the short anthers of the pin plants to the short styles of the thrum plants.**

anthers

style

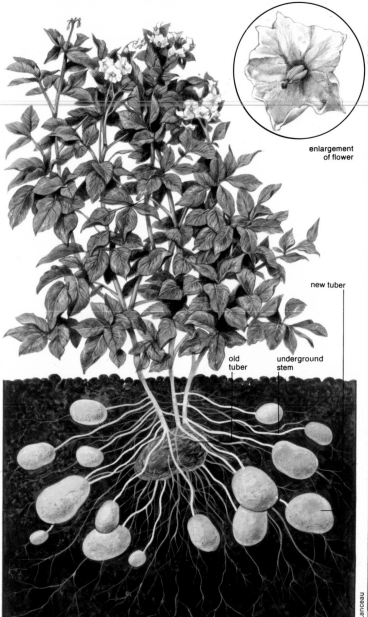

enlargement
of flower

new tuber

old
tuber

underground
stem

Above right: Pumpkins,
Cucurbita maxima, are
members of the cucumber
family, *Cucurbitaceae*.

Above: Potatoes, *Solanum
tuberosum*, are not
roots but swollen
sections of underground
stems, called *stem
tubers*, containing stores
of nutrient which the
plant lays down for its
next year's growth.
The 'eyes' of potatoes
are in fact buds from
which new plants are
produced in the spring.
Potatoes contain a lot
of starch, a little
protein, and a useful
amount of vitamin C
(*ascorbic acid*). Because
of their food value
and because they are easy
to grow, they are a
staple item of diet in
many parts of the world.

Left: Commercial
varieties of potato
produce far more food
than the plants require
for themselves. The
largest potato ever
grown weighed 3.2 kg
(7 lb 1 oz).

Right: Another member
of the same family,
Solanaceae, as the
potato is deadly
nightshade, *Atropa
belladonna*. The plant
contains a poison of
the nervous system.

Solanum tuberosum, tomato, Lycopersicon esculentum, and sweet pepper, Capsicum; wild plants, such as deadly nightshade, Atropa belladonna; and garden plants, like Petunia. The flower structure of this family varies but that of the potato is quite typical, with the white petals joined and spreading, and a group of projecting yellow anthers at the centre.

This family also includes the legendary mandrake, Mandragora officinalis. This is a perennial with bluish flowers, and fruits not unlike yellow tomatoes. The reputation of the plant derives from the taproot, which may be forked and more than 1 m (3 ft) long, so that it bears a distant resemblance to a human body. The root was valued by medieval herbalists as an anaesthetic and aphrodisiac, and the value of the plant may well have encouraged them to exaggerate the risks involved in digging it up. According to legend, the plant is supposed to shriek as the root is pulled out of the ground and the uprooter to be struck dead, so dogs used to be employed for this allegedly dangerous task. Mandrake grows naturally in southern Europe, in stony ground and neglected fields. It makes an interesting, and harmless, garden plant, notwithstanding its magical reputation.

Mints, figworts and lobelias

Though there are several complex regular-flowered families, most complex flowers are zygomorphic—they are symmetrical about only one plane. Three typically zygomorphic families are the mint family, Labiatae, the figwort family, Scrophulariaceae, and the lobelia family, Lobeliaceae.

The mint family includes familiar plants such as dead nettle, Lamium, thyme, Thymus, rosemary, Rosmarinus officinalis, and lavender, Lavandula, as well as many species of mint, Mentha. The plants often have stems with a roughly square cross-section and two leaves, or groups (whorls) of leaves, at each node. Most of the plants also have glands, sometimes seen as minute translucent dots on the leaves, which secrete volatile oils which give each species its own characteristic smell. The flowers, often called two-lipped, have a corolla in which the petals are united into two lobes, above and below the mouth of the flower. Many plants in the family are pollinated by bees. The bees land on the lower lip of the flower before extending their proboscises to reach the nectar deep inside.

The figwort family also has two-lipped flowers, typified by the snapdragon, Antirrhinum. Normally the entrance to an antirrhinum flower is completely blocked by the upper and lower lips of the corolla but humble bees, Bombus terrestris, are heavy enough to depress the lower lip and open the flower. Pollen is deposited on the bees' hairy backs as they feed on the nectar secreted at the bottom of the corolla tube.

The lobelia family includes many garden flowers, typical of which is the cardinal flower, Lobelia cardinalis, with its 1 m (3 ft) spike of scarlet flowers. Other members of the family are even more spectacular although they are never seen in temperate gardens. These are the giant lobelias of East Africa. Many species of these grotesque plants are known, most of them with a very limited distribution. For example, Lobelia telekii is found only in one valley on Mount Kenya, and Lobelia deckenii grows only on Mount Kilimanjaro in Tanzania. This is probably an instance of that common evolutionary phenomenon—the proliferation of new species on islands. In this case, however, the islands are not surrounded by sea, but are high mountains, above 3,000 m (10,000 ft), separated by lowland areas where these very specialized plants are unable to grow. On each separate mountain, adaptation to the local environment has resulted in a species very slightly different from that growing on the next mountain.

Because the East African mountains are close to the equator they receive a great deal of sunshine by day, but, because of their altitude, they quickly cool at night. Only well adapted plants can survive in these extreme conditions and the

Above left: A member of the figwort family, the foxglove, Digitalis. Foxglove leaves contain the chemical digitalin which makes the plant poisonous, though digitalin itself is used to make a drug important in the control of heart disease.

Left: Teasel, Dipsacus. Plants of the family to which teasel belongs, the scabious family, Dipsacaceae, are similar to members of the daisy family, Compositae. Both families have a composite flower head (inflorescence) made up of a mass of tiny individual flowers. Teasels can be distinguished from the thistles (Compositae) which they resemble by the spines (bracts), in a ring called an involucre, which surround the flower head.

Right: A typical composite, marguerite, Chrysanthemum frutescens. This is a common garden daisy. A wild daisy common by roadsides, the ox-eye daisy, Chrysanthemum leucantheum, is also sometimes known as marguerite.

ZEFA

Giuseppe Mazza

69

lobelias have adapted so well that they often grow up to four metres (12 ft) tall, looking like small trees though they are not woody plants.

The stems and growing points of giant lobelias are hidden by a dense growth of leaves, up to 0.25 m (10 in) long, and these leaves protect the stems and growing points by insulating them from the very low night temperatures. For example, in an air temperature of −5°C (23°F) the stem and flower temperature may be 2°C (36°F). Arctic and alpine plants of higher latitudes survive much harsher conditions while they are dormant in the winter but, unlike the giant lobelias, they do not experience extreme fluctuations of temperature every day of the year.

Daisy family

The dicot family with the most highly-evolved flowers is also the largest of flowering plant families. This family, the daisy family, *Compositae*, contains at least 13,000 species, about five per cent of all species of flowering plants. A few species are shrubs or small trees, but most are herbaceous and many are found in man-made habitats—as weeds on agricultural land or growing along roadsides and in abandoned pastures. Among these are the dandelion, *Taraxacum officinale*, the common daisy, *Bellis perennis*, the pineapple weed, *Matricaria matricarioides*, thistles, *Cirsium* and *Carduus*, and groundsels, *Senecio*. Like lobelias, giant groundsels, too, are found in East Africa.

Many other members of the daisy family are familiar as garden plants: Michaelmas daisies, *Aster*, and golden rod, *Solidago*, for example, and also *Chrysanthemum* and *Cineraria*. Not surprisingly, the family supplies food plants as well, and these include lettuce, *Lactuca*, and sunflower, *Helianthus annuus*. Sunflowers are grown for their seeds, from which oil is extracted, while the leaves and stems are fed to cattle, either fresh or made into silage. They are widely cultivated in continental Europe and Russia.

It is not easy to account for the huge success, in evolutionary terms, of the *Compositae*. One reason may be the adaptation of the flower and inflorescence for insect pollination. The family receives its name from the composite flower-head, a kind of inflorescence called a *capitulum*. In each flower the anthers are fused into a tube around the style. They shed their pollen into this tube, and the style, which is often ringed with hairs, then grows up and carries the pollen up above the tube. Any visiting insect becomes dusted with pollen, while at this stage the stigma, at the end of the style, is not exposed and self-pollination is impossible. Later on, the tip of the style divides and the two halves curl back to reveal the stigma which can then be cross-pollinated by another visiting insect. But if insects are lacking, the stigma curls back even further, far enough to collect some of the flower's own pollen. In this way self-pollination is virtually certain to take place if cross-pollination fails.

Another reason for the success of the *Compositae* is their seed dispersal mechanism. The sepals of each flower in the capitulum are often modified into a tuft of fine hairs attached to the seed. These are easily caught and blown away by the wind—as dandelion seed-heads show very well.

Ronan

Above: The mystical and symbolic properties once ascribed to plants often stemmed from improperly understood scientific facts. This seventeenth century illustration describes how the 'magnetism' of the sun makes a sunflower follow the sun—allowing the flower to be used to tell the time of day.

Below: Nutmeg is produced from the dried seed of *Myristica fragrans*. The seed is enclosed inside a fruit consisting of an outer yellow *pericarp*, an inner crimson *aril*, and a thin shell-like *endocarp*. When the fruit is ripe the pericarp splits open revealing the aril. Both the seed and the endocarp are then removed and dried.

Right: Herbs and spices belong to a wide range of plant families but especially to the mints, *Labiatae*. Those here are:
Basil—*Labiatae*
Bay—*Lauraceae*
Mint—*Labiatae*
Oregano—*Labiatae*
Rosemary—*Labiatae*
Cloves—*Myrtaceae*
Coriander—*Umbelliferae*
Ginger—*Zingiberaceae*
Pepper—*Piperaceae*

HERBS AND SPICES

Herbaceous plants are sometimes known simply as herbs, but the word 'herb' is more often used to describe plants whose leaves are used, either fresh or dried, as a flavouring for food. 'Spices' are the dried parts of plants other than leaves.

Right: The seventeenth century herb garden of Altdorf University, Bavaria. The early study of plants was closely associated with their medical and herbal uses.

Basil
Ocimum basilicum

Oregano
Origanum majorana

Coriander
Coriandrum sativum

Jacana

ZEFA

s nobilis

Mint
Mentha

nary
arinus officinalis

Cloves
Eugenia caryophyllata

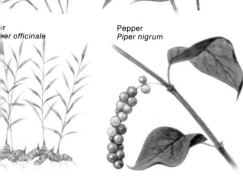

r
er officinale

Pepper
Piper nigrum

Above: Sage, *Salvia officinalis*, was thought to have health-giving properties—hence the Latin name, from *salvere*, to be in good health.

Left: Fruits of cumin, *Cuminum cyminum*. The plant is a member of the parsley family, *Umbelliferae*. It has finely divided leaves and white or yellow flowers. Cumin is widely used in the preparation of curry powder and as a seasoning in both bread and cakes. The seeds also yield an oil which is used in the manufacture of perfume.

Right: Sieving and refining mustard. Mustard is prepared from the powdered seeds of black mustard, *Brassica nigra*. (White mustard, *Sinapis alba*, is the mustard of 'mustard and cress'.) The seeds are first blended and then crushed to separate the husks from the kernels. The kernels are then ground to a powder on rollers and this powder is refined by passing it through a series of silk screens. *Turmeric*, a colouring agent, is then added.

Flowering Trees and Shrubs

The naturally dominant vegetation of any moderately wet and fertile area is forest. Trees are capable of producing a tall leaf canopy which overshadows other plants. In colder northern regions these trees are normally gymnosperms, but in more hospitable warm temperate and tropical areas they are almost always angiosperms. They are dicots, but have retained the tree characteristics which were probably normal among the earliest flowering plants, rather than evolving into herbaceous forms.

The trunks and branches that form the framework of trees and shrubs are built up over years of growth, with a gradual increase in girth. Typically this increase is about 25 mm (1 in) a year (measuring around the trunk at 1.5 m (5 ft) above the ground.) Some species grow much faster than this, in particular species of *Eucalyptus*. Others, including horse chestnut, *Aesculus hippocastanum*, and the common

Above left: Female catkins of the common sallow (goat willow), *Salix caprea*. Members of the willow family, *Salicaceae*, which also includes poplars, *Populus*, have flowers in catkins but each plant has flowers of one sex only. Willows may be large trees, such as the cricket bat willow, a variety of *Salix alba*; shrubby trees, such as osier, *Salix viminalis*; or dwarf shrubs like creeping willow, *Salix repens*. Poplars are often large, fast growing trees, such as some varieties of black poplar, *Populus nigra*.

Left: Cork oak, *Quercus suber*. Its thick rugged bark is the world's principal source of cork.

lime, *Tilia × europea*, grow more slowly. Young trees usually grow more rapidly than average; old trees more slowly.

The growth of a woody trunk or stem involves a process known as *secondary thickening*. In both dicots and gymnosperms there is a ring of vascular bundles in the stem towards the outer surface. In older stems and branches this ring of individual vascular bundles becomes a continuous ring of conducting tissue, with phloem on the outside, xylem on the inside, and a layer of cambium in between. The cells of the cambium continue to divide to produce new xylem and phloem cells and the stem grows outwards by the laying down of successive layers of xylem tissue. In cold and temperate regions the xylem cells produced in spring are relatively large, with thin walls, but as the growing season progresses the new

cells are smaller, with thicker, darker walls. Thus over a number of years the wood comes to have a series of *annual rings*, each being a band of darker *autumn wood* separated by the lighter *spring wood*. When a tree trunk is sawn across, these rings are clearly visible and by counting them the age of the tree can be found. Trees growing in the tropics, without pronounced seasons, have either irregular rings, corresponding to periods of good and bad weather rather than to years of age, or no rings at all.

Increase in the height or spread, rather than the girth, of a tree or shrub takes place by a different process, called *terminal growth*, which occurs at the tips of the branches. In the autumn, growth ceases and *winter buds* form. Each bud consists of a growing point covered by a number of *bud scales* which are modified

leaves. The bud usually contains part or all of the following year's new leaves and flowers, and the bud scales protect them from the extremes of the winter. In tropical and sub-tropical species whose growth continues throughout the year, winter buds do not form.

Temperate tree families

There is no hard-and-fast dividing line between dicot families which include trees and shrubs and those which include only herbaceous plants. Many families include both—suggesting that, if herbaceous plants evolved from woody plants, then this evolution must have taken place on many separate occasions. Nevertheless, many families consist predominantly of trees and shrubs.

The tree family that contains plants probably most similar to the earliest angiosperms is the magnolia family, *Magnoliaceae*. Like the simple herbaceous family, the water-lilies, *Nymphaeaceae*, they have flowers with many separate petals and stamens. The flowers are valued by gardeners for their large size and delicate pink or cream colouring.

Beeches, *Fagus*, sweet chestnuts, *Castanea*, and oaks, *Quercus*, all belong to one family, the *Fagaceae*. These are mostly

Left: The majestic English elm, *Ulmus procera*. Unfortunately elm trees are susceptible to a fungal disease, 'Dutch' elm disease, *Cerotocystis ulmi*, spread by a bark beetle, *Scolytus scolytus*. Periodic outbreaks have killed large numbers of trees. For example, one such outbreak, which started in 1970, killed most of the prominent hedgerow elms in large areas of England. Chemical control of the disease is impracticable for the millions of trees growing in the countryside and in the long term it is probably better to reduce the impact of epidemics by planting different trees to replace the elms.

Right: Common (or European) beech, *Fagus sylvatica*. Beeches, oaks, *Quercus*, and sweet chestnuts, *Castanea*, all belong to the same family, the beech family, *Fagaceae*.

Below: Scanning electron micrograph (about 700 times life size) of the *xylem* (wood) of lupin, *Lupinus*. The thickened rings around the xylem vessels give strength to the wood.

G. R. Roberts

Giuseppe Mazza

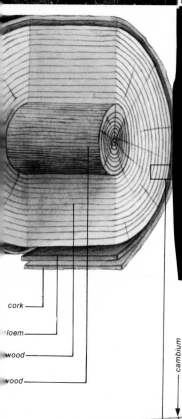

cork
loem
wood
vood

cambium

Wood is made up of annual rings of xylem produced by a thin layer of cells, the *cambium*, between the phloem and xylem. The cells of the xylem continue to function as water-conducting tissue for 20–30 years. During this time, however, they eventually become *lignified*—filling gives strength to the wood but prevents the passage of water. The outer, functional xylem forms a pale zone called the *sapwood*. The central lignified zone, often darker in colour, is called the *heartwood*. The *cork* (bark) is a protective layer of dead impermeable cells.

deciduous forest trees, with simple leaves and separate male and female flowers on the same tree. The flowers are grouped into inflorescences of petal-less flowers, called *catkins*, and appear early in the year, often before the leaves. The pollen is carried by the wind from male to female catkins, making cross-pollination very likely where a number of trees of the same species are present. After fertilization the female flowers produce *nuts*, hard-walled fruits dispersed by the animals which use them as a source of food.

Over 450 species of oak grow in Europe, Asia or America. Two are native to Britain and Northern Europe. The sessile oak, *Quercus petraea*, has acorns carried directly on the twigs (which is what the word 'sessile' means), while the pedunculate oak, *Quercus robur*, has stalked acorns. Pedunculate oak is often planted in areas where sessile oak is the naturally occurring wild-growing species and, since the two species interbreed freely, intermediate types are common.

Beeches, *Fagus*, are also widespread. They are particularly common on steep, chalk-based hillsides, such as the Chiltern hills in southern England, although they are found in most north temperate regions; while a related genus, the southern beeches, *Nothofagus*, are common in the southern hemisphere. Beech nuts (*mast*) are enclosed in a prickly husk. 'Copper beech' is a variety of the most common northern species, *Fagus sylvatica*, but has dark, purplish foliage.

Elms, *Ulmus*, belong to another family, the *Ulmaceae*. They are important timber trees but are perhaps more important for their contribution to the scenery in both Europe and North America. They are particularly common hedgerow trees, and, although elm flowers have inconspicuous greenish petals, the stamens have bright red filaments, so that the branches of an elm in flower appear red at a distance. The flowers are wind-pollinated, and the fruits, consisting of a seed surrounded by a circular papery wing, are dispersed by the wind. However, the fruits are often sterile. Most elm trees originate

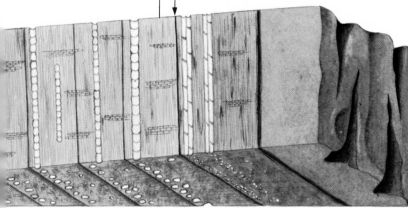

xylem   annual ring   phloem   cork

Sycamore
Acer pseudoplatanus

London plane
Platanus acerifolia

Midland hawthorn
Crataegus oxycanthoides

Above: Trees are capable of enlivening a drab urban scene. These six trees are common in British towns:— *Sycamore* is sometimes regarded as an urban weed as it produces masses of winged seeds which often germinate in unlikely places. *Midland hawthorn* is generally planted as a hedging plant, mainly because of its 3 cm (1 in) thorns. *London plane* for many epitomizes the town tree, thriving in central London. Characteristically the dark soiled bark peels off in strips, revealing pale new bark beneath. *Lime*, though often mutilated and 'lollipopped', is in fact a stately tree with yellow-green, heart-shaped leaves. *Flowering cherry* unfailingly produces a mass of colour in the spring. The variety 'Kanzan' is grown by grafting buds on to a rootstock of wild cherry, *Prunus avium*. *Red horsechestnut* is a hybrid between white horsechestnut, *Aesculus hippocastanum*, and American red buck-eye, *Aesculus pavia*.

Left: A group of alders, *Alnus*, in their most common habitat—beside water. Alders, which are members of the birch family, *Betulaceae*, have two remarkable features: they are the only flowering trees to produce 'cones', and they have symbiotic nodules on their roots. The 'cones' are not true cones as produced by gymnosperms but fruits which develop from the fertilized female catkins. The root nodules, probably formed by an *actinomycetes* fungus, provide the alder with a supply of n[i] which may b[e] supply in the boggy soils i[n] the tree grow[s]

Below: *Antho[...]* the leaves of maples, *Acer[...]* turns them g[...] in autumn. M[...] *Aceraceae*, oc[...] America, As[...] Europe. Sug[...] are native to[...] America, pa[...] New Englan[...] common Eu[...] are sycamor[e] *pseudoplatan[...]* Norway map[le] *platanoides*.

as suckers thrown up by neighbouring trees.

The family with the hardiest of all flowering trees is the birch family, *Betulaceae*, which includes alder, *Alnus*, and birches, *Betula*. One especially hardy birch is the dwarf birch, *Betula nana*, a small shrub with glossy, circular leaves which grows at high altitudes in northern Europe. Birches generally are small, fast-growing trees which are often the first to colonize open areas of land.

A closely related family to the birches is the *Corylaceae*, which includes hornbeam, *Carpinus betulus*, and hazel, *Corylus avellana*. Hornbeam is somewhat similar in appearance to beech, but its leaves have serrated rather than smooth edges, and the fruit is a cluster of winged seeds rather than a nut.

A final family of temperate woody plants is the heath family, *Ericaceae*, important more for shrubs than for trees. Most members of the family are evergreen shrubs, including *Rhododendron*, and many different kinds of heather, *Calluna* and *Erica*. Heathers and other dwarf ericaceous shrubs are the dominant plants over large areas of heathland, a vegetation type that is widespread in temperate areas and which also occurs on mountains in the tropics.

Tropical food trees
Several woody families include tropical plants from which are obtained food or drinks. Tea comes from the shrub *Ca[m]-*

ellia sinensis of the family *Theaceae*. It has been cultivated in China for at least 3,000 years. Both ordinary black teas and green teas are made from its leaves, but by different processes of withering (drying), roasting, fermentation and pressing. Coffee comes mainly from *Coffea arabica* (family *Rubiaceae*) which originally grew wild in Ethiopia. Another species, *Coffea canephora*, produces the inferior 'robusta' coffee. Coffee plants carry red berries, and the 'coffee beans', which are the seeds, are extracted from inside the berries.

Cocoa, a native of tropical America, but now widely grown in West Africa, comes from a small tree called *Theobroma cacao* (family *Sterculiaceae*). The tree is unusual in that the flowers and fruits grow directly from the trunk and main branches rather than on side branches. The cocoa beans, 40-60% is a fat called *cocoa* enclosed in red or yellow pods be processed in several ways cocoa for drinking, in which c[a] the fat is removed; or to make in which case extra cocoa bu[t] and milk are added.

Many tropical trees yield ed[...] but the papaya, *Carica papa[ya]* *Caricaceae*), is unusual in sev[...] The trees grow rapidly from se[...] fruit in the first year. After 3-4 may reach a height of 6 m (20 ft fruit-bearing then declines and be replaced. Male and female borne on separate trees. The f[...] produce an edible fruit, somet[...] melon, which is a greenish-yel[...] but has orange flesh. The s[...] useful. It contains an enzym[...]

Common lime
Tilia x europea

Flowering cherry
Prunus "Kanzan"

Red horsechestnut
Aesculus x carnea

NHPA

Eric Crichton

G. R. Roberts

Left: Two ghost gums, *Eucalyptus papuana,* **growing near Alice Springs in central Australia. The name 'eucalyptus' comes from the Greek** *eu,* **well, and** *kalyptos,* **covered. It refers to the cap, formed from the joined sepals and petals, which covers the stamens while the flower is in bud. This cap falls off when the flower opens.**

Right: Two fruits: (top) sweet chestnut, *Castanea sativa;* **(bottom) mango,** *Mangifera indica.* **The sweet chestnut (family** *Fagaceae***) is a common woodland species in north temperate regions but, although once planted it grows well in northern regions, it is really a warm temperate species—it does not produce ripe seed further north than the Midlands of England. The mango (family** *Anacardiaceae***) is a large evergreen tree up to 27 m (90 ft) tall —though cultivated varieties may be smaller—producing the fruit sometimes known as the 'tropical apple'. The fruit is eaten raw, cooked as an ingredient of chutney, or occasionally canned.**

which can break down protein. Papain is collected on a commercial scale and used, among other things, to tenderize meat.

Tropical and sub-tropical timber trees

Other tropical families contain species which are valuable for their timber. Among the better known of these timbers are mahogany, from *Swietenia mahogani* (family *Meliaceae*), teak, from *Tectona grandis* (family *Verbenaceae*) and ebony, from *Diospyros ebenum* (family *Ebenaceae*). In sub-tropical areas, species of *Eucalyptus* (family *Myrtaceae*) are becoming increasingly important as timber trees. Eucalypts, or gum trees, are native to Australasia, and are unusual in that they have two kinds of foliage. The foliage found on young plants consists of large rounded leaves clasping the stem. The adult foliage has smaller, lanceolate

(long and narrow), stalked leaves. Eucalypts can grow extremely quickly, up to 10 m (33 ft) a year; one species, *Eucalyptus regnans,* grows to more than 105 m (340 ft), making it the tallest of all flowering trees.

The baobab, *Adansonia digitata* (family *Bombacaceae*) does not grow as fast as *Eucalyptus,* but is one of the oddest-looking trees, having a massive trunk up to 40 m (130 ft) in girth, surmounted by a comparatively sparse crown, as if it had been stuck into the ground with its roots waving in the air. For this reason, it is sometimes called the 'upside-down-tree'. The largest baobabs are around 1,000 years old, and old trees are treated with some reverence—but not by elephants, which frequently kill them. The trunks of baobabs store water and may contain over 100,000 litres (20,000 gallons).

Other uses of flowering trees

Flowering trees are important for food and for their timber. They also have a number of other uses, such as the production of cork, rubber and tannin. Further uses are more exotic. Around the Red Sea, for example, a small twisted tree, *Boswellia thurifera,* (family *Burseraceae*) produces a resin which is collected by making an incision in the tree's trunk. As the resin oozes out it gradually hardens and after about three months can be scraped off as hard, translucent lumps, 1-2 cm ($\frac{3}{8}$-$\frac{3}{4}$ in) across. These lumps are the most important constituent of frankincense, which for thousands of years has been an important item of commerce in the Middle East. It is burnt in houses and churches all over the world. A high-yielding incense tree may be the jealously guarded property of a Somali family.

The Rose, Pea and Spurge Families

It is generally recognized that herbaceous dicots have evolved from woody ancestors. But if this is so it must have occurred on many unrelated occasions, for many dicot families contain both herbaceous and woody species. Three such families are particularly important—both because of the number of their species and economically. They are the rose family, *Rosaceae*, the pea family, *Leguminosae*, and the spurge family, *Euphorbiaceae*.

Within these three families evolutionary adaptation to different environments has produced a diverse range of floral and vegetative structure. This is most conspicuous among the *Rosaceae*, which range from trees with complete flowers and simple leaves, such as the apple tree, *Malus*, to herbaceous plants with compound leaves and small flowers which lack petals, such as the lady's-mantle, *Alchemilla*. Nevertheless, despite this range of structure, it is possible to trace patterns of similarity within each family that confirm its common origin. *Rosaceae*, for example, have leaf-like outgrowths, called *stipules*, at the base of the leaves; most of the *Euphorbiaceae* have systems of vessels in their stems which secrete a milky white liquid, called *latex*; and the *Leguminosae* have root nodules containing symbiotic nitrogen-fixing bacteria.

Fruits and seeds

The *Euphorbiaceae* are economically important mainly because the family includes the rubber tree, *Hevea brasiliensis*, while the *Rosaceae* and the *Leguminosae*

Apple
Malus

Almond
Prunus amygdalus

Oak
Quercus

Tomato
Lycopersicon
esculentum

Strawberry
Fragaria

Pomegranate
Punica granatum

Wheat
Triticur
aestivu

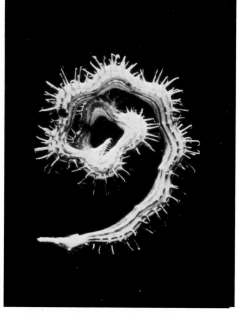

Heather Angel

Left, above and right: To be successful a plant species must ensure that its seeds are widely dispersed. Three types of dispersal are shown here. The raspberry, *Rubus*, (left) is a succulent fruit eaten and dispersed by animals. Medick, *Medicago*, (above) is also dispersed by animals—but in this case by hooks that cling to animals' coats. Dandelion, *Taraxacum*, seeds (right) have a tuft of hairs to aid wind dispersal.

Heather Angel

76

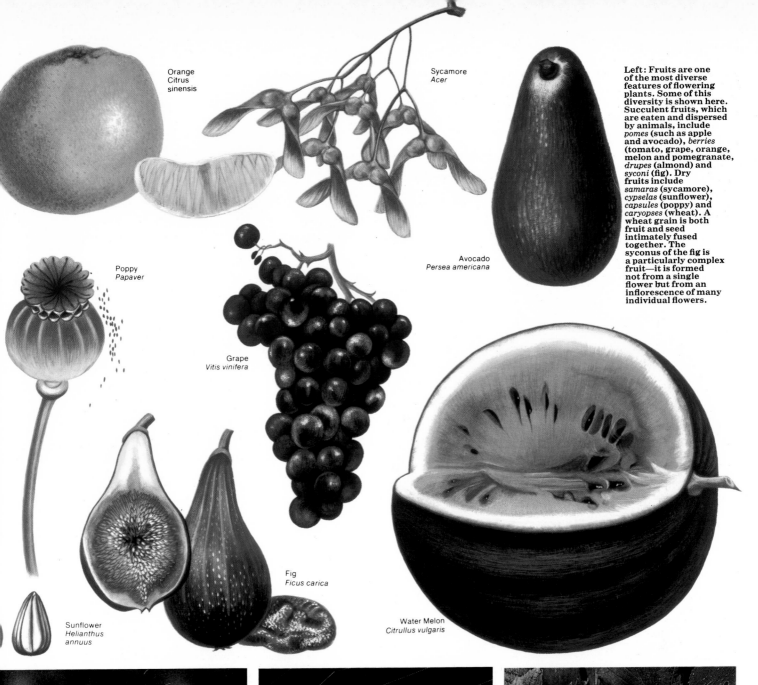

Orange
Citrus
sinensis

Sycamore
Acer

Avocado
Persea americana

Poppy
Papaver

Grape
Vitis vinifera

Fig
Ficus carica

Sunflower
Helianthus
annuus

Water Melon
Citrullus vulgaris

Left: Fruits are one of the most diverse features of flowering plants. Some of this diversity is shown here. Succulent fruits, which are eaten and dispersed by animals, include *pomes* (such as apple and avocado), *berries* (tomato, grape, orange, melon and pomegranate, *drupes* (almond) and *syconi* (fig). Dry fruits include *samaras* (sycamore), *cypselas* (sunflower), *capsules* (poppy) and *caryopses* (wheat). A wheat grain is both fruit and seed intimately fused together. The syconus of the fig is a particularly complex fruit—it is formed not from a single flower but from an inflorescence of many individual flowers.

Left: 'Explosive' dispersal. The fruit of the Mediterranean cranesbill, *Erodium botrys*, has a long 'beak' which twists as the fruit ripens. The beak suddenly breaks, throwing the seed at its tip into the air.

R. G. Milne

Above: Birch, *Betula,* nuts weigh about 0.0002 g (0.000006 oz) and are easily blown long distances by the wind —barring spiders' webs.

Right: A dormouse unwittingly dispersing blackberry, *Rubus.*

Heather Angel

Left: Plums, damsons, apricots, almonds and cherries all belong to one genus, *Prunus*. The wild species from which thay were originally cultivated is unknown, but a relative is the sloe, *Prunus spinosa*. **Above: The Australian desert pea, *Clianthus formosus*. The plant is specialized to survive in a dry habitat.**

Below: In general, rose flowers have five sepals, five petals and many stamens, while the seeds are carried inside a fleshy, urn-shaped *receptacle* at the base of the flower below the sepals. In wild roses, such as *Rosa rugosa x roxburgii*, (shown here) the receptacles turn bright red or orange as the fruits ripen and are called *rose-hips*. Garden roses are often sterile, however, and in these varieties the ripe rose-hips may not form. Garden roses also often have extra petals which obscure the simple regularity of the wild flower. Rose-hips are eaten by birds, so dispersing the seeds which are indigestible.

are important largely because of the use of the fruits and seeds of some member plants as food. Peas and beans (*Leguminosae*) are seeds, while apples and pears (*Rosaceae*) are fruits. There is a distinct difference between seeds and fruits. *Seeds* develop from the female gamete (normally after fertilization) inside the ovary; *fruits* develop from the ovary wall (and occasionally from other parts of the flower as well) outside the seed.

The evolution of fruits is a major reason why flowering plants have become the dominant land vegetation. They have evolved in a number of ways each designed to produce widespread dispersal of the seeds contained inside them. Many have developed wings so that they can be more easily dispersed by the wind; others have developed hooks which attach to passing animals; while a third group, belonging to waterside plants, have developed so that they float on water and can be carried along by water currents.

The most economically important group of fruits, however, produce succulent tissue which is food to animals including man. The seeds, which are normally either inedible or indigestible, are dispersed as the fruits are collected and eaten.

The rose family

The family which is perhaps the most important for its fruit bearing members is the rose family, *Rosaceae*. It includes, among others, apples, *Malus*, pears, *Pyrus*, raspberries, *Rubus*, strawberries, *Fragaria*, plums and cherries, *Prunus*, as well as roses, *Rosa*.

Roses have some of the features which are characteristic of the *Rosaceae*, although few features are common to all of the family's 3,000 species. The only common features, in fact, are leaves with stipules and regular flowers. As well as

these features roses have compound leaves—that is leaves divided into leaflets—and stems which are usually prickly, each thorn being a woody outgrowth of the outer layer of tissue, the *epidermis*. These thorns are modifications of the hairs which are found on the surfaces of most plants. They protect the plant from being eaten by animals.

Roses are most widely grown purely for decoration but they do have a few other uses. Rose fruits, called *hips*, contain ascorbic acid (vitamin C) and are used to make *rose-hip syrup*, and in Bulgaria the damask rose, *Rosa damascena*, is cultivated on a large scale for the manufacture of *attar of roses*, an oil used in perfumery. Some 2,000 rose flowers have to be distilled to yield just 1g (0.03 oz) of the oil.

Brambles, *Rubus*, belong to another genus of *Rosaceae*, and they are often found in habitats similar to those of the roses. Unlike roses, however, they do not have a rose-hip but a composite fruit, typified by the familiar blackberry, which is composed of a lot of small fruits, called *drupelets*.

The common bramble, or blackberry, is also interesting because it shows *apomixis*, a kind of reproduction in which flowers are produced in the normal way but seeds and fruits develop *without* fertilization. This means that the seeds grow into plants that are identical to the parent plant, just as if they had been grown vegetatively from cuttings. In this way minor structural differences between plants are propagated unaltered into succeeding generations. At least 2,000 of these different kinds of blackberries have been given names as separate species, but these names have little meaning or usefulness and the normal practice is to describe the blackberry as an *aggregate species* under the name *Rubus*

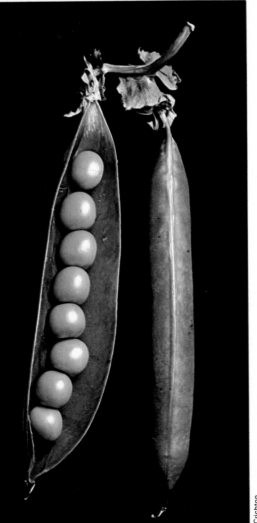

G. R. Roberts

Eric Crichton

Above: A decorative legume—lupin, *Lupinus*. Here garden plants have 'escaped' to grow wild.

Left: The garden pea, *Pisum sativum*. Other cultivated legumes, or *pulses*, are the soya bean, *Glycine max*, chick pea, *Cicer arietinum*, lentil, *Lens culinaris*, broad bean, *Vicia faba*, and several species and varieties of *Phaseolus*, including runner and haricot beans. All are important sources of protein and all, like all legumes, possess symbiotic, nitrogen-fixing bacteria in nodules on their roots. This allows high crop yields to be obtained without expensive dressings of nitrogen fertilizer.

fruticosus. Cultivated brambles include raspberry, *Rubus idaeus*, and loganberry, *Rubus loganobaccus*.

Several other trees and shrubs in the rose family are common wild plants in northern temperate regions. Among these are *Crataegus*, hawthorn, and *Sorbus*, which includes rowan and whitebeam. Herbaceous plants are fewer but one of particular interest is the strawberry, *Fragaria*. Apart from its fruits strawberry can be recognized by its habit of sending out long runners, or *stolons*. The stolons are actually fast-growing horizontal stems which take root and grow into a series of new plants. Cultivated strawberries originated as hybrids between two American species, *Fragaria virginiana* from the east and *Fragaria chiloensis* from the west.

Fruit trees
Like raspberries and strawberries, most common types of fruit tree belong to the rose family. Wild forms of two of these, the crab apple, *Malus pumila*, and the wild pear, *Pyrus communis*, grow wild all over Europe, although the fruits of the wild forms bear little resemblance to the highly selected varieties of apples and pears normally cultivated. These varieties have been developed by gardeners over many thousands of years.

Perhaps the best eating variety, 'Cox's Orange Pippin', was first produced as a seedling from the old variety 'Ribston Pippin' in about 1850. Other old varieties, such as the 'Russets', can also often be bought but modern varieties, such as 'Golden Delicious' and 'McIntosh', crop more heavily, particularly in southern Europe, Australia and North America. Cooking varieties, such as 'Bramley', contain relatively more acid and less sugar, while cider apples have a high tannin content which gives a slight bitterness to the drink.

Plums, damsons, apricots, almonds and cherries all belong to one genus, *Prunus*. As with apples and pears, edible *Prunus* species have been cultivated for at least 3,000 years. Two other small trees in the *Rosaceae* are also cultivated for their fruit, though on a much smaller scale. The quince, *Cydonia vulgaris*, produces a hard yellowish pear-shaped fruit, which is somewhat acid and therefore used for making jam or jelly—the Spanish name of the quince, *marmelo*, is the origin of the word marmalade. The medlar, *Mespilus germanica*, is a small spreading tree with twisted branches. It bears round brown fruits which are eaten when they are half rotten or *bletted*.

The pea family
The most striking characteristic of the pea family is the fruit. It is formed from the cylindrical ovary which splits into two halves to disclose a row of spherical seeds. Typical of such a fruit is the ordinary garden pea pod. The pod is called a *legume*, and plants of this family are often referred to as 'legumes'.

Many crop plants are legumes. Particularly important is the groundnut, *Arachis hypogaea*, which is grown all over the tropics and sub-tropics, and also in the US as far north as Virginia. Sometimes called the peanut or monkey-nut, it is an 79

G. Mazza

G. Mazza

Above: *Acalypha hispida,* an ornamental member of the spurge family, *Euphorbiaceae. Acalypha hispida* and its close relative, *Acalypha wilkesiana,* are widely cultivated for their long, flaming red inflorescences. Some varieties also have *variegated* leaves—that is leaves partly lacking chlorophyll.

Above: African acacias, like *Acacia xanthophloea* (shown here), possess spines which develop from modified stipules at the bases of the leaf stalks. Spines protect the acacias from animals such as antelopes. In Australia, however, there are few large grazing animals and Australian acacias, or *wattles,* lack spines.

annual plant which grows either into a small bush, 45 cm (18 in) high, or trails over the ground. It has small yellow flowers, which are usually self-pollinated. After pollination the flower stalks elongate, pushing the developing seed pods into the soil, and the nuts ripen underground.

Groundnuts, removed from their fibrous pods, are an important food in much of the world, because they contain 30 per cent protein and from 40 to 50 per cent oil, as well as vitamins B and E. They can be eaten raw, cooked, or ground to make peanut butter. Groundnut oil is used as a cooking oil and for making margarine.

As well as pulses (legumes with edible seeds, like peas, beans and lentils) the pea family contains about 13,000 other species and is often divided into three sub-families, only one of which, the *Papilionoideae* (meaning 'butterfly flowers'), has the characteristic pea flowers. These irregular (*zygomorphic*) flowers have ten stamens and five petals. The uppermost petal is large and spreading, the two lateral ones are narrower and directed forwards, and the two lowest are partly fused and enclose the ovary and stamens. Nine of the ten stamens are also fused to form a trough surrounding the ovary, but the uppermost one is free.

This distinctive flower structure encourages cross-pollination by long-tongued insects, such as bees, which are also heavy enough to depress and force apart the petals enclosing the stamens. Having done this, a bee can then reach the nectar which is secreted into the trough formed by the fused stamens. In the process, pollen is dusted on to the hairs of the bee's body by the free stamen and is carried to other flowers, so promoting cross-pollination, for most insects tend to visit a number of plants of the same species in succession. Despite this,

Above: The castor oil plant, *Ricinus communis,* showing flowers and fruit. Inside the fruit are three seeds from which castor oil is obtained. Medicinal castor oil must be extracted from cold seeds, otherwise it is poisonous. The seeds themselves are also poisonous—eating more than three may be fatal. The industrial oil, obtained from heated seeds, is used in hydraulic fluids.

however, many species are self-pollinated.

Pulses belong to the *Papilionoideae* as do several common wild flowers including gorse, *Ulex,* broom, *Cytisus,* and birdsfoot trefoil, *Lotus.* Two other *Papilionoideae,* lucerne (alfalfa), *Medicago sativa,* and clover, *Trifolium,* are common forage plants.

The two other sub-families of *Leguminosae* grow mainly in tropical and subtropical regions and are mostly trees or shrubs. The largest of the two, the *Mimosoideae,* has eight clusters of small regular (*actinomorphic*) flowers, and numerous stamens that project beyond the petals, giving the clusters a feathery appearance. One genus of *Mimosoideae, Acacia,* is especially common in South and Central America, Africa and Australia. These trees are interesting because

of the spines which generally develop from modified stipules at the base of the leaf stalks. In some species, called *ant-acacias,* the bases of the spines are inflated and hollow, and inhabited by ants. These ants help the tree to survive. They feed on sugar secreted by the tree but also eat any other plants which grow nearby.

The third sub-family of the *Leguminosae,* the *Caesalpinioideae,* is smaller than the other two sub-families but includes one of the most spectacular tropical flowering trees. *Amherstia nobilis* is a small tree, growing to 10 m (33 ft). It is pollinated by birds which it attracts with clusters of between 20 and 30 large flowers, each about 70 mm (3 in) across.

The spurge family

There are some 3,000 species in the spurge family of which about a third belong to one genus, *Euphorbia,* which contains many plants which contain compounds with a purgative action—hence the name 'spurge'. Most plants in this family are poisonous. Other family characteristics include single-sexed flowers which lack petals, three-celled ovaries, and the production of latex.

Species of *Euphorbia* have several male flowers and one female flower clustered together into an inflorescence, called a *cyathium,* which is surrounded by small flat petal-like structures. The cyathium is the one common characteristic of *Euphorbia;* it links together what is otherwise, both structurally and ecologically, a very diverse collection of plants. For instance, temperate euphorbias, such as sea spurge, *Euphorbia paralias,* which grows on beaches and sand dunes, are mostly herbs or shrubs, while in Africa many *Euphorbia* species in dry areas look like cactuses, having swollen succulent stems with spines and no leaves.

Grasses

About 80 per cent of all known flowering plant species are dicots. The remaining 20 per cent (about 55,000 species in all) belong to the other major group of angiosperms, the *Monocotyledonae*, or more simply the *monocots*. The monocots are generally recognized as being the most highly evolved of all plants and they include orchids, lilies and irises as well as grasses, sedges and rushes. It is the grass family which provides man with his most valuable food and forage crops.

In the 65 million years since they first evolved the monocots have developed along two main and diverging pathways. One of these, typified by the orchids, *Orchidaceae*, is towards extremely elaborate and specialized flower structures to promote cross-pollination by insects. The other, typified by the grasses, *Gramineae*, it towards simplified flowers, often with the petals and sepals missing altogether.

It is the second of these groups, the grasses, which is probably the most important of all plant families. Grasses, either as cereals or as forage for livestock, are the basic source of food for most of the world's population. No other plant family is cultivated to anything like the same extent. The grasses are also one of the larger families of flowering plants, containing more than 8,000 species in over 600 genera. They provide one quarter of the world's vegetation cover.

Despite their importance, however, grasses are rarely conspicuous: different species often look very much the same. The major reason for this uniformity is that grasses have no need for sepals, petals or other brightly coloured structures to attract pollinating insects. Instead the flowers of grasses are very well adapted for wind-pollination. They have three stamens, and a single ovary—containing a single ovule from which develops the *grain*, or seed—with two styles. Each style terminates in a feathery

Above: The most important food crops are cultivated grasses or *cereals*. The most important tropical and sub-tropical cereal is rice, *Oryza sativa*. The rice plant has a loose, open head of many small one-flowered spikelets and is usually grown in flooded fields. The stems are hollow—allowing oxygen to pass down to the roots which would otherwise be deprived of oxygen by the waterlogging of the soil. These terraced fields are in the Phillipines.

Below: Sugar, *Saccharum officinarum*, is another tropical cereal. This is a 1725 illustration of a West Indian plantation.

stigma which provides the largest possible surface area for catching pollen grains as they blow past in the air.

The individual grass flowers, or *florets*, which are often very small, are grouped into inflorescences, called *spikelets*, containing up to twenty flowers packed tightly together. (Occasionally these spikelets may contain only one flower but they are still normally considered as inflorescences). The spikelets themselves are then arranged in a head which may be very compact, as in the fox-tail, *Alopecurus pratensis*, or loose and widespreading, as in wavy hair-grass, *Deschampsia flexuosa*.

Other characteristics of grasses are their tufted growth style and their hollow circular stems and long narrow leaves. The lower part of each leaf is wrapped around the stem. In many species individual plants increase in size from buds at the base—a process known as *tillering*. Additionally new plants may be produced by spreading horizontal underground stems (*rhizomes*) from which new plants grow up at intervals. It is the ability of grasses to grow from the base, combined with their ability to colonize bare areas rapidly from seed, that has resulted in their extraordinary success. They are able to survive grazing and burning better than any other group of plants.

Cereals

The most important of all food plants are the *cereals*, cultivated members of the grass family. About 12 species of cereals provide the staple diet of most of the world's population. These species have evolved as a result of cultivation and the deliberate selection of characteristics.

Remy

ZEFA

ZEFA

Left, above and right:
Three temperate cereals:
rye, barley and oats.
Rye, *Secale cereale*,
(left) has flower-heads
similar to wheat but
the spikelets contain
only two florets
rather than wheat's
five. There are two
species of barley:
two-rowed, *Hordeum
distichon*, (above)
and six-rowed, *Hordeum
vulgare*. The names
refer to the apparent
number of rows of grain
on the head. Both
species have spikelets
in groups of three in
two rows, one each side
of the flower head. In
six-rowed barley each
spikelet is fertile,
while in two-rowed
barley only one in three
is fertile. Oats, *Avena*,
(right) have spikelets
containing 2-4 drooping
florets.

The most important temperate crop species is bread wheat, *Triticum aestivum*. There are a large number of varieties of this species but most have a spikelet of five florets, of which three are fertile and develop grains. Furthermore, the main stalk of the ear of wheat remains intact while the grains are shed. In related wild grasses, the stalk shatters, making the separation of the grain and chaff much more difficult.

Wheat species are among the earliest plants to have been cultivated by man. A species called emmer, *Triticum dicoccum*, was found by archaeologists to have been cultivated at Jarmo, in Kurdistan, around 5000 BC. It is likely that ancient wheat species originated in this area from artificial crosses between two wild grass species.

The other major temperate cereals are barley, *Hordeum vulgare* and *Hordeum distichon*, grown for animal feed and as a source of malt for brewing; durum wheat, *Triticum durum*, whose flour contains a high proportion of *gluten*, the component of flour which becomes sticky and elastic when wetted, so that it is ideal for making pasta; rye, *Secale cereale*; and oats, *Avena*. Both rye and oats probably grew as weeds in fields of wheat and barley, but were recognized by early cultivators as useful plants in their own right. The wild oat, *Avena fatua*, is still an extremely troublesome weed of cereal crops. It is particularly difficult to eliminate because it is so similar in development and physiology to the cereals among which it grows.

Whereas wheat is the main temperate food species, another grass, rice, *Oryza sativa*, is the staple food for tropical and sub-tropical areas in large parts of Africa and Asia. It is also increasingly grown in other parts of the world, such as Australia and southern Europe. It was first cultivated about 3000 BC, and, because of its value as a food plant, within only 1,000 years was being grown throughout China, India and South-East Asia.

The third major cereal is maize, *Zea mays*. It is the only cereal to have originated in the New World—it was first cultivated between 4500 and 3500 BC—but is now a major crop throughout tropical and sub-tropical areas of the world. It is also quite widely grown in temperate regions. The ripe grain can be ground into meal, or, if grown in countries, such as Britain, where the summer is too short for ripening, the whole plant can be harvested and made into silage.

Other tropical and sub-tropical cereals include sorghum, *Sorghum vulgare*; sugar cane, *Saccharum officinarum*; and many kinds of millet, *Panicum*. A few other rarer cereal species are grown only in one area. For example, teff, *Eragrostis teff*, is the most commonly grown cereal in the upland areas of Ethiopia but is hardly grown at all anywhere else.

Bamboos

Although most grasses are herbaceous, one group of grasses, the bamboos, which grow mostly in tropical and sub-tropical regions, have remained woody. Because of this, and because some species have fleshy fruits, they are regarded as the most primitive kind of grasses. Some species grow tree-like to more than 40 m (130 ft), with stems up to 20 cm (8 in) in diameter, although there is no secondary thickening.

Below: Modern cereals are the result of thousands of years of selection and breeding. In the past this was done with little knowledge of the underlying genetics but in modern times these have been extensively studied. This maize cob is the result of a cross between purple-seeded parents which each contained a recessive gene for yellow seeds. The result is a ratio of three purple seeds to one yellow.

Right: Two other monocot families, rushes, *Juncaceae*, and sedges, *Cyperaceae*, are grass-like. One sedge, papyrus, *Cyperus papyrus*, (shown here) was cultivated in Egypt to make paper.

Biophoto Assoc./Carolina Biol. Supply Co.

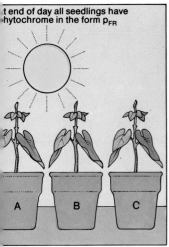

t end of day all seedlings have phytochrome in the form p_{FR}

4 normal nights

4 nights with short period far red light- P_R formed

red light reverses the effect of far red - P_R returns to P_{FR}

all plants have normal days and nights for several days

no elongation

P_R causes stem to elongate

no elongation

Courtesy Scientific American

PLANT HORMONES

auxins

gibberellins

abscisic acid

eythlene

cytokinins

1 *Auxins* produced in the growing point of the stem control stem elongation, the dominance of the main bud, and the formation of roots.
2 *Gibberellins* produced in the growing point control cell division in the growing point.
3,4 *Ethylene* produced in fruits and leaves controls fruit ripening and leaf senescence.
5 *Cytokinins* produced in fruit control fruit development.
6,7 *Abscisic* acid produced in leaves controls senescence and stomata opening.

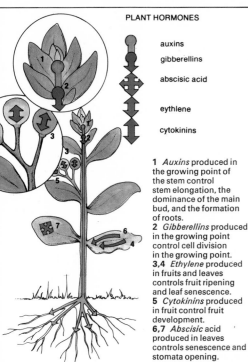

Ann Ronan Picture Library

Left: Some of the effects of hormones. *Ethylene* is a special case. It is unknown whether it is itself a hormone or a by-product of hormone action.

Above: The response of plants to light is partly due to a chemical, called *phytochrome*, which exists in plants in two reversible forms P_R and P_{FR}. Red light in daylight converts P_R to P_{FR} but light of a longer wavelength (*far red light*) converts P_{FR} back to P_R. One effect of phytochrome (on stem elongation) and the reversible nature of the P_R/P_{FR} system are shown here. Three bean seedlings were first grown under normal conditions.

G. R. Roberts

Plant A remained in these conditions but plants B and C were given a period of far red light every night for 4 nights and then normal nights. Plant C was also given a period of red light immediately after the far red light. At the end of the experiment some days later only plant B had elongated. This was due to P_R formed by the far red light. Far red light encourages stem elongation so that plants grow up out of the shade of other plants. Beneath a leaf canopy there is more far red than red light.

Left: The vitality of a growing plant: *Eucalyptus* devouring a fence post.

THE CONTROL OF GROWTH IN PLANTS

The growth of plants from germination to flowering and eventual death is controlled by both genetic and environmental factors. The final shape and nature of an individual plant is the result of the modification of its fundamental hereditary constitution (called the *genotype*) by environmental influences. Exactly how this happens is not fully understood. Nevertheless, it is known that many features of plant growth and development are controlled by *hormones*.

The first plant hormone to be isolated was *indole-3-acetic acid* (IAA), one of a group of plant hormones called *auxins*. It appears to have a general role in controlling the development of plant tissues in conjunction with two other groups of plant hormones called the *cytokinins* and the *gibberellins*. The correct combination of these three hormones can cause isolated plant cells, suspended in tissue culture solution, to develop into complete plants. A fourth plant hormone, *abscisic acid*, is involved in the control of leaf-fall and bud dormancy in deciduous woody plants.

Germination and growth

A seed contains a *dormant* plant embryo in which normal physiological processes, such as respiration, operate at a very low rate while cell division and growth are completely stopped. The seed also contains a store of nutrient, either as *endosperm* or in swollen seed leaves (*cotyledons*). Until the seedling starts to photosynthesize, it is dependent on its stored reserve.

After the seed is shed from the plant, it remains dormant for anything from a few hours to many years until it receives an external stimulus which triggers germination. This stimulus varies from one species to another, but it is generally a favourable combination of day-length, moisture and temperature, following a suitable additional stimulus, such as exposure to cold, during the dormant period.

When the seed germinates a root grows out first, enabling the seedling to obtain water and mineral nutrients. The cotyledons appear as the first green leaves of the seedling, unless they are swollen with food reserves (as in the runner bean, *Phaseolus coccineus*) in which case they remain below ground.

Growth of the seedling involves a rapid increase in the numbers of cells in localized regions called *meristems* (by the process of *cell division*). The meristems are found at the tips of the stem and roots. After dividing, the cells elongate and *differentiate*, developing the structures, such as vacuoles, which are typical of mature, specialized plant cells. For example some of the cells develop the special features of *xylem* and *phloem*.

Tropisms

The direction in which a plant grows is influenced by light and gravity. The effect of light was first investigated by Charles Darwin. He showed that the *coleoptile* (growing shoot) of a grass seedling bends towards light; this is called *positive phototropism*. Plants also show several other tropisms: stems are *negatively geotropic*, that is they tend to grow upwards against gravity, even in the absence of light, while roots are *positively geotropic*. All these changes in the direction of growth are caused by the cells on one side of the stem or root elongating more than those on the other side as a result of hormone action.

Tropical Monocots

Tropical vegetation contains many strange forms of plant life. This is especially true of tropical monocots, many of which have features of structure or habit unknown in plants of temperate regions. In particular, many grow into tree-like forms superficially more like dicot trees (such as oak or elm) or gymnosperm trees (such as pines) than the herbaceous plants which are the more typical form of monocots.

Palms and screwpines

Although many tropical monocot families have some tree-like species, only two families, the palms, *Palmae*, and the screwpines, *Pandanaceae*, are chiefly composed of large trees. Of these the palm family is by far the larger and more important, containing some 2,500 species. Different species of palm supply food and shelter for millions of people in the tropics.

Palms and screwpines are trees, but their development and structure are quite different from that of dicot trees. A palm seedling grows for several years with its stem *apex*, or growing point, at ground level. This produces leaves but makes no upward growth until the apex has enlarged to a certain width, which varies from species to species. Once this width has been reached, which may take

Above, right and below: Palms, *Palmae*, are most often associated with the desert, camels and oases (right, a Tunisian oasis). However, they are an extremely important tropical and sub-tropical family. The most important cultivated palms are the date palm, *Phoenix dactylifera*, the oil palm, *Elaeis guineensis*, and the coconut palm, *Cocos nucifera* (below), all of which form the basis of major industries. Others are rarer and exotic. The coco-de-mer, *Lodoicea maldivica* (above), whose massive fruits may weigh up to 20 kg (45 lb), is found on only two islands in the Seychelles.

Jean-Pierre Bourret

G R Roberts

Dr Giuseppe Mazza

Left: Many bromeliads, like *Fascicularia bicolor* (shown here), are epiphytes in which the leaf bases form a rosette in which a pool of water collects. The plants use this pool as a supply of water and also the dead leaves and insects, which collect and decompose in it, as a supply of nutrients. Bromeliads can therefore flourish on the branches of trees where other plants would die from lack of nutrients and water.

Above right: The upside-down inflorescence of the banana, *Musa*.

Below: Many tropical monocots are familiar house plants. This is *Maranta leuconeura*.

up to 12 years, no further lateral growth occurs no matter how tall the palm grows. The trunk of a palm is generally the same diameter from base to crown. There is none of the *secondary thickening* that gives strength to dicot and gymnosperm trees.

Despite the lack of secondary thickening, palms can grow to quite considerable heights. One species of wax palm, *Ceroxylon*, which grows high in the Andes, can grow to 60 m (200 ft) or more though most palms only grow to less than half this height. The trunk is supported by the woody, vascular bundles which, as in all monocots, are distributed evenly across the width of the trunk. In the coconut palm, *Cocos nucifera*, there are about 18,000 vascular bundles in a trunk about 30 cm (1 ft) in diameter. For all palms, additional support is provided by fibres which run alongside the vascular bundles.

Other palms, the rattans, such as *Calamus* species, have relatively slender stems and are climbing plants. They are particularly common in South-East Asia and grow up into the forest canopy, attaching themselves by hooks and spines which cover their stems and leaves. This method of growth is an adaptation to the intense competition for light in tropical rain forests.

Palms grow upwards at a rate of anything from 20 cm (8 in) to 1 m (3 ft) per year, producing a succession of new leaves. There are two types of palm leaf. In a *pinnate*, or feather, leaf, like that of the oil palm, *Elaeis guineensis*, the leaflets are attached in pairs at intervals along the axis of the leaf; in a *palmate*, or fan, leaf, the leaflets radiate outwards

from a point. In both cases, in the bud, the young leaves are not divided but folded in a corrugated pattern. As the leaf expands it splits along these corrugations. When a new leaf unfolds the oldest one dies off, so that the total number of leaves on the plant remains the same.

Screwpines, which are not as widely distributed as palms—they are not found at all in America—generally have branched trunks with several heads of undivided leaves. Palm trunks, except in the genus *Hyphaene*, are never branched and palm leaves are normally divided into leaflets.

Flowering and fruiting

The flowering and fruiting of palms can be a spectacular affair. For instance the talipot palm, *Corypha umbraculifera*, cultivated in Ceylon but not found in the wild at all, flowers only once when the tree is 50 to 70 years old, and then dies. This is not surprising as the inflorescence is 6 m (20 ft) high and 10 m (30 ft) across, with half a million fruits ripening as the tree dies.

In other palms the inflorescences are smaller, and many species flower repeatedly. The flowers have three small white, green or yellow sepals, three similar petals, and anything from three to over 1,000 stamens. The ovary has three cells, each containing a single ovule. Sometimes the flowers are unisexual, in which case the male and female flowers may be either on the same tree, possibly in different inflorescences, or on different trees. Little is known about pollination: some species may be pollinated by wind, others by insects.

85

Palm fruits contain a single large seed, and may be coconut-like, with a dry outer skin covering a thick fibrous husk and the 'nut' within, or date-like, where the stone is enclosed in a fleshy, often brightly coloured, layer containing up to 70 per cent sugar. Succulent, date-like palm fruits are clearly intended for dispersal by animals, which eat them and pass the stones undigested through their guts. Exactly how dry, inedible fruits of the coconut type evolved, however, is not so clear. Many are dispersed by rolling along the ground, or by water, but in some cases, neither of these methods seems very practical. For example, the fruits of the coco-de-mer, *Lodoicea maldivica*, which take six years to ripen and weigh 15 to 20 kg (30 to 45 lb), sink in water and are too heavy to do anything except roll downhill. The distribution of these enormous plants is correspondingly limited. They are found only on two islands in the Seychelles.

Other tropical monocots

Three other important tropical monocot families are the agave family, *Agavaceae*, the bromeliad family, *Bromeliaceae*, and the banana family, *Musaceae*. The first of these, the agave family, includes several species which are fairly characteristic of dry tropical and sub-tropical regions. The plants consist of a clump of many stiff, sword-shaped leaves at the top of a short woody stem. Most members of the family are relatively small, but some species, particularly in the genus *Dracaena*, produce branched stems reaching to heights of 10 m (30 ft) or more.

Agave and *Yucca* species are found from the southern US down into South America. Many species of *Agave* have very long life cycles, growing for 60 to 100 years before flowering and dying, hence their common name of 'century plants'. *Yuccas* have a special pollination mechanism, involving moths of the genus *Pronuba*. The moth lays its eggs in the ovary of the yucca flower, and then deposits pollen, previously collected from another plant, on the stigma. It thus ensures that enough ovules develop both to feed its caterpillars and to perpetuate the yucca, which can only be pollinated by the moth. Neither the moth nor the yucca can survive without the other.

Bromeliads are similar in general appearance to the agave family, but are mostly found in tropical forests in South America. Many are *epiphytes*, growing for support on other plants, but the commercially important pineapple, *Ananas comosus*, is a bromeliad that grows on the ground. Its complex fruit is formed from the amalgamation of all the individual fruits in the inflorescence.

The banana family contains a number of herbaceous plants that build up massive stems and attain the height of small trees. The commercial banana, *Musa*, is fairly typical of these plants. It builds up a tall stem, 3 to 10 m (10 to 33 ft) high, from the overlapping leaf bases. From this a spike of flowers eventually grows out and bends over to hang downwards. The male flowers are at the tip of this 'upside-down' inflorescence, with the female flowers above them. In cultivated bananas the fruits develop from the female flowers without fertilization, so that ordinary bananas for eating are seedless. After fruiting, the whole stem dies and a new one grows up to replace it.

Dr Giuseppe Mazza

Above: The bird of paradise flower, *Strelitzia reginae* **(family** *Strelitziaceae***), is so named because the inflorescence is said to resemble a bird's head. It is also remarkable as it is pollinated by sun-birds (***Nectarinidae***) and has two petals fused together to form a 'bird-perch'.**

Below: The bromeliad *Tillandsia cyanea,* **which is grown as a house plant for its flowers. Another** *Tillandsia,* **Spanish moss,** *Tillandsia usneoides,* **grows as a wild epiphyte in the American continent. Its long festoons of thread-like stems and leaves are often seen hanging from telegraph wires.**

Dr Giuseppe Mazza

Ann Ronan Picture Library

Pl ·12

Fig: 26.

Fig: 25.

S.

WATER AND NUTRIENT TRANSPORT IN PLANTS

A growing plant needs a constant supply of water and nutrients, which must be transported through the plant to the tissues where they are used. Water has five main functions in a plant. Firstly, all cells need to maintain a certain water content because biochemical reactions take place between compounds in solution. Secondly, the water content of plant cells holds them in shape; a plant that is short of water wilts. Thirdly, a plant must have a film of water over the surfaces of the *mesophyll* cells in the leaves; carbon dioxide dissolves in this water film and diffuses into the cells, where photosynthesis takes place. This water is constantly evaporating and has to be replaced from within the plant. Fourthly, a small amount of water is used up in the basic chemical reaction of photosynthesis. And finally, both organic and mineral nutrients are transported within the plant while dissolved in water.

A plant needs to transport both organic and mineral nutrients. Organic nutrients have to be transported from the leaves, where they are photosynthesized, to other parts of the plant, where they are used either as building blocks in the synthesis of more complex chemicals or as sources of energy. Additionally, in plants with storage organs such as tubers or bulbs, nutrients must be transported to and from these reserves so that they can be mobilized for the rapid growth of new leaves, stems and roots when conditions are favourable. Mineral nutrients, such as nitrate and potassium, are taken up by the roots from the soil, and have to be transported upwards to the above-ground parts of the plant.

Transport in the plant occurs in the *xylem* and *phloem* tissue. Xylem and phloem have different functions related to their different structures. The xylem is concerned with the *passive* transport of water and mineral nutrients up the plant. The plant expends energy to transport mineral nutrients from dilute solution in the soil across the cell membrane into the more concentrated solution within the root cell. Water, on the other hand, enters the roots without the need for the plant to expend energy. This is done by the physical process known as *osmosis* (by which water will pass through a membrane from a weak solution to a more concentrated one).

After entering the root, however, both water and mineral nutrients are then carried up the plant primarily by the suction formed as water is continually *transpired* from the leaves—the xylem acting merely as a pipe. In a tall tree the pressure difference between the crown of the tree and the roots may be as much as 30 bars (430 psi).

As an indication of the quantities of water involved, a large tree may lose 50 kg (110 lb) of water in a day by transpiration. The amount of water lost, and hence the rate of water flow up the xylem, is controlled by the *stomata* of the leaves. If the soil becomes dry, or if the roots cannot absorb water fast enough on a sunny day, the stomata close to prevent the further loss of water. Closure of the stomata is achieved by two cells, known as *guard cells*, which collapse when short of water, so blocking the stomatal pores.

The phloem, unlike the xylem, is concerned with the *active* transport of organic nutrients especially sugars. The nutrients are transported in the *sieve tubes* of the phloem, and although the mechanism of transport remains a mystery, it is likely that the energy required to transport them is obtained by respiration in the *companion cells* adjacent to the sieve tubes. The contents of the sieve tubes, the plant *sap*, consists of water containing a high concentration of sugars, mainly sucrose. This sugar can be used commercially. In the sugar maple, *Acer saccharum*, the bark is tapped in spring when the phloem is carrying nutrients up to the crown, before the new leaves expand. The sap which oozes out is collected and evaporated to yield *maple syrup*.

I told you not to overdo the nutrients in the hydroponic garden."

Below left: Early experiments into the use of water by plants were conducted by Stephen Hales and published in his book 'Vegatable Staticks' 1727. The apparatus at the top here is an early *potometer* which measures the rate at which a plant takes up water. The water taken from the tube on the left is equal to that transpired by the plant through the leaves.

Above: Soil is not necessary for plant growth—it merely acts as a supporting medium from which water and nutrients can be extracted. The growing of plants in a soil-free medium is called *hydroponics*.

Below: Transpiration, and hence the rate of water flow up the xylem, is controlled by the stomata which close when the plant is in danger of wilting so preventing further water loss from the intercelluar spaces in the leaves. Stomatal closing is achieved by *guard cells*. They collapse when short of water and block the stomatal openings.

Below: Plants can have too much water. Some, like maize, *Zea mays* (shown here) excrete excess water through glands (*hydathodes*) on the leaves. This is known as *guttation* and occurs when too much water enters the roots by osmosis.

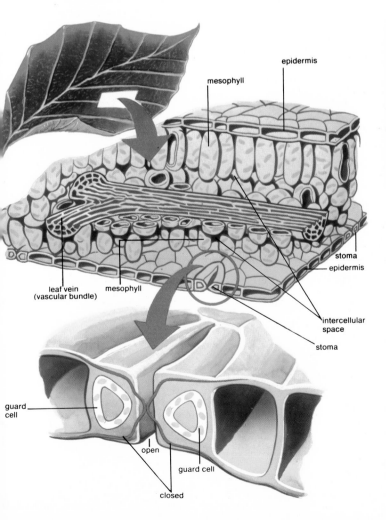

epidermis

mesophyll

stoma

epidermis

leaf vein (vascular bundle)

mesophyll

intercellular space

stoma

guard cell

open

guard cell

closed

87

Gymnosperms

Few plants have captured the imagination of botanists as have the maidenhair tree, the dawn redwood of China and the giant coastal redwoods of Pacific California. These exotic trees all belong to a relatively small, but economically important, group of plants known as the *Gymnospermae* or more simply as gymnosperms. This name comes from the Greek *gymnos*, meaning naked, and *sperma*, meaning seed. The gymnosperms are the naked seeded plants.

Most gymnosperms are evergreen trees or shrubs and they characteristically have eggs, *ovules*, which are in direct contact with the air so that pollen can fall directly on to them. Male and female plants are generally separate and typically have reproductive organs borne in cones, *strobili*. The male cones produce great quantities of tiny pollen, some of which is blown by the wind to the cones of female plants to fertilize their eggs.

Many groups of gymnosperms are now extinct and have been so for millions of years. Five groups still have living representatives. These are the cycads, *Cycadales*, maidenhair trees, *Ginkgoales*, yews, *Taxales*, conifers, *Coniferales*, and finally a mixed group, called *Gnetales*, which includes the twitch plants, *Ephedra*, and the extraordinary *Welwitschia bainesii* of the Kalahari Desert in south-west Africa.

Cycads and maidenhair trees

Most cycads are small trees rarely reaching 10 m (33 ft) high. Less commonly they have short subterranean stems with a rosette of leaves at or above ground level. They are sparsely but widely distributed throughout the tropics and the southern hemisphere. Tree cycads closely resemble palm trees at first glance though their reproductive structures are quite different. In most cycads both male and female plants bear cones which are a metre (3 ft) high and 50 cm (20 in) in diameter in some species. The cones are borne in the centre of the plant and are surrounded by palm-like leaves arranged in a spiral from the top of the stem.

Few trees have gained the popularity and mystique reserved for *Ginkgo biloba*, the maidenhair tree, so-called because of the resemblance of its leaves to those of the popular house plant, the maidenhair fern. Extinct, or almost so, in its native China, it was cultivated for its beauty and also for its edible fruits in the royal palace of Peking, from where the first seeds were introduced into Europe in 1762. It is now a prize addition to many parks and large gardens.

Yews and cow-tail pines

Another small, but quite distinct, group of gymnosperms, *Taxales*, includes the yew tree, *Taxus*, and its distant Asiatic relatives, the cow-tail pines, *Cephalotaxus*. One of three gymnosperms native to Britain (the others are the Scots pine, *Pinus sylvestris*, and the juniper, *Juniperus communis*), mature yews have enormous trunks many metres in circumference crowned with a mass of dark green foliage. Yews are unlike conifers in having no female cone. Instead they have a fruit, the *aril*. Female trees in fruit are quite beautiful, as the bright red

A-Z Collection

Above: Leaves and fruit of a female maidenhair tree, *Ginkgo biloba*. **Ginkgo trees may grow to 30 m (100 ft) or more high, are deciduous and characteristically branch low down so that two or more leading shoots are present. Both male and female trees are widely grown, but male trees are more popular as females produce great quantities of olive-like fruits which smell of rancid butter when ripe.**

Below: The exception in the cycads, *Cycas* **itself. Unlike other cycads, female** *Cycas* **plants do not bear cones but have reproductive structures which more closely resemble a small leaf. This species is** *Cycas revoluta*.

Giuseppe Mazza

Right: The fruit (*aril*) of the yew tree, *Taxus baccata*. **The aril is sweet and attractive to birds which eat the fruits whole. The seeds inside the fruits are indigestible and pass through the birds' digestive system unharmed. They may be excreted many miles away, so dispersing the yew trees.**

Far right: The biggest trees in the world are the Wellingtonias, *Sequoiadendron giganteum*. **One Wellingtonia, known as** *General Grant*, **is 91.5 m (267 ft) high and 24.3 m (79 ft) in girth 2.4 m (7 ft) above the ground. Coast redwoods,** *Sequoia sempervirens*, **are generally taller but are not as massive. The tree with the largest girth, however, is a specimen of Spanish chestnut,** *Castanea sativa*, **which had a girth of 51 m (167 ft) when measured in 1972.**

Herve Chaumeton/Jacana

The Scots Pine (*pinus sylvestris*) is closely related to the giant redwoods of California, and is one of only three gymnosperms native to Britain.

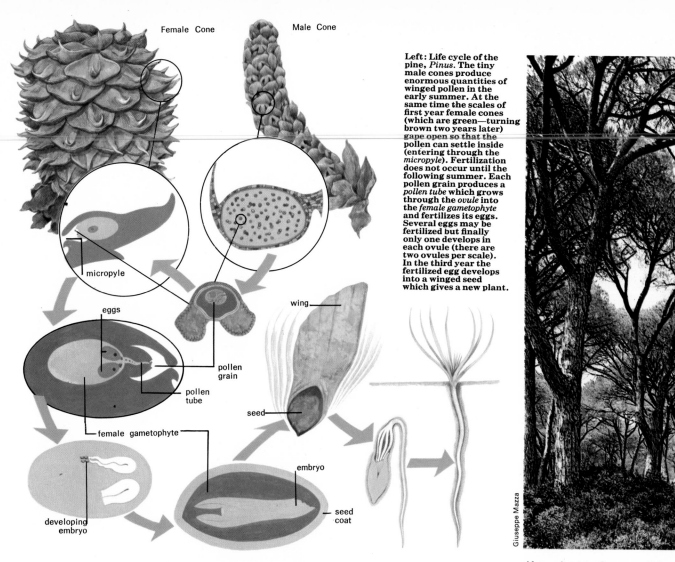

Female Cone

Male Cone

micropyle

eggs

pollen grain

pollen tube

seed

wing

female gametophyte

embryo

developing embryo

seed coat

Giuseppe Mazza

Left: Life cycle of the pine, *Pinus*. The tiny male cones produce enormous quantities of winged pollen in the early summer. At the same time the scales of first year female cones (which are green—turning brown two years later) gape open so that the pollen can settle inside (entering through the *micropyle*). Fertilization does not occur until the following summer. Each pollen grain produces a *pollen tube* which grows through the *ovule* into the *female gametophyte* and fertilizes its eggs. Several eggs may be fertilized but finally only one develops in each ovule (there are two ovules per scale). In the third year the fertilized egg develops into a winged seed which gives a new plant.

fleshy aril around each seed contrasts markedly with the dark green leaves.

Conifers

By far the largest living group of gymnosperms is the conifers, *Coniferales*. Not only are there many species of conifers but many have great economic importance. Some may be numbered among the most important cash crops in the world. This is particularly true of many of the species of pine, larch, spruce, fir, podo and monkey-puzzle, all of which are important timber trees often grown in vast plantations.

For convenience, conifers can be divided into two groups, those which are predominantly of north temperate distribution and origin and those which are predominantly from the southern hemisphere. The northern hemisphere group consists of the pine and its relatives, *Pinaceae*, the swamp cypress and its relatives, *Taxodiaceae*, and the cypress and its relatives, *Cupressaceae*.

The red-barked Scots pine, *Pinus sylvestris*, is perhaps the best known member of the *Pinaceae* but it is only one of some 200 species in this family. There are also some 80 species of the genus *Pinus*, one of which, the bristlecone pine, *Pinus longaeva*, is the oldest living tree in the world with a specimen 4,900 years old. Pine species are distinguished by many characters of the wood, bark and cone but particularly by the number of needle-like leaves in the bunches on the short side shoots of each branch. Most species have either two, four or five needles per bunch but higher numbers are known in some species.

Related to the pines are several other familiar plantation trees such as spruce, *Picea*, silver fir, *Abies*, larch, *Larix*, hemlock, *Tsuga*, Douglas fir, *Pseudotsuga*, and cedar, *Cedrus*. Spruces and silver firs are often confused but may be readily distinguished for spruces have pendulous cones and, when their leaves fall, peg-like projections are left behind on the stem, while the cones of silver firs are upright. Larches are easily recognized as, unlike most gymnosperms, they are *deciduous*, that is they lose their leaves in the winter. The Douglas fir, *Pseudotsuga menziesii*, is a superb species with specimens over 90 m (300 ft) tall having been recorded from the Pacific coast of North America.

The largest trees, however, belong to a different group, *Taxodiaceae*, which is a small family, totalling only 14 species, but which includes two of the most famous of all trees, the coastal redwood, *Sequoia sempervirens*, and the legendary dawn redwood, *Metasequoia glyptostroboides*.

The coast redwood, and its close relative, the Wellingtonia or big tree, *Sequoiadendron giganteum*, are both natives of Pacific North America. The former is confined to a narrow coastal belt from Oregon to southern California whilst the latter grows at between 1,500 m and 2,500 m (5,000-8,000 ft) altitude in the Sierra Nevada in California. The tallest living tree in the world is a specimen of coast redwood, 112.4 m (368 ft) high, known as the *Howard Libbey* tree. Wellingtonias fall a few metres short of this in height but are generally much more massive trees.

Above: A grove of Mediterranean pines, *Pinus pinea*. Unlike most conifers, these trees have branched trunks.

Below: The juniper, *Juniperus communis*, is a small shrub which belongs to the cypress family. Its berries are used to flavour gin.

Herve Chaumeton/Jacana

Related to the redwoods are the swamp cypresses, *Taxodium*, of the southern USA and Mexico. Growing in swampy ground, such as the Everglades in Florida, these trees develop roots which project, peg-like above the water around the base of the tree. Swamp water contains little dissolved oxygen and these roots, called *pneumatophores*, can absorb oxygen from the atmosphere. The swamp cypresses are also rather unusual among the conifers as they are deciduous.

Another deciduous conifer is the dawn redwood. This extraordinary species was known as a fossil from the Tertiary period before being discovered living in a very restricted area of east Szechwan and north-east Hupeh in China in 1941. Seeds were distributed to European and American botanic gardens and parks in 1948 and its growth has been so rapid that specimens over 27 m (90 ft) tall had been recorded both in Britain and in the USA by 1977. This is an annual increase in height of nearly 1 m (3 ft), an astonishing rate of growth.

A final group of northern hemisphere species is the cypress and its relatives, *Cupressaceae*. Two genera are both commonly given the name 'cypress'; these are the true cypresses, *Cupressus*, and the false cypresses, *Chamaecyparis*. Nevertheless, the two genera can be easily distinguished at a glance, for, despite the characteristic shape of the trees, the true cypresses have branches growing in all planes around the main shoot whilst the false cypresses have their branches all in one plane.

Two families of conifers are native to the southern hemisphere, the monkey-puzzles, *Araucariaceae*, and the podos, *Podocarpaceae*. Both are rarely planted in the northern hemisphere, but one species, monkey-puzzle or Chile pine, *Araucaria araucana*, is very commonly planted in front gardens. Its whorls of slightly drooping branches covered by spirals of triangular, sharply pointed leaves are an exotic sight in many suburban streets. In Chile and Argentina, however, the Chile pine is an important timber tree forming large forests.

The other group of southern conifers is known in the timber trade as *podo*. Their most remarkable feature is the female fruit. In many ways it resembles the fruit of the yew but the fleshy aril is white and the shiny black seed sits on top of it, instead of inside it as in the yew.

History and importance

The gymnosperms are an ancient group of plants, which can be recognized in fossil deposits 300 million years old and are common constituents of the coal measures of the Carboniferous period. For 120 million years, from 220 million years ago to 100 million years ago, they formed the dominant vegetation of the Earth, to be challenged for supremacy only by the rise of the flowering plants during the Cretaceous period. The heyday of the gymnosperms is now over but many species continue to survive, though many are mere relict populations. Others still form the major constituent of the vegetation over great tracts of the Earth's surface. As timber trees they are of massive importance—their straight stems are particularly suitable to the timber industry.

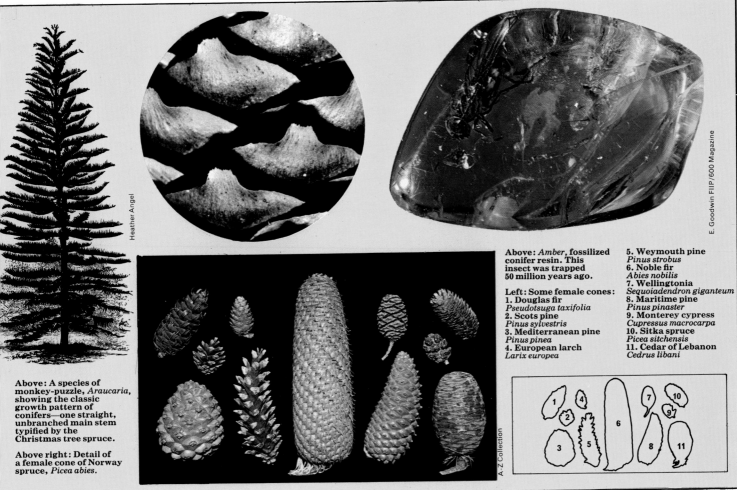

Heather Angel

E. Goodwin FIIP/600 Magazine

A-Z Collection

Above: A species of monkey-puzzle, *Araucaria*, showing the classic growth pattern of conifers—one straight, unbranched main stem typified by the Christmas tree spruce.

Above right: Detail of a female cone of Norway spruce, *Picea abies*.

Above: *Amber*, fossilized conifer resin. This insect was trapped 50 million years ago.

Left: Some female cones:
1. Douglas fir
Pseudotsuga taxifolia
2. Scots pine
Pinus sylvestris
3. Mediterranean pine
Pinus pinea
4. European larch
Larix europea
5. Weymouth pine
Pinus strobus
6. Noble fir
Abies nobilis
7. Wellingtonia
Sequoiadendron giganteum
8. Maritime pine
Pinus pinaster
9. Monterey cypress
Cupressus macrocarpa
10. Sitka spruce
Picea sitchensis
11. Cedar of Lebanon
Cedrus libani

Plant and Animal Habitats

The Saguaro cactus, *Carnegiea gigantea.*
This specimen was photographed in
New Mexico, in the south-western area
of the United States, where it is a
common feature of the landscape.

Moorland and Heath

Since prehistoric times man has felled trees and burned vegetation to clear land for cultivation and grazing. The regions which have been primarily used to support herds of sheep and cattle have become, over the centuries, the uncultivated, treeless moors and heaths we know today.

In everyday speech the words 'moor' and 'heath' are often used to mean the same thing. Ecologists, however, reserve the term *heathland* for areas in which trees or tall shrubs are entirely absent or only very thinly distributed, and the dominant plants are evergreen dwarf shrubs, typically members of the heath family, *Ericaceae*. The looser term *moorland* describes any area with wet, acid soils, usually more than 300 m (1,000 ft) above sea level. Such conditions often lead to the formation of *peat*, a layer of partly decomposed dead plant remains over the surface of the ground. Many areas of moorland support heathland vegetation, while others are *bogs* in which the dominant plant is the moss *Sphagnum*. Grasses, sedges and rushes are also common moorland plants.

Heathlands

The most characteristic lowland heaths are found in Western Europe, from northern Scandinavia to Spain. They flourish in an oceanic climate, with abundant rainfall and lacking extremes of temperature at any time of the year. The soils are typically *podsols*, that is to say well-drained, often sandy soils where rainwater has dissolved the nutrients in the surface layer and deposited them lower down.

Formed from rocks which lack nutrient elements such as calcium, these soils are usually acid. A normally fertile soil develops by the mixing of the surface layer of organic matter with the underlying mineral layer. Under acid conditions, however, few earthworms are present to mix the organic and mineral components of the soil so that the plant litter remains as a separate layer on the soil surface, and decomposes only very slowly.

In Europe, the common heathland shrubs include the common heather or ling, *Calluna vulgaris*, and various species of *Erica* such as bell heather, *Erica cinerea*, and cross-leaved heath, *Erica tetralix*. These genera are not found in North America, but others such as *Vaccinium*—for example cowberry, *Vaccinium vitis-idaea*—are found in heathland plant communities throughout the Northern Hemisphere. Other typical heathland shrubs are bearberry, *Arctostaphylos uva-ursi*, and crowberry, *Empetrum nigrum*.

As their common names imply, the fruits of many of these dwarf shrubs are succulent berries, attractive to animals which disperse the seeds in their droppings. Apart from reproduction by seed, most of the dwarf shrubs also spread by creeping stems, so that one seedling may grow into a mat-like plant covering a wide area. Some of these stems, because they are partly buried, will survive fires, so that burnt areas are re-colonized.

Robin Fletcher

Below right: Two of the most common heathland plants—a lichen of the genus *Cladonia*, and the bearberry, *Arctostaphylos uva-ursi*, recognized by its red-brown leaves.

Below: The growth of a heather plant can be traced through four distinct phases. In the *pioneer phase*, which lasts between three and six years, compact clumps grow from seedlings or from buried stems. This is followed by the *building phase*, in which the plants grow outwards to cover the ground. After about 15 years they enter the *mature phase* during which they reach their greatest height, but growth slackens. After another 15 years or so the plants become *degenerate*.

P. Morris

pioneer

building

mature

degenerate

Heather Angel

Left: Desolate, treeless moorland in the north of Scotland. This sort of terrain is inhabited by the red deer, *Cervus elephus*, and is often misleadingly termed 'deer forest'.

Right: The most common herbivores of the heathland are insects like this leaf-hopper nymph, *Fileno spumario*, which lives in a frothy secretion of bubbles. A variety of insects feed on the young shoots and leaves of heather plants, among them thrips, springtails, mites, moth caterpillars and heather beetles. These in turn provide food for animals like shrews, lizards and insectivorous birds such as the meadow pipit.

Below left: Deliberate burning of heather in Scotland. Younger heather plants are more palatable to animals and contain more nutrients, so periodic burning (typically every ten years or so) improves the quality of the grazing for sheep and game birds such as grouse. Normally the heather is burnt in patches and only a proportion of the area is burned each year.

Giuseppe Mazza

Left: A froghopper, *Cercopis vulnerata*, a typical heathland species. The insect's bold colour and marking probably serve as a warning to potential predators that it would make an unpalatable meal (or make it look like an unpalatable species). Insects form vital links in many heathland food chains. This froghopper, for example, might be eaten by a grouse which could then fall prey to a top carnivore such as a fox, an eagle or a wild cat.

Below: The emperor moth, *Saturnia pavonia*, is another heathland insect. Clearly visible are the 'eye spots' on the wings. These resemble the eyes of a larger animal and so help to deter predators.

Heather Angel

Robin Fletcher

Other plant species are found growing among the dominant shrubs. Most conspicuous are the lichens, especially *Cladonia*, some species of which have bright red spore-bearing organs. One species of lichen, *Parmelia physodes*, actually grows on the stems of old heather plants. There are also grasses, such as wavy hair-grass, *Deschampsia flexuosa*, with its conspicuous silvery flower heads. Herbaceous dicotyledonous plants, however, are rare.

Comparable plant communities are found in other parts of the world, for example in some of the 'pine barrens' of the eastern US and Canada, at the extreme southern tip of South America and on some southern Atlantic islands including the Falkland Islands. At extreme northern and southern latitudes, the climate becomes too harsh for shrub species, and heathland gives way to tundra where mosses and lichens predominate. Heathlands are also found on mountains, for example in East Africa, South Africa and in Australia and New Zealand. Tree heaths, such as *Erica arborea*, are found on the East African mountains, but they grow to more than 10 m (30 ft), forming a forest rather than a heathland habitat.

The origin of heathland

The history of vegetation can be investigated by *pollen analysis*. Cores are taken from deep peat deposits or lake sediments, and by laboriously counting the pollen grains of different plant species it is possible to discover the abundance of different types of plants at different times in the past. In some cases, recognizable fragments of plants are found as well as pollen grains, and also layers of ash indicating the burning of the vegetation. The age of different layers in a core can be found by radiocarbon dating. As a rough guide it takes about 1,000 years to form a 1 m (3 ft) depth of peat.

Evidence of the original forest cover of heathland is provided by the appearance in the cores of pollen of trees which once lived in the area. In some places clearance took place in Mesolithic times (around 4000 BC), but the main change from forest to heath began in the Neolithic period (3000 to 2000 BC). Forest clearance resulting in the spread of heathland has continued into modern times.

Once cleared, the forest did not return. Part of the reason may have been the climatic change in Western Europe towards a cooler, wetter climate less favourable for tree growth. Another possibility is that the removal of the trees caused an irreversible deterioration of the soil, resulting in the infertile podsols. However, the main factor—and one which can to some extent be controlled once its effects are properly understood—was grazing. Although tree seedlings are eaten by herbivores such as deer, rabbits and voles, in natural conditions enough survive for forests to regenerate. In contrast, heavy grazing by domestic sheep and cattle can stop any seedlings at all from growing into trees. The absence of trees from large areas of heathland and moorland may therefore be explained by the fact that the main use of these areas in Europe, since early medieval times, has been as grazing for sheep and cattle.

The growth of heather plants generally follows a fixed pattern, ending, after about 30 years, with the plants becoming degenerate. The central branches die, while the outer branches collapse outwards often lying flat on the ground like the spokes of a wheel, There is then an open space at the centre of each plant, in which lichens flourish and where new heather seedlings can germinate to replace the dying plants.

Moorlands

Although many moorland areas can be considered as heathlands, other kinds of vegetation may have originated as a result of overgrazing or excessive burning. Unpalatable plants such as mat-grass, *Nardus stricta*, and bracken, *Pteridium aquilinum*, are common. In other cases, poor drainage and high rainfall create conditions in which heather grows badly, and here the dominant plant is often *Sphagnum*.

Sphagnum bogs are of three types. *Valley bogs* occur where water drains into a valley or depression. This water brings with it nutrients leached from the land around, so a fair variety of plants may be found in such bogs, including the soft rush, *Juncus effusus*. *Raised bogs* develop on top of valley bogs, and have a convex surface, with a thicker layer of peat at the centre than at the edges. The peat is formed of the dead, partly decomposed *Sphagnum*, while the living *Sphagnum* forms a continuous cover over the surface of the bog. *Blanket bog* describes large areas of *Sphagnum* covering flat or gently sloping land. Raised and blanket bogs are both dependent on a continual supply of rainwater, and so the finest examples are found in the west of Ireland, in Connemara and western Mayo, where the rainfall is up to 250 cm (100 in) a year.

The vegetation of wet moorlands is quite varied: in addition to the ever-present *Sphagnum*, there are usually small hummocks colonized by plants of drier habitats. Very often bell heather is found in the drier patches, while cross-leaved heath can grow in the wetter depressions. Among the typical plants of bogs and wet moors are bog asphodel, *Narthecium ossifragum*, with star-like yellow flowers, two sedges called cotton grass, *Eriophorum*, and deer grass, *Scirpus cespitosus*, and the aromatic shrub *Myrica gale*, bog myrtle. The commonest grass is purple moor-grass, *Molinia caerulea*, and there are also the insectivorous plants sundew, *Drosera*, and butterwort, *Pinguicula*. These supplement the inadequate nutrient content of the moorland soils by catching and digesting insects.

Animals of moor and heath

Moorlands and heathlands are not noted for their diversity of animal species, possibly because they are man-made habitats and therefore of recent origin by evolutionary standards. A hectare of typical moorland in Scotland is likely to have only three species of birds: curlew, *Numenius arquata*, red grouse, *Lagopus lagopus scoticus*, and meadow pipit, *Anthus pratensis*. These are all birds which nest on the ground. More species are found where there are trees nearby, and reafforestation causes a great increase in the diversity of birds and other animals.

Frogs and newts are common on wet moors, while the drier lowland heaths provide an ideal habitat for snakes and lizards. Moorland areas with warm, wet

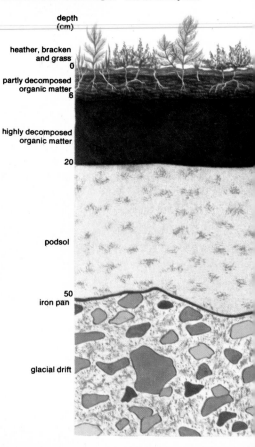

P. Morris

Above: Many moors and heaths owe their existence to the clearing of woodland by man and subsequent grazing by domestic animals. Sheep can thrive on poor pasture and so are suited to such habitats.

Below: Heathland soils are often *podsols*. Formed from rocks which lack nutrient elements such as calcium, they are usually acid. An acid environment discourages **bacteria as well as invertebrates such as earthworms and snails, so decomposition of plant litter is slow and there is little mixing of the soil layers.**

depth
(cm)

heather, bracken and grass
0

partly decomposed organic matter
6

highly decomposed organic matter

20

podsol

50
iron pan

glacial drift

Below: The red grouse, *Lagopus lagopus scoticus*, is found only in Britain and Ireland. It is a close relation of the willow grouse found in other parts of northern Europe. Its diet consists chiefly of heather.

A. Winspear Cundall/Natural Science Photos

Varin-Visage/Jacana

Bryn Campbell/Transworld

Above: The nightjar, *Caprimulgus europaeus*, is an inhabitant of heath and open woodland. By night it hunts large flying insects, especially beetles and moths, while by day it lies motionless on the ground or in a tree.

Below: A typical moorland blanket bog in Snowdonia, Wales. Visible in the picture are dark green heaths of the family *Ericaceae*, paler green mosses, *Sphagnum*, and the white fruiting heads of cotton grass, *Eriophorum*.

Right: Deerstalking in the Highlands of Scotland. Each year many thousands of red deer are killed, about 15 per cent of the total population in the Highlands. Even so, the deer population is on the increase.

Heather Angel

summer weather, such as the west of Scotland, may be infested with biting flies, including midges, *Ceratopogonidae*, and clegs, *Haematopota pluvialis*, a species of the horse-fly family.

The herbivore species have adapted to the extensive areas of moorland to be found in the British Isles. The red grouse, found only in Britain and Ireland, is closely related to the willow grouse found in other parts of northern Europe. Unlike the willow grouse, which has a varied diet of young shoots and willow, birch and bilberry fruits, the red grouse eats mainly heather.

The cock grouse occupy and defend territories, and only those which can obtain territories are able to breed. The rate of increase of the grouse population is therefore limited by the size, and hence the number, of territories. Grouse feed largely on young heather shoots, and after a season of good heather growth the territories may become smaller—down to about 2 hectares (5 acres)—allowing more birds to breed. This is an example of population regulation by the behaviour of an animal, which is interesting because it means that grouse should never become so numerous that they are short of food.

The red deer, *Cervus elaphus*, is found in forests all over Europe, but in Britain it has become a moorland species, smaller and lighter than the original forest deer. Red deer are particularly common in Scottish 'deer forests', which are not forests at all but desolate, treeless moorland. There are about 10,000 sq km (4,000 sq miles) of deer forest in Scotland, although this area is constantly being reduced by the appearance of new forest plantations.

Deserts

Although most of the land surface of the Earth is covered by vegetation there are large areas with only scattered plants or no plants at all. In tropical and sub-tropical regions, high temperatures all the year round mean that water from rain evaporates rapidly and an annual rainfall of less than 20 cm (8 in) results in a *hot desert*, in which plant and animal life is severely restricted by shortage of water. Similarly barren arid areas, but with cool winters, are found in higher latitudes; the plants and animals of these *cold deserts* have to endure low winter temperatures as well as scarcity of water.

Climate

Taking average figures for a number of years, all deserts are seen to have a low annual rainfall. The pattern of rainfall, however, varies widely from one desert to another. Some deserts, such as the central Sahara, have no rain at all in many years, while others, like the Sonoran desert on the Mexican-US border and the Karroo desert of South Africa, may have two rainy seasons in a year. But however often the rain falls, in most deserts even the low annual rainfall figures recorded (often about 5 mm, 0.2 in, a year) exaggerate the amount of rain likely to fall in any one year. They are the result of averaging, say, one heavy shower over several years. Desert rainfall is unpredictable but in most years it is significantly less than the average.

Natural Science Photos

Above: The starkness of the Namib Desert in southern Africa. Desert habitats can be defined as areas where the overriding ecological consideration is shortage of water.

Below: Deserts are not always hot. Occasionally they can even be cold enough for snow. This is the Mojave Desert, high in the Sierra Nevada of California.

Desert plants

Only specialized plants are able to survive the chronic water shortage of deserts. Different species are adapted in different ways, but perhaps the simplest adaptation is a physiological ability to withstand long periods in which the water content of the plant falls to a very low level. Plants which can do this include lichens as well as flowering plants, such as the creosote bush, *Larrea divaricata*, which grows in the deserts of North and South America. The leaves of a well-watered creosote bush contain about 55 per cent water but this can fall to around 30 per cent during a drought. If the drought is prolonged, the older leaves die while the immature leaves and buds turn brown, losing the ability to photosynthesize but not dying. When rain comes the leaves turn green and the plant starts to grow again.

Other plants, called *succulents*, store water for use in time of drought. The water is stored either in swollen stems, as in the cactus family, *Cactaceae*, and the spurge faily, *Euphorbiaceae*, or in both stems and leaves, as in the stonecrop family, *Crassulaceae*. To eke out what water they can obtain most desert plants have mechanisms for cutting down the amount of water that they lose by transpiration (through the stomata) or by evaporation (through the cuticle).

Water economy is achieved in a number of ways. To reduce transpiration the stomata may be sunk beneath the leaf surface or the leaves may be rolled up with the stomata on the inside. Sunken stomata and rolled-up leaves reduce transpiration because the stomata are then surrounded by a stable layer of air which, because it is in intimate contact with the inter-cellular spaces within the leaf, is far more humid than the dry desert air. Water loss by evaporation through the cuticule may be cut down by reducing the surface area of the plant relative to its volume (by having small leaves or no leaves at all—in

Photri

Camels have adapted thoroughly to desert life. Long eyelashes and muscular nostrils keep out windblown sand, and the camel feeds mainly on plants with a high water content.

From 'Desert Animals' by K. Schmidt-Nielsen, Oxford University Press

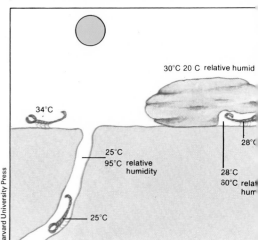

37°C 40°C 35°C 40° 70° 38°C 70°C

Harvard University Press

30°C 20 C relative humid

34°C

25°C
95% relative
humidity

28°C

28°C
80°C rela
hum

25°C

Left: Many desert plants survive dry periods as seeds. There may be 25,000 per square metre (2,500 per square foot) of soil. After rain they germinate, transforming barren areas into colourful meadows. They must, however, flower and reproduce before the soil dries again.

Below: Birds' eggs fail to hatch if left unprotected in the desert sun. They are therefore normally laid in the shelter of bushes, holes, caves or under rocks. The elf owl, *Micrathene whitneyi* (shown here) has an ideal solution. It nests in the abandoned holes formed by woodpeckers in the giant saguaro cactus, *Carnegiea gigantea.*

which case the stem is used for photo-synthesis) or by increasing the thickness of the layer of waxes on the cuticle.

These adaptations of the above-ground parts of the plant are complemented by root systems able to collect such small amounts of rain as do fall. Many desert plants have root systems which extend over large areas. For example, the roots of the bean caper, *Zygophyllum dumosum*, may cover an area of 35 square metres (400 square feet), although the plant itself is no more than 2 m (6 ft) across. It follows that such plants must grow well spaced out from their neighbours, and it is common in desert areas to see shrubs, like the creosote bush, growing several metres apart with more or less bare ground between them.

Instead of rooting outwards, other desert plants send down deep roots, as far as 4 m (12 ft) or deeper, to take advantage of the fact that heavy rain often finds its way, as *surface run-off*, into drainage channels or wadis. Immediately after rain these channels become short-lived rivers, but even after the surface water has disappeared large amounts of water remain deep in the soil. Furthermore, where permanent rivers flow through deserts, there is often underground water for some distance away from the river. Additionally, water flowing down from high plateaus may flow under the desert floor and be reached by deep growing roots. Both river banks and apparently dry drainage channels often support lush vegetation quite different from the barren areas around them.

All the ingenious adaptations of desert plants have but one purpose—they either reduce water loss or increase water up-

Photri

Frank Lane

Left: The extraordinary desert gymnosperm, *Welwitschia bainesii*, of the Namib and Kalahari Deserts of southwest Africa. Many Namib plants obtain moisture from sea fogs but *Welwitschia* most often grows in drainage channels and probably obtains most of its water from the soil.

Right: During the hottest weather, some animals like this desert tortoise, *Gopherus agassizi*, aestivate—a process not unlike hibernation but at a higher temperature.

Below: Saharan camels, *Camelus dromedarius*.

Bottom: The gecko, *Palmatogecko rangei*, has webbed feet to prevent it sinking in soft sand.

Above left: The coat of a dog or other hairy animal not only keeps it warm in cold climates but also cool in hot climates. The temperature at the surface of the coat can be very high in comparison with the skin temperature of a man. Although both dog and man gain heat by radiation from the sun and the ground, only man gains significant heat from the air because his skin temperature is lower than that of the air. Loose-fitting clothes will keep him cool in a similar way to the dog's coat.

Left: Invertebrates survive in the desert by hiding in burrows or under stones where the microclimate, both in terms of temperature and relative humidity, is usually far more amenable. This experiment shows how the body temperature of a typical desert dweller, a scorpion, depends on whether it is inside a burrow, under a stone, or directly in the sun.

take, and so allow the plant to continue to transpire when other plants would have to close their stomata because of water shortage. Any plant can reduce its rate of transpiration to zero by closing its stomata, but by doing this it also stops itself from photosynthesizing. This happens because the stomata are not only concerned with transpiration: carbon dioxide required for photosynthesis enters the plant through the stomata as well.

Perhaps the most highly adapted desert plants, mainly members of the stonecrop family, such as *Kalanchoe*, have to some extent mastered even this problem. They have a different kind of photosynthesis which allows them to absorb carbon dioxide at night and to store it as organic chemicals, such as malic acid, which are converted in the daytime to carbohydrates by the normal photosynthetic reactions. These plants can thus close their stomata during the daytime without stopping growth. When their stomata are open at night the lower night temperatures and higher night humidities reduce the rate of water loss.

A final group of desert plants avoid altogether the problem of trying to grow without water. Most of them are annuals and remarkably they germinate only when sufficient rain has fallen for them to grow from germination to seed dispersal before the ground dries again. Others, often members of the lily family such as the desert tulip, *Tulipa amphiophylla*, are able to survive dry periods as underground storage organs, such as bulbs.

Desert animals

The basic problem faced by desert animals is the same as that for desert plants—the 101

NHPA

NHPA

Oxford Scientific Films

need to maintain the water content of their tissues. An animal can obtain water from three sources. The surest of these is *metabolic water*, produced as a by-product of the biochemical reactions of respiration. The amount produced is small, about 0.5 g for each gram of carbohydrate used in respiration, but for some desert animals it is the main source of water. Others rely on eating food containing water: either succulent plants, in the case of herbivores, or other animals, in the case of carnivores. Finally, a few desert animals obtain most of their water by drinking from open water, although this is only useful if they can exist for several days without drinking or if they can travel long distances to water as some birds do.

Set against these three sources of water are the three ways in which an animal loses water. Exposed to the sun, and surrounded by air at temperatures of up to 45°C (110°F), mammals and birds need to regulate their body temperature at a roughly constant value, usually in the range 35 to 40°C (95 to 105°F). This is chiefly achieved by the evaporation of water—about 600 calories of heat are lost when 1 ml of water evaporates. Water can be lost either by sweating or by panting. In panting the animal takes very rapid breaths to increase the evaporation of water from the membranes of the lungs and from the moist surfaces of the tongue and mouth.

As well as losing water to keep cool, animals also cannot avoid losing water in their faeces and urine. The faeces of a cow, for example, contain about 85 per cent water. This would be an excessive waste of water for a desert animal, and in desert

NHPA

species much of this water, instead of being excreted, is extracted from the intestinal contents. For instance, a camel without access to water produces faeces with only 45 per cent water. Similarly, desert animals excrete relatively small amounts of urine containing high concentrations of salts and urea. The salt concentration of man's urine is about four times that of the blood plasma; in the camel the urine concentration is eight times that of plasma.

As well as reducing the amount of water lost in excretion, concentrated urine also increases the number of water sources available to the animal. Because the kidneys of desert animals can excrete high concentrations of salt they can drink salt water and eat plants with a high salt content. This is important, because desert soils in dry water channels often contain large amounts of salts, left behind when the water in which they were dissolved evaporated. Birds and desert reptiles go a stage further, and do not excrete urine at all. Instead they excrete *uric acid*, which is almost insoluble and is produced as a semi-solid paste with a very low water content. Nevertheless, this cannot really be considered as a desert adaptation for *all* birds and most reptiles excrete uric acid.

Camels
The camel, *Camelus*, is a very good example of how a large mammal can adapt to desert conditions. The facts about the ability of camels to go without water are remarkable, although often exaggerated in travellers' accounts. There is no doubt, however, that camels can travel across the waterless desert of Saudi Arabia, a distance of about 900 km (550 miles), in 21 days without drinking.

This is done without any special water storage organ—the hump consists mainly of fat—and the ability of camels to survive results from a combination of subtle modifications of normal mammalian physiology. As well as producing dry faeces and concentrated urine, camels also reduce the amount of water which must be lost in body cooling by allowing their body temperatures to increase by up to 6°C (11°F) during the day, cooling down at night.

Other animals
Another factor which works in the camel's favour in the desert is its size. Because an animal in a hot environment gains heat energy through its body surface, the amount of water needed for cooling is greater, relative to body weight, in a smaller animal since a smaller animal has a larger surface to volume ratio. To avoid overheating on a typical summer day in the desert a camel needs to evaporate an amount of water equivalent to only 1 per cent of its body weight every hour; for a mouse the equivalent figure is 15 per cent.

Smaller animals are forced to hide from the heat of the daytime sun in order to survive. Most commonly they spend the hot daylight hours in burrows or under stones and come out to feed only at night.

Many nocturnal rodents, for example the kangaroo rats, *Dipodomys*, from the deserts of the southwestern US, survive indefinitely without drinking. Their diet consists solely of dry seeds and other dry plant material. Their nocturnal habit thus allows them to survive on the little water in their food supplemented by the metabolic water produced during respiration.

So long as they can find an adequate supply of prey, carnivores have less of a problem of water supply than herbivores, since meat typically contains 60 to 70 per cent water. Nevertheless, the same basic adaptations for avoiding water loss are found in carnivores as in herbivores. In particular, many of them are active at night—although it is possible, of course, that this simply reflects the nocturnal habits of their prey.

Among nocturnal carnivores which range far into the desert in search of prey are the jackal, *Canis aureus*, the fennec, *Fennecus zerda*, of Africa, and the kit fox, *Vulpes velox*, of Mexico and the southern US.

Invertebrates
Whereas the most striking desert animals are the large mammals, the most numerous, as in most other habitats, are the invertebrates, particularly insects and other arthropods. These animals do not need to maintain their body temperatures within such strict limits as mammals, but they too must conserve water to avoid becoming desiccated. They survive by the same sorts of adaptations as those of smaller vertebrates. In addition, arthropods have an impermeable exoskeleton which reduces water loss to a minimum, and they can also tolerate a large degree of dehydration. By making use of metabolic water and by taking full advantage of the cool, humid *microclimates* found under even small stones or within the rosettes of plants, small invertebrates can live in the hottest and driest deserts virtually uninhabited by larger animals.

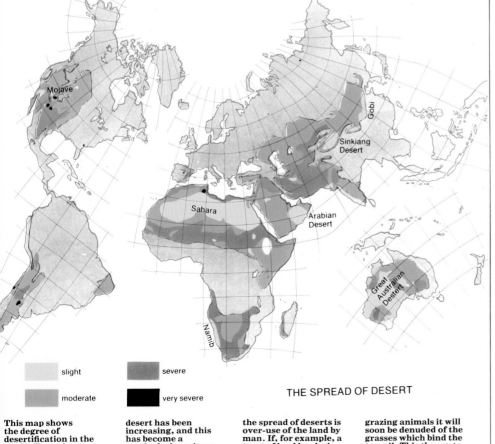

THE SPREAD OF DESERT

slight

moderate

severe

very severe

This map shows the degree of desertification in the world. For at least 1,000 years the total land area covered by desert has been increasing, and this has become a particularly serious problem in recent years. The chief reason for the spread of deserts is over-use of the land by man. If, for example, a tract of land bordering a desert region is used to support too many grazing animals it will soon be denuded of the grasses which bind the topsoil. This then gets stripped away by wind and water erosion.

H. E. Dregne, Texas Technical University

103

The Arctic and Antarctic

Among the most inhospitable areas of the world are the cold polar regions of the Arctic and Antarctic. They are popularly thought to be icebound wastes inhabited by a very few hardy beasts, such as polar bears in the Arctic and penguins in the Antarctic, able to eke out an existence in the intense cold. In fact this is far from the case. The poles themselves are indeed virtually lifeless areas but the polar regions as a whole support an astonishingly large number of plants and animals, especially around the edges of the two regions where the climate is not so extreme.

Differences between the two poles

Both Arctic and Antarctic are cold in relation to tropical and temperate regions but, other than this, differences between them are numerous. Many of these differences spring from the fact that the Arctic is an ocean surrounded by land whereas the Antarctic is a continent surrounded by ocean.

Antarctica has an area of 140 million sq km (5.5 million sq miles), most of which is covered by permanent ice that in places reaches a depth of 3,600 m (12,000 ft)—the average depth being around 1,800 m (6,000 ft). In contrast, the Arctic Ocean is covered by just a few metres of floating ice and has no large ice-covered land areas,

apart from Greenland which has only a tenth as much ice as that of Antarctica. The greater mass of Antarctica makes it many degrees colder than the Arctic which has its climate further modified by the inflow of warm water to the Arctic Basin from the Pacific and Atlantic Oceans. In consequence the cold influence of the Antarctic spreads much further north than the influence of the Arctic does south.

Paradoxically, the Antarctic is a continent but the Antarctic ecosystem derives most of its primary energy from the sea, while the Arctic is a sea whose ecosystem derives most of its energy from the land. This is not surprising, however, when it is realized that both of the polar regions are importers of energy from the milder, more productive areas to the north and south. The Arctic imports from the tundra and forest areas of the American and Eurasian continents, while the Antarctic imports from the highly productive Southern Ocean.

Arctic and Antarctic plants

The *tundra* of the Arctic consists of an area of flat, nearly treeless country which extends from the edge of the northern coniferous forest to the permanent pack ice of the pole. In winter it is covered by snow, but in summer the land thaws to a depth of about half a metre (20 in), although the soil below this remains permanently frozen and is called the *permafrost*. The melting snow reveals a variety of habitats from bare rock to swamp.

The dominant vegetation in the tundra are lichens, particularly reindeer 'moss', *Cladonia*. In addition, algae and moss are common. There are also about 100 species

Suinot/Jacana

Above: The remarkable emperor penguin, *Aptenodytes forsteri*. **These birds breed in the late winter— when it may still be continuously dark—so that the chicks will fledge when their food is most abundant.**

Left and below left: Some typical Arctic animals.

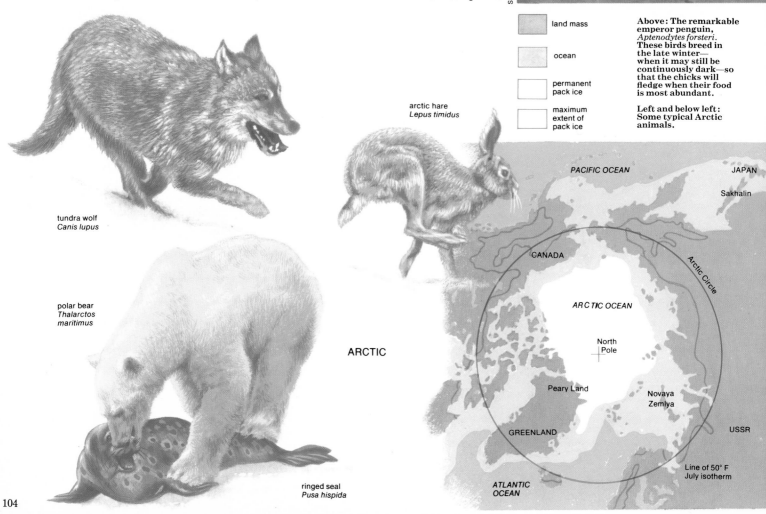

tundra wolf
Canis lupus

polar bear
Thalarctos maritimus

arctic hare
Lepus timidus

ringed seal
Pusa hispida

land mass

ocean

permanent pack ice

maximum extent of pack ice

PACIFIC OCEAN

JAPAN

Sakhalin

CANADA

Arctic Circle

ARCTIC OCEAN

North Pole

ARCTIC

Peary Land

Novaya Zemlya

GREENLAND

USSR

ATLANTIC OCEAN

Line of 50° F July isotherm

of flowering plant, including cranberries and bilberries, *Vaccinium*, the stichwort, *Stellaria crassiflora*, and the dwarf birch, *Betula nana*. Most of the flowering plants grow in a low cushion-like manner which makes them self-sheltering thus reducing the chilling effects of the wind. They are also often dark in colour to better absorb solar radiation.

There are few plants in the Antarctic but the commonest are again the lichens. These plants grow on nearly all rocky faces free of snow. They are often brightly coloured but their most remarkable feature is their ability to tolerate the harshest possible conditions, although they do not grow quickly. Their growth rate is so slow as to be almost undetectable and some colonies are thought to be as much as 4,000 years old.

In more sheltered Antarctic areas, where a minimum of soil has accumulated and a little water is available, mosses develop; and in favourable areas, such as the South Orkney Islands, banks of moss peat several metres deep have been found. In the most favourable habitats just two flowering plants may also occur. These are a grass, *Descampsia antarctica*, and a pink, *Colobanthus quitensis*.

Land animals

Because of the severity of the climate, and because Antarctica has no land connections with more temperate continents over which animal species could migrate, there are very few true land animal species in the Antarctic. They are limited to a species of springtail, *Cryptopygus antarcticus*, several species of mites and a wingless fly, *Belgica antarctica*. In addition the lakes contain a few species of copepod, and a fairy shrimp, *Branchinecto gaini*. Semi-aquatic soil-dwelling protozoa and nematode worms are also fairly common.

In contrast, animal life in the Arctic summer is abundant. Many crane flies, *Tipulidae*, hover flies, *Syrphidae*, and butterflies, *Lepidoptera*, feed on the summer flowers. The butterflies spend the winter as caterpillars, some of which burrow into vegetation and others into rock crevices where they lie dormant until the first warmth of spring. Mosquitoes, *Culicidae*, are also extremely common.

The tundra also supports many land dwelling mammals, though there are none in the Antarctic. The larger mammals include the musk ox, *Ovibos moschatus*, and the caribou (or reindeer), *Rangifer tarandus*. The musk ox is so well protected against the cold that it is able to winter in the Arctic. Caribou migrate to less harsh southern areas for the winter.

On a smaller scale Arctic hares, *Lepus timidus*, lemmings, *Lemmus lemmus*, and voles, *Microtus*, are common. As a regular food source cannot be guaranteed these animals exploit a wide variety of different foods. Lemmings, for example, will eat lichen, fungi, moss and carrion.

Lemmings and voles form the major food source for carnivores such as wolverines, *Gulo gulo*, brown bears, *Ursus arctos*, and Arctic foxes, *Alopex lagopus*. The most aggressive Arctic carnivore, however, the wolf, *Canis lupus*, also preys on herds of caribou and musk ox. Wolves go around in family packs, following the herds on which they feed.

Fred Bruemmer

Below: The Arctic and Antarctic Circles are of little use in defining the limits of the polar ecosystems. The north polar ecosystem is better defined by the 10°C (50°F) *July isotherm* which is a line connecting all those places where the maximum temperature in July is 10°C. It corresponds closely with the northern limit of trees. The southern polar ecosystem is best defined by the *Antarctic convergence* which is where cold water flowing northwards from Antarctica dips below warmer water flowing southwards from the great oceans.

Above left: The edge of the tundra. It stretches from the northern limit of trees (shown here) to the pack ice of the pole.

Right: Tundra fruits—the crowberry, *Empetrum nigrum*.

Right and below right: Some typical Antarctic animals.

SOUTH ATLANTIC OCEAN

South Georgia Islands

Antarctic Circle

Falkland Islands

Weddell Sea

South America

Graham Land

South Pole

Ross Sea

ANTARCTIC

INDIAN OCEAN

wandering albatross
Diomedea exulans

SOUTH PACIFIC OCEAN

Line of Antarctic convergence

Fred Bruemmer

Fin Whale
Balaenoptera physalus

Tundra mammals have evolved in several ways to enable them to survive the harshness of the winter. Some adaptations, such as the reduced ears of the Arctic hare and the development of thick winter coats, are anatomical, while others are behavioural. For example, lemmings bury themselves under the snow. Many others, such as caribou and brown bears, migrate south to the coniferous forest during the winter.

Perhaps the most important migratory animals, however, are the birds. Many species (a high proportion of which are water-feeding birds taking advantage of the poorly drained tundra) migrate northwards in the spring to feed and nest. A few birds survive in the tundra throughout the winter. These include two species of ptarmigan, *Lagopus*, the raven, *Corvus corax*, the snowy owl, *Nyctea scandiaca*, and the gyrfalcon, *Falco rusticolus*. The owls feed primarily on lemmings and their population fluctuates in response to that of the lemming. The gyrfalcon feeds on ptarmigan, neatly avoiding competition with the owl.

Sea and shore animals

Unlike terrestrial animals, most sea and shore-dwelling polar animals live in the Antarctic. They are more numerous than those of the Arctic because the Southern Ocean is far more productive than the Arctic Ocean—much of which is permanently covered with ice. The high productivity of the Southern Ocean is due to the constant upwelling of bottom water containing plant nutrients, resulting in a large phytoplankton population. This is especially the case around South Georgia

Right and below: Because of its severe climate and because the Antarctic has no land bridges, connecting it with more temperate continents and over which animals could migrate, there are no large land animals in Antarctica. In the Arctic, however, there are several, including large herbivores like the musk ox, *Ovibos moschatus* (right, shown in defensive formation) and the caribou (reindeer), *Rangifer tarandus* (below). In the Arctic winter the musk ox move to high ground where deep snow cannot accumulate and in the worst storms huddle together in groups to keep warm. Caribou migrate south to warmer areas instead.

Below right: One way of surviving in even the harshest environment is to be parasitic. These are warble fly larvae, *Oestridae*, feeding on the skin of a caribou.

Fred Bruemmer

Fred Bruemmer

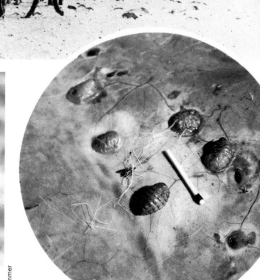

Fred Bruemmer

Left: A leopard seal, *Hydrurga leptonyx*, surprising a group of Adélie penguins. All penguins lay two eggs (except emperor penguins which lay only one) from which hatch the helpless down-clad young.

Below: The largest of the Antarctic petrels, the giant petrel, *Macronectes giganteus*, feeding on a dead penguin. Petrels feed mainly on plankton and krill but most will scavenge when the opportunity arises.

Benoit Tollu/Jacana

S. Bougaeff/Explorer

106

Fred Bruemmer

Above: An Arctic fox in its white winter coat which provides excellent camouflage against the snow. The summer coat is purple-brown. A rare form, however, much hunted for its beautiful fur, is smoke grey throughout the year.

Left: A white Arctic fox caught by an Eskimo trapper on the edge of the northern forest. There is no native human population in Antarctica but the Arctic has both Eskimos and Lapps. While the Eskimos traditionally hunt and trap animals, the Lapps have semi-domesticated the caribou and follow its herds on migration.

Below: Today, however, Antarctica is not uninhabited—several hundred scientists visit it each year. This experiment is to discover how the long-suffering Adélie penguin keeps warm.

Nicholas Devore/Bruce Coleman Ltd

S. Bougaeff/Explorer

and that area is particularly rich in animal life.

The most important organisms which feed on the phytoplankton are the euphausid crustacea known by the Norwegian name of krill, of which *Euphausia superba* is the most important. These animals are perhaps best known as the food of the great whalebone whales, *Mysticeti*, but the importance of krill does not stop with whales for it is also directly responsible for supporting large populations of fish, penguins, seals and flying birds.

One of the interesting aspects of the polar seas as a habitat is their uniformity. In contrast to the wide variation in temperature experienced over the year by animals on land, those in the sea experience only 2 to 3°C (3 to 5°F) difference between winter and summer. The minimum temperature the sea reaches before freezing is around —1.8°C (29°F), varying with its salt content, while in summer the seas are kept cold by the melting ice. Rises of more than a few degrees above freezing are rare.

Nevertheless, several species of Arctic and Antarctic fish experience winter temperatures below the 'normal' freezing point of their blood. To combat this they employ a number of anti-freeze mechanisms most of which are based on increasing the concentration of salt or protein molecules in the blood which lowers its freezing point. Even so, some species, such as the Antarctic cod, *Notothenia neglecta*, still spend part of the winter in a supercooled state in which they will freeze if they come into contact with ice.

Fish provide food for the best known Antarctic animals, the flightless shore-dwelling penguins. These animals are superbly adapted to dive and 'fly' underwater where they feed on fish and krill. The most numerous species are the chinstrap, *Pygoscelis antarctica*, Adélie, *Pygoscelis adeliae*, and macaroni, *Eudyptes chrysolophus*, which may be found in colonies numbering millions of pairs of birds.

Another well known group of fish-eating carnivores are the seals, *Phocidae* and *Otariidae*. Species of seal live in both the Antarctic and Arctic regions but their close relatives the walruses, *Odobenidae*, are confined to the Arctic. Seals provide food for the best known Arctic animal, the polar bear, *Thalarctos maritimus*. This is one of the few animals which lives permanently on the Arctic pack ice.

Sea-birds are also common in both the Antarctic and Arctic. The Arctic is home for auks, *Alcidae*, puffins, *Fratercula arctica*, and eider ducks, *Somateria;* while in the Antarctic are found the magnificent albatrosses, *Diomedidae*, which feed in the open sea taking squid, fish and crustacea. Recent studies have shown that the various species of albatross are highly specific in the type of food they take, thus avoiding competition.

A few birds are common to both polar regions. For example the Dominican gull, *Larus dominicanus*, is the southern counterpart of the lesser black backed gull, *Larus fuscus*. But the Arctic tern, *Sterna paradisaea*, is probably the most interesting of these species. It spends the northern winter migrating to the Antarctic and back. The Antarctic tern, *Sterna vittala*, however, remains in the Southern Hemisphere throughout the year.

Mountains

ZEFA

The plant and animal life of the world's mountains reflects the unusual climatic conditions which prevail in these regions. Because air pressure decreases with height, the air at high altitudes is thin and absorbs little of the sunlight which passes through it. As a consequence, much of the radiant energy of the sun reaches the ground, and so the surface of a mountain can be quite warm while the air temperature is low. However, at night or when the sun is hidden, the surface temperature drops sharply. Night frosts are common in mountainous areas, even in the tropics. The fluctuation of a mountain's surface temperature can be very high over a 24 hour period, but it is usually equalized to a large extent by the wind, and may even be less than on nearby lowland areas.

When an airstream is deflected upwards by a mountain, it becomes cooler and as a result some of its moisture falls as rain. Rainfall therefore tends to increase with altitude on windward slopes, although occasionally low altitude rain belts do form (as on Mount Kilimanjaro and in the Andes) above which the climate is dry. On leeward slopes the descending airmass rewarms, and since it is now dry it has a marked desiccating effect on both vegetation and soil.

Mountain zones

Even when it rises in a tropical rainforest, a mountain, if sufficiently high, can be capped with permanent snow. The nineteenth century scientist and traveller Alexander von Humboldt (1769-1859) noticed that the vegetation changes encountered on a journey from the equator to the poles were similar to those seen on climbing from the tropical base to the icy summit of mountains in Ecuador. At least five vegetation zones could be recognized on these mountains, roughly corresponding to the main lowland climatic types.

The *Arctic zone* occurs above the permanent snow line, above which the snow never melts. In the tropics this occurs at above 4,500 m (15,000 ft), but the snow line is found at progressively lower altitudes as one travels towards the poles, and is also dependent on such factors as the climate and topography of the mountain.

The *alpine zone* lies between the snow line and the tree line, and in many respects corresponds to the tundra. The environment is characteristically cold and moist with melted water, and the growing season is short. However, major differences between the tundra and the alpine zones of mountains at lower latitudes are the lack of a long dark winter and the greater intensity of the sunlight. Also, while the tundra is continuously cold in winter and continuously mild in summer, the daily temperature range is much greater in the alpine zone, particularly if the mountain is in the tropics. Temperatures may reach 30°C (86°F) at midday and fall below freezing at night. Such extreme conditions result in some bizarre adaptations.

At altitudes over about 3,000 m (10,000 ft) in the East African mountains, tree daisies, *Senecio*, reach a height of 5 m (16 ft). These curious plants have cabbage-

Above: Alpine scenery is as impressive as any in the world. This is a view of the Dolomites, a group of mountains lying in the eastern section of the Italian Alps. Plants in this region include the mountain pine, *Pinus mugo*, and the alpine rose, *Rhododendron hirsutum*. One of the most typical animals of the region is the alpine marmot, *Marmota marmota*, a ground squirrel which can weigh as much as 8 kg (18 lb). It feeds mainly on roots, herbs and grasses.

Right: A forest of tree rhododendrons *Rhododendron arboreum*, growing at 2,500 m (8,200 ft) in Nepal. Rhododendrons are members of the heath family, *Ericaceae*, and they thrive in a cool, damp atmosphere.

Below: One of the larger alpine mammals is the ibex, *Capra ibex*, a wild goat. There are various sub-species of the ibex to be found in the Alps, the Caucasus and parts of the Middle East. Once nearly extinct, there are thought to be about 10,000 alpine ibexes living today.

Keith Gunnar/Bruce Coleman Ltd

Ermie/Jacana

Jeff Foott/Bruce Coleman Ltd

Left: A clubmoss, *Lycopodium*, growing out from a granite rock at an altitude of 3,300 m (11,000 ft). Clubmosses are common in mountain habitats—they are the only living descendants of a group of plants which flourished some 250 million years ago.

Below: The vegetation changes seen on a journey from the equator to the poles are similar to those encountered on climbing a high mountain in the tropics, although the zones are rarely quite as clear cut as suggested in this diagram. Trees may be absent, for example, in a valley which acts as a wind trap, and deep hollows can trap cold air producing conditions colder than would otherwise be expected.

MOUNTAIN ZONATION

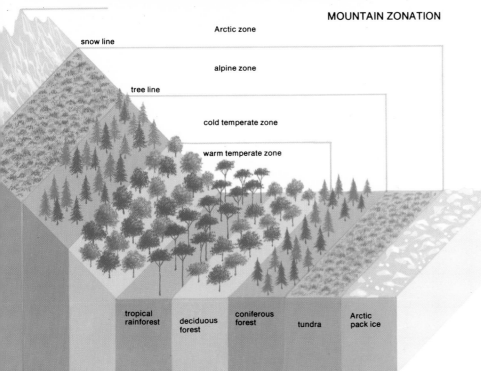

snow line

Arctic zone

alpine zone

tree line

cold temperate zone

warm temperate zone

| tropical rainforest | deciduous forest | coniferous forest | tundra | Arctic pack ice |

Left: Stemless trumpet gentians, *Gentiana clusii*. About 400 species of gentians are distributed in alpine habitats throughout the Northern Hemisphere and in South America, New Guinea and New Zealand. They are normally pollinated by insects.

Far left: A golden eagle, *Aquila chrysaetos*, with its victim, a jack rabbit, *Lepus alleni*. The golden eagle is found in mountainous regions of North America, Europe and Asia (this picture was taken in Idaho, US). In Europe the golden eagle is one of the few remaining large predators of mountain habitats. Once it competed for prey with mammal carnivores like lynxes, bears and wolves, but man has eliminated these creatures from many of their former ranges. In Europe the golden eagle feeds chiefly on such animals as grouse, hares and marmots as well as the young of larger animals such as ibexes and chamois. In the mountains of the Americas, the puma or mountain lion, *Felis concolor*, is a fairly common predator.

like heads of leaves which open during the day but close at night to insulate the growing point and flowers from as much as 4°C (7°F) of frost. A silvery reflective layer of hairs on the backs of the leaves helps to reduce heat losses by radiation. Because the tree daisies only grow at high altitudes they have evolved in isolation, probably from a common lowland ancestor, and mountains such as Mount Elgon, Mount Kenya and Mount Kilimanjaro have their own separate species.

Despite the differences between the climates of the tundra and the tropical alpine zone, the temperate alpine vegetation has many similarities to that of the tundra. Many European alpine plants, such as the purple saxifrage, *Saxifraga oppositifolia*, the golden saxifrage, *Saxifraga aizoides*, the mountain avens, *Dryas octopetala*, the dwarf birches and willows, *Betula nana* and *Salix herbacea*, the mountain sorrel, *Oxyria digyna*, and the alpine grasses *Poa alpina*, *Phleu alpinum* and *Deschampsia alpina*, are also widespread in the Arctic. Some of these species occur in the mountains as far south as the Pyrenees and are also found in North America.

Like the tundra vegetation, temperate alpine plants are typically low, compact, ground-hugging species often forming mats (grasses and sedges) or dense cushions (mosses) which can take advantage of warm patches and hollows exposed to sunlight but protected from the wind. Taller plants would be clipped back by the wind and are generally less well protected from frost. Where there is enough moisture, and especially where the rocks are alkaline, such as limestone, there are abundant wild flowers—for example, mountain speedwell, *Veronica fruticans*, Alpine fleabane, *Erigeron borealis*, campanulas, *Campanula*, primulas, *Primula*, and the mountain azalea *Loiseluria procumbens*.

The *cold temperate zone* forms the lower edge of the alpine zone and the division is marked by the upper tree line, above which conditions become too severe for trees to grow. Below the tree line there is typically a zone, about 50 m (160 ft) wide, of stunted wind-clipped trees and shrubs. Lower still is an uninterrupted belt of coniferous forest. In the American Rocky Mountains this belt is rich in Engelmann spruce, *Picea engelmannii*, and alpine fir *Abies lasiocarpa*, while in the montane coniferous forests of Europe species of fir, *Abies*, predominate. Firs also occur in the Himalayas, Asia Minor, Indochina and Central America. Pines, *Pinus*, are most common in the lower reaches of the coniferous forest zone.

In the Southern Hemisphere the upper forest limit is often formed by evergreen broadleaved trees such as the southern beeches, *Nothofagus*. In New Zealand the black beech, *Nothofagus sclandri*, forms pure forests up to the snow line, and beech forests are also important in the Andes of Argentina.

In the tropics the coniferous forest zone begins in the dry region above the cloud level and *Podocarpus* is probably the most widely distributed genus. Towards the upper forest limit the trees become progressively more branched and stunted, forming a habitat known as *elfin forest*.

The *warm temperate zone* of mountains in the tropics coincides with the cloud belt and an extremely moist habitat

MOUNTAIN IN NORTHERN HEMISPHERE

shallow angle
weak sunlight
large shadow

90° angle
strong sunlight
small shadow

NORTH

SOUTH

Norman Tomalin/Bruce Coleman Ltd

known as *cloud forest* develops, usually between 1,000 and 2,500 m (3,300 to 8,200 ft). These forests are luxuriant and rich in epiphytic plants such as Spanish moss, *Tillandsia*, and orchids, mosses and ferns, especially the filmy ferns, *Hymenophyllaceae*. The canopy is more open than in the lowland tropical rain forest and the floor is carpeted with mosses and *Selaginellas*. In higher latitudes, the montane warm temperate zone contains broad-leaved tree species, especially birches, *Betula*, and poplars, *Populus*.

Mountain animals

Many lowland animal species inhabit or visit mountains, but there are a number of species which are especially adapted to the mountain environment. In North America the wolverine, *Gulo gulo*, and other members of the weasel family, *Mustelidae*, inhabit alpine regions of the Rocky Mountains, and the snow leopard *Panthera uncia*, lives in the mountains of Central Asia and the Himalayas above about 2,500 m, feeding on wild sheep and goats. Otherwise most of the larger alpine mammals are herbivorous.

The bighorn or Rocky Mountain sheep, *Ovis canadensis*, is renowned for its agility in rock climbing and jumping, using soft pads on its feet to absorb shock and to provide grip. Many other species of sheep and goats are mountain inhabitants, including the argali, *Ovis ammon*, a close relative of the bighorn from Central Asia, the markhor, *Capra falconeri*, a mountain goat from the Himalayas, the Rocky Mountain goat, *Oreamnos americanus*, from North America and the chamois,

Rupicapra rupicapra, and ibex, *Capra ibex*, from the mountains of Western Europe. The only member of the ox subfamily which inhabits mountains is the yak, *Bos grunniens*, a long-haired animal of Tibet which has extreme resistance to exposure, living at heights from 4,000 to 6,000 m (13,000 to 20,000 ft).

In the alpine zone of temperate regions insects are extremely seasonal, perhaps only appearing for two months of the year. Insectivorous bird species are therefore rare, and most alpine birds are either ground-living species such as the partridges, *Phasianidae*, and grouse, *Tetraonidae*, birds of prey such as the golden eagle, *Aquila chrysaetos*, or carnivorous scavengers such as the Lammergeier or bearded vulture, *Gypaetus barbatus*, which is an inhabitant of high mountains in Europe and flies up to 6,000 m in the Himalayas. Certain members of the crow family, *Corvidae*, live as scavengers on mountains: the raven, *Corvus corax*, for example is distributed throughout Europe and North America living in rocky areas. The most successful smaller birds of the alpine zone in Eurasia are omnivorous species like the accentors of which the hedgesparrow, *Prunella modularis*, is a common member.

Cold-blooded animals, such as insects, reptiles and amphibia have no temperature control mechanisms so their body temperatures are dependent on those of the surroundings and on the amount of solar radiation. They are therefore active only for short periods of the year in alpine regions, except in the tropics where the daily temperature cycle allows some activity each day. Almost all insect groups are represented in the alpine fauna.

All the reptiles and amphibia of alpine zones, including the European salamander, *Salamandra atra*, the European viper or adder, *Viperus berus*, and the common lizard, *Lacerta vivipara*, are ovoviviparous—their eggs develop within the body of the female. This protects the eggs both from predators and from the extremes of cold and heat.

Marion Morrison

Top left: The amount of radiation received by a mountain depends on the angle of its slopes and the direction they face. In the Northern Hemisphere, a given area on a south-facing slope receives sunlight at angles close to 90° and therefore maximum intensity. Shadows are small. On a north-facing slope the angle of the sunlight is shallow so the same area receives less radiation.

Top right: A snow leopard, *Panthera uncia*. These creatures inhabit the central Asian highlands, from the Himalayas north to the Altay, where they feed on wild sheep and goats, large rodents and birds. An adult snow leopard may measure 2 m (6.5 ft) from nose to tail and reach a height of 60 cm (2 ft) at the shoulder.

Left: A herd of llamas in a village high in the Bolivian Andes. The llama was domesticated thousands of years ago from the guanaco, *Lama glama guanicoe*, a South American member of the camel family, *Camelidae*. The llama is used as a pack animal at altitudes up to about 4,000 m (13,000 ft).

The Sea

No man, animal or plant is an island. Each one is part of a community, every member of which is influenced by the others and by the external environment. The study of the inter-relationships between living things and their environment is called *ecology*. It is the study of the biological whole rather than its individual parts.

The place where a particular community of plants and animals lives is called its *habitat*. For example, a habitat may be a forest, a desert, a coral reef, or a freshwater pond. But by far the largest habitat in the world is the open sea—it covers some 70 per cent of the Earth's surface and provides a home for vast numbers of individuals and species.

The Sun as an energy source

Every living community ultimately depends on an external energy source. Energy is needed to build up the organic chemicals which make up the bodies of living things and to allow movement. In the sea, as in most other communities, the external energy source is the Sun. Plants trap this energy in the process of photosynthesis. Animals then feed on these plants and on each other, but at each stage of such a *food-chain* most of the energy is lost as heat. Plants thus make an energy profit which the rest of the community gradually dissipates.

However, the light rays on which the community depends do not penetrate far

Bruce Coleman

Above right: 70% of the Earth's surface is covered by sea—making this the biggest ecological habitat in the world and home to countless living things. The temperature is generally stable—so most members of the sea community do not need to control their body temperatures—and all the materials which plants and animals need for their growth and good health are dissolved in the water around them.

Below: The smallest animals in the sea are *Protozoa* like this radiolarian, *Acanthometron*. Radiolarians have an intricate skeleton of glass-like minerals.

Right: In the shifting oceans, plants are generally unable to grow to any great size and many are very small indeed, falling in the size range 1 μm to 1 mm. Planktonic plants shown: diatoms *Thalassiosira* (1), *Biddulphia* (2) and *Chaetoceros* (3), and dinoflagellates *Noctiluca* (4) and *Ceratium* (5 and 6).

PHYTOPLANKTON

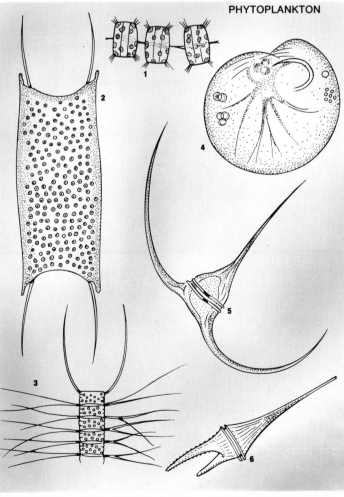

Giuseppe Mazza

into the sea because they are absorbed by water. In turbid water, for instance near the coast, they are absorbed even more rapidly than in the clearer waters of the open sea, and the stronger light in the tropics penetrates deeper than the weak light towards the poles: but even in clear tropical seas there is little light below a depth of 100 m (330 ft). In temperate seas in early summer this depth is nearer 30 m (98 ft). Below it plants can do no productive work. Since the average depth of the sea is 3.5 km (2.3 miles) it is evident that plant life will be confined to a very small fraction of the total volume—the rest of the sea being pitch black except for the faint light which some deep sea organisms produce themselves. This productive upper layer, on which all sea life depends, is called the *euphotic zone*.

The different colours which make up white light are not all absorbed by water at the same rate. The longer wavelengths (red light) are absorbed best, then the shorter green waves and finally blue. These differing absorbtion rates have important consequences to the plants which inhabit the euphotic zone. Plants have pigments with which they trap light in the first step of photosynthesis, and different pigments use different parts of the spectrum. Many marine plants have adapted to the marine environment by producing pigments which absorb the shorter wavelengths present at greater depths. In particular many are brown due to a high concentration of the pigment *xanthophyll* which can absorb green light.

Nevertheless, chlorophyll is essential to all plants. It is the only pigment which can actually carry out chemical synthesis. Energy trapped by the other pigments has to be passed on to chlorophyll before it can be used. All marine plants therefore possess chlorophyll but they also have a higher concentration of other pigments than land plants.

Plant types

The plants which live in the euphotic zone and incorporate light energy into the community are generally microscopic and are called the *phytoplankton*. They are mostly tiny *algae* varying in size from 1 μm (a millionth of a metre) to 1 mm. Most of the larger plants of the phytoplankton belong to two groups of algae, the diatoms, *Bacillariophyta* (*Chrysophyta*), and the dinoflagellates, *Pyrrophyta*. In addition there are large numbers of smaller plants, including flagellates, blue-green algae and bacteria, about which little is known.

The range of a particular species depends on light intensity, the availability of nutrients, temperature and the number and type of plant-eating animals (*herbivores*). Of these, temperature is a particularly important factor. Although the temperature range found over the world is not as extreme in the sea as on land, there is still considerable variation. The surface layers in the tropics are at about 30 °C (86 °F), whereas at the poles near ice they can be as cold as —2 °C (28 °F). In addition, each great ocean current has its own characteristic temperature which can produce large local fluctuations.

A radical change in the species composing the phytoplankton occurs with these temperature variations, so it appears that temperature is of prime importance in limiting the range of many

Dr. Georg Gerster/John Hillelson Agency

P. Morris

Left: Some species of phytoplankton carry out 'chemical warfare' against other species. Some dinoflagellates in particular produce powerful poisons which, if concentrated because of an 'algal bloom', may result in a 'red tide' as shown here. These can kill large numbers of fish and can severely damage fisheries.

Right: One notable feature of ocean life is the vertical migration which many animals undertake every 24 hours. The reasons for this are not well understood, but it is possible that by feeding near the surface only at night they can successfully avoid predators which hunt chiefly by sight.

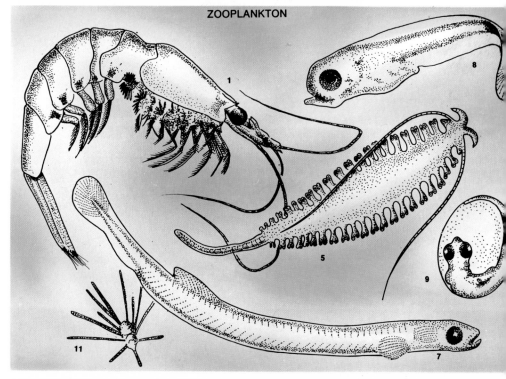

ZOOPLANKTON

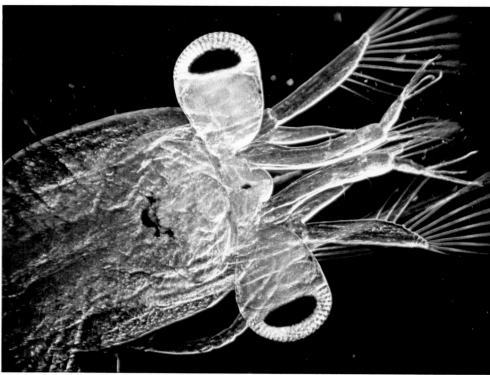

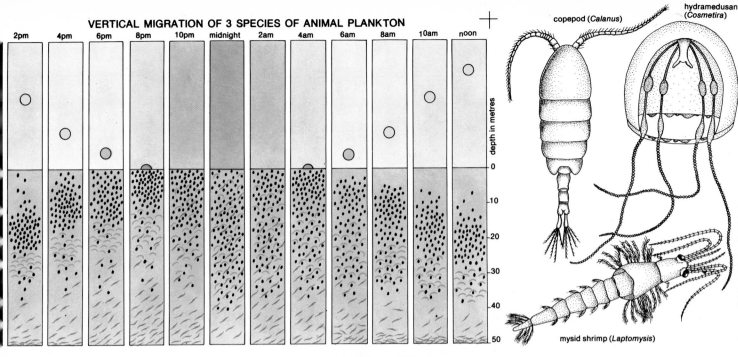

VERTICAL MIGRATION OF 3 SPECIES OF ANIMAL PLANKTON

2pm 4pm 6pm 8pm 10pm midnight 2am 4am 6am 8am 10am noon

depth in metres

0 -10 -20 -30 -40 -50

copepod (Calanus)

hydramedusan (Cosmetira)

mysid shrimp (Laptomysis)

Courtesy of Sir Frederick Russell. Originally published in 'The Seas' (Frederick Warne)

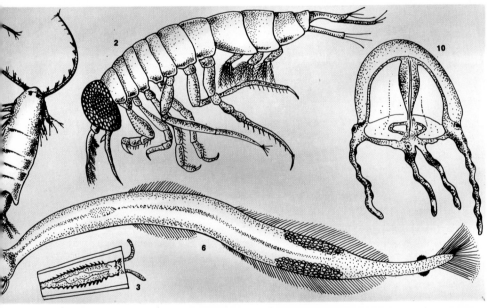

2 10

6

3

Above: Although whales, the largest animals, live in the sea, most marine animals are smaller than 1 cm (0.4 in) and are called the *zooplankton.* **These particular animals are:**

1. euphausiid *Meganyctiphanes norvegica*
2. amphipod *Parathemisto abyssorum*
3. polychaete worm *Lanice conchilega*
4. copepod *Labidocera wollastoni*
5. polychaete worm *Tomopteris helgolandica*
6. arrow worm *Sagitta elegans*
7. teleost fish larva *Sprattus sprattus*
8. teleost fish larva *Gadus morhua*
9. teleost fish egg *Gadus morhua*
10. hydromedusan *Sarsia exima*
11. sea urchin *Echinocardium cordatum*

Left: Many species in the plankton are the immature stages of larger animals. This is the larva (*zoea***) of the hermit crab,** *Eupagurus.*

Right: The coral-eating crown of thorns starfish *Acanthaster planci***, which has destroyed much of the Great Barrier Reef off eastern Australia.**

Bruce Coleman

species. On the other hand, however, laboratory experiments often indicate that particular species have wider temperature tolerances than their natural range seems to imply. Other factors are therefore involved. Ecologically, the effect of single factors is almost always modified by interactions with other effects. In the seas the effects of temperature interact with other environmental factors, such as salinity, in determining the species present in any area.

Cycles of productivity

The interaction of environmental factors can be clearly seen when seasonal changes in the population of phytoplankton are examined. In temperate latitudes, such as the North Sea, a regular cycle of changes in plankton numbers occurs each year. The numbers are low in winter, start to increase in March and reach a peak towards the end of April. They then fall dramatically and remain low throughout the summer, until there is another rapid increase in the autumn—but the autumn peak is lower than the spring peak. The numbers then gradually return to their low winter level.

The causes of this *cycle of productivity* are now fairly well understood. During the winter the limiting factor for photosynthesis and plant growth is lack of sunlight. In spring, as both the intensity of sunlight and day length increase, this limitation is removed. The algae grow and reproduce rapidly. At the same time, the temperature of the surface water increases. The density of water depends on its temperature—warm water is less dense than cold water—so warming of the surface establishes a layer, about as deep as the euphotic zone, of less dense warm water above the cold body of the ocean. Within this upper layer water mixes freely, but it no longer mixes with the deeper water from which it is separated by the lower boundary of the warm layer, called the *thermocline* or *discontinuity layer.* There is no mixing across the thermocline.

At first, the presence of the thermocline accelerates phytoplankton production because it prevents the algae from being carried beyond the depth at which light penetrates. But it also isolates the surface waters nutritionally from the sea

113

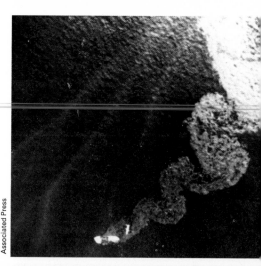

Left and right: Man and the sea. Technological advances, particularly in diving equipment, have allowed man to obtain a greater understanding of the animal and plant life of the sea. (This diver, left, is exploring the beauty of a coral reef). It has also brought the risk of catastrophes big enough to upset the ecological balance even of as large a habitat as the sea. This aerial photograph (right) taken from 1,680 m (5,500 ft) shows part of the huge slick—estimated at 155 million litres (7.6 million gallons) and 161 km (100 miles) long—produced when the Liberian oil tanker *Argo Merchant* foundered off the North American coast during late December 1976.

Above and right: Two rare fish. Brilliantly coloured *Pseudochromis fridmani* (right) is found only in the Red Sea, while the Antarctic ice fish, *Chaenocephalus aceratus*, (above) is peculiar because it has no *respiratory pigment* which other animals use to transport oxygen in the blood.

below. Essential nutrients, particularly phosphate and nitrate, are used up by the expanding plankton community and cannot be replaced. Dead organisms and faecal pellets sink through the thermocline, taking their materials with them to the sea bed. There is no way by which these lost nutrients can be reclaimed from the depths where they accumulate.

It was once thought that the resulting nutrient deficiency caused the decline of phytoplankton in early summer. Yet it is now known that numbers begin to fall when nutrients are still adequate, so the beginning of the decline cannot be caused by the lack of nutrients. In fact the decline is probably started by the grazing of herbivores, whose numbers have increased in the wake of the algal bloom. But once the number of algae has begun to fall their further decline continues because of lack of nutrients.

As the summer progresses, these two factors—the level of nutrients and the grazing of herbivores—interact to produce a stable plant population, and the situation remains largely unchanged until the autumn. Then, the cooling of the surface layers begins to reduce the stability of the thermocline and it is eventually destroyed by the gales which come with autumn. The gales thoroughly mix the various water layers and phosphate and nitrate are returned to the surface. This allows growth to be resumed leading to the second peak. Finally, winter sets in. There is less light and plant numbers fall back to their original level.

Throughout the seasons different species of phytoplankton succeed each other within the main cycle of numbers.

Smaller diatoms are prominent in the early spring. Larger species, which take longer to multiply, become dominant later. Dinoflagellates are much more numerous than diatoms during the summer. Diatoms become numerous again in the autumn. The causes of this succession are complex and are not well understood, although there is some evidence that dinoflagellates are more tolerant of a shortage of phosphate than are diatoms.

The same factors which occur in temperate seas also occur in the tropics but in the tropics the thermocline is permanently stable. This explains why tropical seas have a far lower phytoplankton population—there is a chronic shortage of nutrients. The thermocline is normally only broken by an upwelling of bottom water caused by such factors as the trade winds which drive the surface waters away from the west coasts of South America and Africa. In such circumstances the surface waters are replaced from the deeps by water rich in nutrients and a large phytoplankton and dependent fish population can grow up. Such a system is responsible, for instance, for the huge anchovy hauls off Peru.

Animals

The animals of the sea do not themselves need the surface light but can live at all depths. However, herbivores do have to feed in the euphotic zone and they are followed there by their predators. Most marine animals then, like the plants on which they depend, live near the surface. From the surface a steady rain of organic debris falls to support a smaller population of scavengers and their predators in the deeps. Quite large populations, how-

Below: The fate of the Peruvian anchovy fishery is a good example of how the combination of overfishing and adverse environmental factors can reduce a seemingly inexhaustible supply. In 1970, 13 million tonnes were landed, but by 1973 the figure was only two million tonnes. One cause of this dramatic drop in catch was the intrusion further south than normal of the warm water current, *El Nino*. This upset the mixing of nutritionally rich bottom waters with the surface layers —the basis of this fishery. Restrictions imposed by the Peruvian Government and the retreat of *El Nino* have since prevented further falls in yield.

American Museum of Natural History

Ronan

Above and above left: Some deep sea fishes. All deep sea animals are either scavengers —feeding on organic matter falling down from above—or carnivores feeding on other members of the bottom community. These fish are *Anomalops catopton* (above left), *Eurypharynx pelecanoides* (top) and *Nemichthys scolopacus* (above).

Left: Stories of sea monsters often have their beginnings in exaggerated accounts of real events. This illustration is of an occasion in December 1906 when a French fishing boat landed a catch of some 1,500 octopuses. The fishermen saved themselves by cutting the trawl rope and losing the net.

(*cilia*) whereas the massive baleen whales (*Mysticeti*) swim through the water and collect krill on a complicated barricade called the *baleen*. In all cases of filter feeding, however, there is no selection between plant and animal material by the feeder. Filtering involves the selection of food only by size, although a filter with a small mesh size will tend to catch plants, whereas larger meshes, such as are found in whales and herrings, will trap mainly animals.

Finally, besides the filter feeders, there are many carnivores which feed by attacking and gripping individual prey. These range in size from carnivorous protozoans, through arrow worms, *Chaetognatha*, up to sharks, *Selachii*. Large predators, such as sharks and man, represent the last link in the food-chain of the sea.

Food-chains

In a simple food-chain, herbivores eat the plants and carnivores eat the herbivores. Each of the links in the chain is called a *trophic level*. In the seas, however, it is difficult to assign species to a particular trophic level, both because food-chains tend to be long and complex and because the feeding habits of many species change with their age and size.

Nevertheless, whatever the exact composition of a food-chain, most of the energy bound up in the bodies of animals and plants is lost when they are consumed by animals belonging to the next trophic level. As a general rule, only 10% passes up from one trophic level to the next. Thus it takes 1,000 tonnes of plant material to produce just 1 kg (2.2 lb) of great blue shark, *Prionace glauca*.

ever, can live in the deeps—baited cameras on the sea bottom reveal that large crowds of scavengers can assemble remarkably quickly.

A community consists of the *producers* (the plants), the *primary consumers* (the *herbivores*), and various subsequent levels of *higher consumers* (the *carnivores*). In the euphotic zone the primary consumers consist of protozoans (especially tintinnids, *Tintinnidae*, radiolarians, *Radiolaria*, foraminiferans, *Foraminifera*) and copepods, *Copepoda*, of various kinds, which are all less than 2 cm (0.8 in) long. The group *Copepoda* (class *Crustacea*) has been outstandingly successful in the sea. Samples of animal plankton (*zooplankton*) usually consist of between 50 and 80 per cent copepods. In the North Atlantic the commonest species is the

copepod herbivore *Calanus finmarchicus*.

In a slightly larger size range is another very successful group of crustaceans, the euphausiids, *Euphausiidae*. The best known example is the krill, *Euphausia superba*. This animal is about 4 cm (1.6 in) long and forms the staple diet of the great filter feeding whales of the Antarctic—including the largest animal that has ever lived, the blue whale, *Balaenoptera musculus*.

Filter feeding is a very common form of feeding of marine animals. Most of the food in the euphotic zone consists of small organisms, suspended in the water, and these can be most easily removed by filtering. Techniques for achieving this vary from species to species. For example, tintinnid protozoans create water currents towards their bodies by tiny hairs

115

The Seashore

The seashore is home to an enormous variety of living organisms, among them bacteria, seaweeds, barnacles, limpets, oysters and sea anemones as well as visiting sea birds such as gulls and terns. It provides a wide range of habitats, from sand, shingle, boulders and continuous sheets of rock to muddy beaches and salt marsh.

To the organisms colonizing a shore, the particle size of the beach (that is to say whether it is composed of sand, shingle or rocks) is of great importance. Species which thrive among boulders do not necessarily flourish in sand. Particle size is partly determined by whether the shore is exposed or sheltered. Exposed shores pounded by waves are often rocky and steep, while the sand and shell fragments ground off such shores are carried into sheltered coves for beach building.

The tides

Tides, which cover the shore with sea water every 12 hours 20 minutes, make the seashore a relatively hostile environment. Its inhabitants have to be able to withstand the rigours of both aquatic and terrestrial life: at low tide, for example, they risk desiccation in dry weather whereas in rain they need protection against the fresh water which might dangerously dilute their body fluids. At high tide, on the other hand, they are covered by salt water which, although of a much more uniform temperature than the surrounding air, has a much lower oxygen content.

In general, the most hostile part of any seashore is the region near the high tide line, for it is here that organisms are exposed to the air for the longest time. It is a characteristic of all environments that the more hostile they are, the fewer the number of species within them, even though those few may be abundant. This is true of the seashore; there is a reduction in the number of species as one works one's way up from the mid-tide line.

The zones of the seashore

The result of this gradation of shore conditions is that there are a number of distinct zones, each one at a different level up the shore. Each zone has a characteristic set of organisms living in it which are adapted specifically to tolerate conditions at that level.

Below the average low tide line, the *sublittoral fringe*, of a typical rocky shore in Britain is found the seaweed *Laminaria*, the largest of the brown algae, which grows to a length of 4 m (13 ft). In addition there are many red algae, such as *Rhodymenia palmata*. These species are well adapted to thrive when covered by a layer of deep and turbid water which only transmits light of rather short wavelength, and they have a high proportion of pigments capable of absorbing light of of this kind.

In the *eulittoral zone*, the term given to those parts of the shore that are uncovered and covered by the tide every day, is found the seaweed *Fucus serratus*, which gives way to *Fucus vesiculosus* further up the beach, followed by *Fucus spiralis* and finally *Pelvetia canaliculata*. At the upper limits of the eulittoral zone, algae are

Georg Gerster/John Hillelson Agency

unable to survive unassisted and we find the symbiotic partnership known as a lichen, in which an alga and a fungus combine. The black *Verrucaria maura* leads into the *littoral fringe* which is characterised by the silver lichen *Ramalina* and the orange *Xanthora parietina*, both of which extend up the cliff face.

Examination of the animals living on the shore shows a similar zonation. Some, like the limpets, *Patella*, simply follow the algae on which they feed, whereas others are limited by their tolerance of high temperatures, desiccation or lack of oxygen. A good example of an essentially marine creature which has adapted to spend long periods in the open air is the star barnacle, *Chthamalus stellatus*, a suspension feeder. It survives in the open by drawing gaseous oxygen through its *micropyle* (a small aperture). However, allowing oxygen to flow over a moist respiratory surface inevitably entails an undesirable loss of water by evaporation, so the creature has developed an alternative method of respiration. If it loses more than 0.5 per cent of its body weight by evaporation, it closes the micropyle completely and relies on the energy released by *anaerobic* respiration to supply its basic living requirements, so avoiding

Above: Algae are among the most universally successful of the shore plants, and as primary producers are vital to the ecosystem. They can reach a great size; the common seaweed *Laminaria* grows to four metres off Britain. This aerial view shows algal growth on the Sinai peninsula (Gulf of Eilat).

Right: The fauna and flora of a rocky shore is related to the severity of wave action it suffers. On an exposed headland (1) barnacles predominate. Algal growth increases with increasing shelter and becomes predominant on sheltered lee shores (3 and 4). Intermediate shores (2) contain both barnacles and algae.

any further loss of water.

Living further down the shore is the common barnacle, *Balanus balanoides*. This species is less good at surviving extremes of environment, but it does better than *Chthamalus* when they are matched in a straight competition for space. In the slow process of growth, *Balanus* slowly undercuts *Chthamalus* until the latter is knocked off by the waves. At the bottom of the shore another barnacle, *Balanus perforatus*, is found, which is in turn supplanted by *Balanus crenatus* under overhanging rocks.

One strategy which animals use to populate a particular zone is to lay eggs within the zone where the parents have lived. The eggs are firmly fixed to the rock and have enough food reserves to develop to the stage when the young can

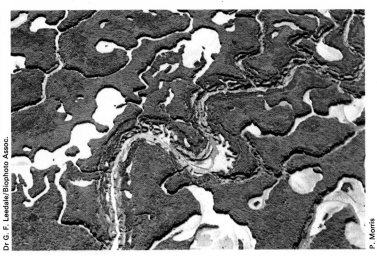

Above: Flowers of the seashore serve the function of binding the sand. They must be able to tolerate a high level of salt and have the ability to conserve valuable fresh water. In order to adapt to their environment, many have reduced leaf size as a protection against evaporation. The flower shown here is the salt-tolerant sea lavender, *Limonium pectinatum*.

Below: An inhabitant of the seashore, and a victim of oil pollution which kills countless birds every year and pollutes increasing numbers of beaches. This oil-covered bird is a Magellanic penguin from Patagonia.

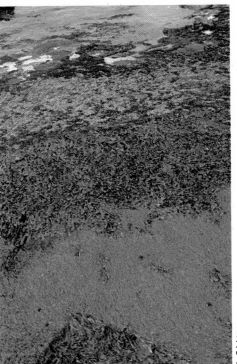

Left: Algae, or seaweeds, are the dominant shore plants, starting at the sublittoral fringe and moving up the shore in zones. Each zone is dominated by the alga best adapted to its conditions. Among the seaweeds on this British shore are *Laminaria*, *Corallina*, *Fucus*, *Pelvetia* and *Enteromorpha*.

Above: Marshes along flat sea coasts are subject to tidal action and because of evaporation the salinity can be even higher than in the open sea. They provide one of the harshest environments for marine animals. The picture shows an aerial view of a salt marsh on the Essex coast of Britain.

maintain their position on the shore. The various species of periwinkle, *Littorina*, do this. In spite of the fact that their eggs cannot drift with the currents, periwinkles are among the most widely dispersed genera of the shore.

In contrast, most shore creatures, especially the immobile ones like barnacles and oysters, have what appears to be a stage specifically adapted for dispersal. In many marine organisms the eggs are released into the planktonic community, where they drift with the vagaries of the ocean current, until the larvae which hatch from the eggs are ready to settle.

The shore community

The organisms found on the seashore make up a community whose members are all affected to a greater or lesser degree by each other's activities. They may be divided into a number of different levels according to their position in the food chain. These are called *trophic levels*: plants (producers) occupy the first trophic level, herbivores (grazers) the second and so on.

At the bottom of the food chain, green plants use the energy of sunlight to photosynthesize new tissue. The food created in this way then passes to the remaining community members by one of two routes: either the plant is eaten by a grazing animal, such as a limpet, or it eventually dies and provides food for saprophytes, such as heterotrophic bacteria. Eventually both pathways lead to carnivores, but not always the same carnivores, at the top of the chain.

On rocky shores, the producers are mainly the various seaweeds which are firmly attached to the rocks by means of *holdfasts*. Various animals graze on these plants, including limpets, chitons and the numerous snail-like molluscs, such as the periwinkle, which are common on most shores. On rocky shores, however, many of the animals are suspension feeders, filtering edible particles out of the water. Barnacles are the most striking of this group. They can take in food particles measuring only 30 µm (millionths of a 117)

exposed rock	encrusting lichen, *Verrucaria*	seaweed *Fucus*
barnacles *Chthalamus and Balanus*	seaweed *Pelvetia*	seaweed *Laminaria*

THE EFFECT OF WAVE ACTION

Brian Seed/John Hillelson Agency

P. Morris

Right: A common inhabitant of tropical beaches is the ghost crab, *Ocypode*. It feeds at night on other animals such as newly hatched turtles.

Left: An extreme example of man's contribution to a shore environment. Surprisingly, quite a number of animals can survive in the sort of conditions prevailing on this polluted beach in Viareggio, Italy. Many European countries enforce legislation to prevent such pollution.

Below right: Man as a visiting predator, with a net on the oyster beds at Bassin d'Arcachon in France.

Below: A generalized diagram of a simple ecosystem showing the flow of energy and the transference of nutrients. Large arrows show directions of energy flow and small arrows indicate the transference of nutrients. The system is divided into a grazing food chain and a detritus or decomposer chain, with corresponding trophic levels. Solar energy is absorbed by primary producers, follows the two chains and is finally lost as radiant heat to the atmosphere. Nutrients are recycled within the system by death, bacterial decay or excretion. Much is deposited outside the system but under balanced conditions an equal amount enters. Thus other ecosystems share the nutrient pool to the mutual advantage of all.

Erich Lessing—Magnum/John Hillelson Agency

metre) across, so that among other things they are likely to ingest single-celled plants, such as diatoms. Diatoms are really a part of the ocean community, so suspension feeders in fact import some material from outside their own community.

Whatever the origin of the producers, the secondary consumers are often permanent residents on the seashore. One example is the dog whelk, *Thais*, which feeds mainly on barnacles and mussels, and, nearer low tide, starfish such as the European starfish, *Asterias rubens*. Besides these permanent residents of the rocky shores, there are a number of visitors which can join one of the various trophic levels for a while and may leave their faeces or corpses on the shore. They are, however, more likely to be exporters than importers of energy. Oyster catchers, gulls and crows may feed on mussels and limpets, and also on such secondary consumers as dog whelks and starfish.

On sandy shores, where there is no firm, stationary surface material, most animals live below the surface. In the more productive shores, which consist of a mixture of sand and mud, there are probably three principal groups of producers. Firstly, the remains of seaweeds and animals which have been torn from rocky shores in storms and deposited on sheltered sandy beaches—in this respect the community of the sandy shore is parasitic on the rocky shore community. Secondly, numerous single-celled plants, such as diatoms and dinoflagellates, lying on or near the surface of the muddy sand. And thirdly, various species of *chemotrophic* bacteria living some distance below the surface of the sand in a black layer al-

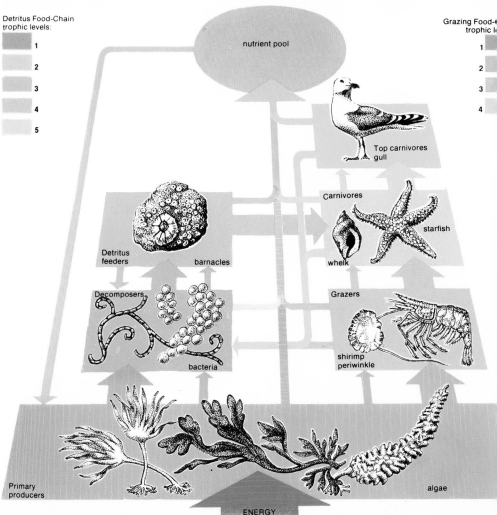

Detritus Food-Chain
trophic levels:

1
2
3
4
5

nutrient pool

Top carnivores
gull

Carnivores

starfish

whelk

Detritus feeders

barnacles

Decomposers

bacteria

Grazers

shirimp
periwinkle

Grazing Food-
trophic le

1
2
3
4

Primary
producers

algae

ENERGY

118

Right: Molluscs have various methods for attaching themselves to their habitats, against such threats as pounding waves or predators. Here, the common mussel, *Mytilus*, is putting out sticky 'guy ropes' with its foot.

Below: Acorn barnacles, *Balanus crenatus*, mating. Barnacles are common among shore animals.

Bottom: These white-fronted terns, *Sterna striata*, are among the predators which visit the shore at low tide to feed on the carnivores such as limpets and mussels. They may leave their faeces or corpses on the shore, but chiefly export energy from the ecosystem.

Jeffrey Goodman

Heather Angel

Heather Angel

most devoid of oxygen.

Chemotrophic bacteria obtain their energy by oxidizing simple inorganic compounds such as hydrogen sulphide, and so they provide a direct energy input for the whole of the food chain. Nematode worms graze on the bacteria, and these in turn are eaten by animals such as ragworms which are part of the diet of bottom dwelling fish.

Heterotrophic bacteria need complex organic compounds from other living things for food, and are therefore ultimately dependent on green plants for their energy. They are found in huge numbers on the particles of sand near the surface of the beach and are responsible for breaking down much of the flotsam which is deposited on the beach.

Considering the abundance of these surface bacteria, it is not surprising that mud flats are usually packed with animals that feed on the bacteria by swallowing the sand on which they grow. Such animals are called *deposit feeders*. One common British deposit feeder, the spire shell snail, *Hydrobia ulvae*, can reach a population density of as many as 60,000 animals per square metre of muddy beach. Another, the peppery furrow shell, *Scrobicularia plana*, a bivalve mollusc, spends its life burrowing in the sand. It has two siphons extending to the surface, one of which moves over the surface like a vacuum cleaner while the other acts as an exhaust pipe.

The other large group of burrowing molluscs are the *filter feeders*, such as the soft-shelled clam, *Mya arenaria*. Like the deposit feeders they have two siphons, but these are bound together along much of their length, and are not manipulated separately. Particles of food suspended in the water are drawn in through the inhalant siphon and trapped in the mucus overlying the ciliated gills which create the current.

The whole of the shore community then is powered by green plants such as seaweeds and diatoms, chemotrophic bacteria and flotsam brought in by the tide. The material passes to grazers, to heterotrophic bacteria (which are consumed by deposit feeders) or to suspension feeders. These creatures in turn are preyed on by carnivores such as starfish. Ultimately some of these carnivores may themselves fall prey to visiting vertebrates such as fish which come in with the tide or seabirds which feed when the tide is out. When these creatures die their bodies provide food for the humble heterotrophic bacteria and so the cycle repeats itself.

119

Ponds, Rivers and Streams

It is generally believed that life began in the sea and spread from there to the land. At first glance an obvious first step in this progression appears to be the colonization of freshwater habitats. But the transition from a salt to a freshwater environment is not as easy as it appears. In fact relatively few organisms have managed this step. Rather than land animals and plants evolving from freshwater organisms the reverse is often true.

Chemical factors

The major difference between the stable and cosy environment of the sea and the inhospitable world of freshwater ponds, rivers and streams is the lack of nutrients. Freshwater contains less than one gram per litre of dissolved mineral salts whereas the sea contains about 35 grams per litre. This lack of nutrients effects freshwater organisms in two ways. Plants have difficulty acquiring sufficient salts for growth and animals have difficulty in maintaining their internal salt concentrations above that of the surrounding water.

Chemically, freshwaters can be divided into two types, *acid* or *soft* waters and *calcareous* (calcium-rich) or *hard* waters; though, of course, there are many streams and ponds which fit in between these two categories. In both types of environment the most important organisms in breaking down organic matter—and so releasing the nutrients locked up inside—are bacteria. These simple plants cannot survive in acid conditions and so acid waters have sparse aquatic communities because the breakdown of organic matter cannot take place. (This is why plant material may remain undecayed for centuries in the acid conditions of peat bogs.) In calcareous waters, however, bacteria can break down plant and animal remains, and so plants can thrive because they have the necessary nutrients for growth.

Consequently, lakes and streams in chalk or limestone areas, rich in calcium, have the largest aquatic communities, both in the numbers of individuals and of species. Acid moorland ponds and streams, on the other hand, contain very few organisms and usually have accumulations of undecomposed organic matter.

Rivers and streams

A community of organisms in which the individuals interact with each other and with their environment is called an *ecosystem*. Most ecosystems are *closed* systems in which nutrients and other materials are constantly recycled between the plants and animals within the system. Streams and rivers, however, are *open* systems. Materials are constantly carried downstream and there is no way in which they can be returned. Hence a community at any place in the stream can only use nutrients once—after that they are lost to the next community further down the stream. In contrast, a lake is a closed system in which nutrients are constantly recycled.

Because they are constantly losing material, stream and river ecosystems

Above: Fresh water at its most spectacular— 2,800 cubic metres (100,000 cubic ft) flow over Niagara Falls every second during the day. (The flow is reduced at night to produce hydroelectric power.) Turbulence is important in freshwater ecosystems. It causes life-giving oxygen to dissolve into the water.

Right: In stiller waters oxygen is obtained from photosynthesizing plants. This is water crowfoot, *Ranunculus aquatalis*.

Below: In many lakes and streams plant growth is limited by shortage of inorganic nutrients. If these are added, for example from fertilizer leached from surrounding fields (as here), massive algal growth can result.

Reeds growing in Wicken Fen, Cambridgeshire. Because its water level is artificially maintained the Fen provides a controlled habitat for birds, insects and plants, particularly willow and alder.

rely on a continual input of organic and other nutrients in order to survive. These materials are largely obtained from animals and plants along the banks. Inorganic nutrients are constantly dissolved from the rocks along the banks and organic nutrients are obtained from both the vegetation and the animals that live on the bankside.

River and stream plants
Very little of the input into a fast flowing stream or river community is produced by aquatic plants within the community itself. This is particularly true of upland streams where plants are few because the swift current makes rooting difficult. Only mosses, particularly *Fontinalis*, and algal films, like *Periphyton*, can survive.

More plants grow in wider streams and rivers where sluggish water flows along some banks and silt and mud are deposited. In such places plants like water milfoil, *Myriophyllum*, and water crow-foot, *Ranunculus*, can take root. Once some plants have rooted they slow the current down further so that more silt and mud is deposited and more plants can grow. In slow-flowing water, too, other, non-rooting plants, such as water hyacinth, *Eichhornia crassipes*, are able to grow. Most importantly the number of *phytoplankton*, minute algae, particularly *diatoms* and *dinoflagellates*, can increase and supply food to the smallest animal herbivores.

River and stream animals
Fast flowing water also presents a problem to stream and river animals. They must prevent themselves being washed downstream, away from their habitat and out to sea. To do this they have evolved three main adaptations. They may be flattened or streamlined to present less resistance to the water, they may have behavioural adaptations, such as *positive rheotaxis* (continuous swimming upstream), or they may have suckers or hooks to attach them firmly to stones. Furthermore, most animals which live in fast flowing turbulent streams are bottom living (*benthic*). Here stones provide shelter and the water current is less because of friction between the water and the stream bottom.

Many benthic animals are young stages (*larvae*) of insects which later emerge from water as winged adults of short lifespan, living only to breed. For example, may-flies, such as *Ecdyonurus* and *Rithrogena*, live for just one day, during which they mate and lay their eggs in flowing water. Immature mayflies (*nymphs*), on the other hand, live for anything from one to three years depending on the species. They are flattened, scarcely 2.5 mm (0.1 in) thick, and have claws which enable them to cling to stones. Other animals which also attach themselves to stones include stone-fly nymphs, *Plecoptera*, leeches, *Hirudinea*, flatworms, *Planaria*, and molluscs, such as freshwater limpets, *Ancylastrum*.

Animals which maintain their station in the stream by swimming against the current include the freshwater shrimp, *Gammarus*, commonly found in crevices between stones, and most species of fish. In temperate streams the dominant group of fish are members of the salmon family, *Salmonidae*, particularly brown trout, *Salmo trutta*, in Europe, and brook trout, *Salvelinus fontinalis*, in North America. These fish require cool well-aerated water, typical of upland streams.

Heather Angel

Left: The freshwater shrimp, *Gammarus*. This animal prevents itself being swept downstream by a behavioural adaptation, called *positive rheotaxis*, which compels it to swim continuously upstream against the current. Its body is also flattened from side to side so that it presents less resistance to the water. Nevertheless, it cannot withstand a current greater than 45 cm per second (18 in/sec) and is found only where currents are slower among stones and weeds.

Right: Caddis fly larvae of the genus *Phryganea* protect themselves by building cylindrical cases from rectangular pieces of plant material arranged into a spiral.

Below: As a stream gradually widens out into a river there is a profound change in the nature of the ecosystem it provides. In streams less than 2 m (6 ft) wide, 99 per cent of primary food comes, not from plants within the stream, but from the surrounding banks. Leaves, in particular, are constantly being blown into the stream. As the stream widens, however, the influence of the banks slowly decreases and much of the food is produced by plants, particularly planktonic algae, within the river. The range of animals present also varies, determined by the type of food available in the stream or river.

Right: The still water of ponds and lakes allows a stable surface layer to develop on the water. This is the home of many animals. Insect pupae and snails live just below the surface while pond skaters, *Gerris*, (shown here) live on top of it.

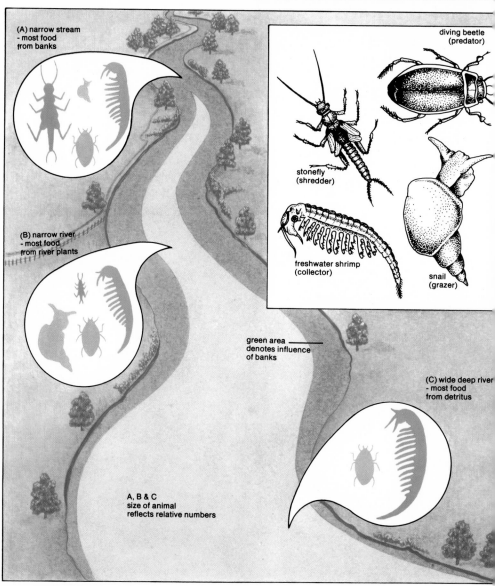

(A) narrow stream - most food from banks

(B) narrow river - most food from river plants

diving beetle (predator)

stonefly (shredder)

freshwater shrimp (collector)

snail (grazer)

green area denotes influence of banks

(C) wide deep river - most food from detritus

A, B & C size of animal reflects relative numbers

Heather Angel

Because plants are few, most stream animals feed on decaying organic debris (*detritus*) swept down in the current from vegetation overhanging the bank. Both caddis fly larvae and some mayfly nymphs are *filter feeders*, feeding on detritus. Many stonefly nymphs, however, are *shredders*, eating large bits of decaying organic matter—not for the plant material itself but for the bacteria and fungi growing on it. Shredders break down big pieces of organic matter into small pieces that can be ingested by filter feeders.

Less common are animals that rely on food produced by the stream community itself. Algae provide food for *grazers*, such as limpets and flatworms, while fish feed by maintaining station in the stream and catching drifting animals. Such drift is greatest at dawn and dusk.

Slow-flowing rivers

In wider, more sluggish rivers and streams, the deposit of silt and mud produces a different habitat from that of fast flowing streams so it is not surprising that different animals live there. Few animals, however, actually live in the mud. This is because the mud, particularly if rich in detritus, supports a large population of decomposers, especially bacteria, which use up the available oxygen making it uninhabitable for all but those animals, such as *Tubifex* worms and midge larvae, *Chironomidae*, which can survive where there is little oxygen.

Instead, most animals are found on the mud surface. These include grazers, like the snails *Valvata* and *Bithynia*, detritus feeders, like the water louse, *Asellus*, and predators such as alder fly larvae, *Sialis*.

Right: A trout leaping against the current. Most members of the trout and salmon family, *Salmonidae*, migrate away from their normal habitats to spawn. Some species, especially the Atlantic salmon, *Salmo salar*, migrate many hundreds of kilometres from the sea to spawning grounds in upland streams.

Below: A shoal of tadpoles, *Rana*. Many freshwater animals are the immature stages of land species.

Jeffrey Goodman

Dr G. F. Leedale/Biophoto Assoc.

Popperfoto

P. Morris

Above: The grayling, *Thymallus*, a trout-like fish of the family *Salmonidae*. It is found in cold, fast-flowing and well-aerated rivers in North America, Europe and Asia, but is greatly affected by pollution. In North America, in particular, pollution has reduced the numbers of this fine game fish.

Left: An illustration from *The Compleat Angler* by Isaak Walton and Charles Cotton entitled 'Landing the Grayling'. There is no doubt that primitive man obtained food by fishing but the development of the

long rod—allowing bait to be cast into deeper water away from the bank—is comparatively recent. Probably the earliest reference to the rod is in the work of the Roman writer Martial, who died in AD 104.

Below: Different species of fish occupy different parts of a large pond or lake depending on their feeding habits. This diagram shows the habitats of some characteristic species of temperate lakes in summer. Most fish, however, move out into deeper water to escape the cold of winter.

Where water weeds have managed to gain a footing an even richer fauna can develop. In such areas dragonfly and damsel fly nymphs, *Odonata*, aquatic spiders, and diving beetles, *Dytiscus*, are common. These are all relatively bulky animals which cannot survive fast water currents because of the resistance of their bodies to the water. They are also all predators, feeding on smaller animals, such as insect larvae and fish fry.

The commonest fish in slow-flowing streams are members of the carp family, *Cyprinidae*, such as roach, *Rutilus*, bream, *Abramis*, and carp, *Cyprinus*. These fish require shallow weeds on which to lay their adhesive eggs and they feed on insects living among the organic debris on the stream bottom and in the mud. Cyprinid's mouths have specialized (*prehensile*) lips which allow them to scoop up mud and silt and sift out the animals contained in it. They are themselves preyed on by large fish predators, such as pike, *Esox*, pike-perch, *Stizostedion*, and perch, *Perca*.

Ponds and lakes

Unlike rivers and streams, ponds and lakes provide most of their own food and are much less reliant on the bank vegetation. In a large lake, 90 per cent of the plant material which supports the community is produced by algae and pondweeds. Algae are fed on by filter feeders, such as the water flea, *Daphnia*, which are in turn eaten by insects or fish. Large pondweeds, however, are rarely eaten directly, and the food they contain usually becomes available only when they die. So the food chain here runs from dead plant to decomposer (bacteria), to insect, to

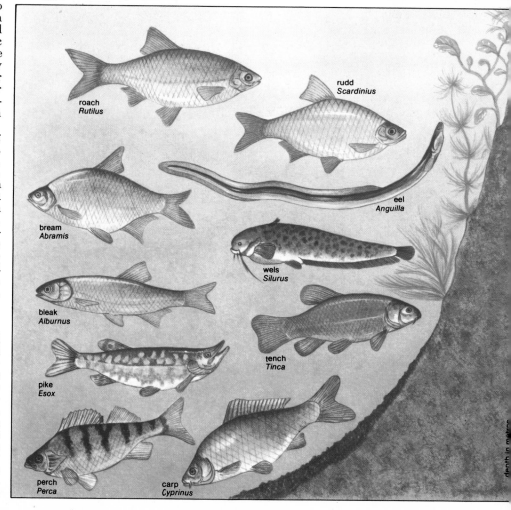

roach *Rutilus*

rudd *Scardinius*

eel *Anguilla*

bream *Abramis*

wels *Silurus*

bleak *Alburnus*

tench *Tinca*

pike *Esox*

perch *Perca*

carp *Cyprinus*

Brian Seed/John Hillelson Agency

Oxford Scientific Films

Above: The flamingo, *Phoenicopterus,* **is a filter feeder—it stirs up muddy water and then sieves out small animals, particularly crustaceans and molluscs, with its bill.**

Right: The great crested grebe, *Podiceps cristatus,* **on its nest. The feet of this bird are set well back on the body allowing it to obtain greater speeds when diving under water, a tactic it uses to escape from predators.**

Left: The rat-like water vole, *Arvicola amphibius,* **one of the few mammals in the freshwater habitat.**

Stephen Dalton/N.H.P.A.

snail, to worm and finally to fish.

Generally the main algal and water-weed production occurs in the upper layer of a lake where it is warm and light. This layer is called the *epilimnion* and is separated from a colder, heavy and deep layer, called the *hypolimnion*, by a boundary called the *thermocline*. Plants release oxygen as they photosynthesize so that the epilimnion always contains dissolved oxygen. This is not the case in the hypolimnion. Here sinking dead animals and plant remains collect and are fed upon by decomposers. These fungi and bacteria use up the oxygen resulting in low oxygen levels. This lack of oxygen restricts most other organisms to the epilimnion.

The amount of life in a lake is largely determined by the concentration of nutrients, particularly phosphates and nitrates. Lakes containing a low concentration of nutrients are called *oligotrophic* (little food) while those which are nutrient-rich are called *eutrophic* (good food). Oligotrophic lakes occur where the rocks of the surrounding area are hard and little weathering takes place to release the essential salts. Alpine lakes are a good example. Eutrophic lakes occur on soft rocks, such as limestone, which weather easily so releasing minerals into the water. Eutrophic lakes are also associated with a rich vegetation both in the water and on the surrounding banks. The decomposing vegetation releases nutrients into the water.

Algae (*phytoplankton*) and small animals (*zooplankton*) are the dominant groups in open water. The numbers of phytoplankton fluctuate during the year in a similar way to the plankton of the sea. During the winter, the water is thoroughly mixed by winds. Nutrients released by organic decay are brought up to the surface. Then, in the spring, algae rapidly consume this food supply and grow in numbers until an *algal bloom* occurs. This sometimes causes the water to turn green. Algal diatoms, such as *Asterionella*, are typical of these spring blooms.

The numbers of zooplankton are closely related to those of the algae on which they feed. As algae numbers increase in spring the numbers of zooplankton also increase but lag behind those of the algae. When most of the algae die the zooplankton switch to feeding on the bacteria which live on the dead algae. Common in the zooplankton are freshwater crustaceans, such as *Daphnia* and the pear-shaped *Cyclops*. Both of these animals feed on algal remains and on the bacteria associated with them.

Other animals live on the mud which collects at the bottom of lakes. These include midge larvae, water louse, and cased caddis larvae, *Trianodes* and *Phryganea*. But probably the commonest mud dwellers are mosquito larvae, such as *Culex* and *Anopheles*.

In temperate lakes and ponds the commonest fish species are carp, sticklebacks, *Gasterosteus* and *Pungitius*, and tench, *Tinca*. These fish breed and feed in the shallows but move out into the deeper water—over 2 m (6 ft)—in the winter to escape the cold. Ice forms on the surface of water, but because water is at its most dense at 4°C (39°F) the deepest water tends to be at this temperature during the winter. This unusual property of water—most other liquids are at their most dense immediately above their freezing point—is important in the survival of freshwater organisms. Without it lakes, and to a lesser extent rivers, would freeze solidly from the bottom upwards, killing all of the organisms in them except those that produce spores or other protective structures.

An interesting difference between lake and river fish is the size of the offspring (*fry*) they produce. Pond fish lay small eggs which hatch into small fry. In still lakes there is a plentiful supply of plankton for small fry to feed on. In rivers, where plankton is scarce, fish lay larger eggs hatching into larger fry which can cope both with the insect food available and with the water flow.

The number of fish species in a lake depends on the richness of the flora and on geography. Eutrophic lakes may contain from eight to ten fish species in temperate regions or many hundreds in Africa. Oligotrophic lakes, however, may contain only one species.

The number of fish species is also low in small lakes and ponds unable to support many breeding populations. Often the only species present is a large predator, like perch. Predators are able to survive in the absence of other fish to eat by eating their own young. The young perch feed on zooplankton, such as *Daphnia*, and in this way a food chain is formed in which algae are fed on by *Daphnia* which are fed on by young perch which are fed on by adult perch. Cannibalism can thus prevent the extinction of the species when food is short. The adult perch are too large to feed directly on zooplankton themselves and if they did not eat their young they would starve and the species would die out in that particular pond.

125

Grasslands

One plant family, the grass family, *Graminae*, has attained an economic and ecological importance unsurpassed by any other. Grasses are the dominant feature of a type of ecosystem which now extends over 45 million sq km (18 million square miles). Apart from the sea, only forest ecosystems exceed grasslands in extent; but grasslands far exceed forests in economic importance. The grasses owe their success to structural and physiological characteristics which allow them to withstand, better than other plants, semi-arid climates, poor soils, grazing by animals and burning.

The leaves of grasses are unique. They are produced from a growing point (*meristem*) located not along the stem of the plant, as in most other plants, but at the stem base. Few plants can survive the repeated destruction of their meristems and if they are grazed or cut they die. Because the meristem of a grass, however, is near its base it can be grazed close to the ground and yet grow back new leaves remarkably quickly.

Also important is the volume and aggressiveness of the root systems of grasses. They are large and extensive in proportion to the volume of the shoot—four fifths of living grass is root. Because they have no tap roots this large volume of root can be produced quickly from the base of the stems. They can rapidly absorb most of the available water when it rains in semi-arid areas.

Grasses are also herbaceous plants. With the exception of bamboos, they rarely exceed a metre (3 ft) in height and are often only a few centimetres tall. Because they do not produce permanent woody tissue they can grow up rapidly from seed. They can quickly recolonize land left bare after burning.

Natural grasslands

Grasslands occur wherever low rainfall, poor soil, grazing and burning have prevented the growth of other plant types—particularly trees. They are found in two areas of the world: in temperate regions, where they are called *prairie* or *steppe*, and in tropical regions, where they are called *savanna*. Grasslands reach their maximum extent in continental interiors between humid forests and arid deserts, and they tend to occur on rolling plains or plateaus.

The French gave the name 'prairie' (or meadow) to the North American grasslands while the name 'steppe' is derived from the name of the commonest genera of grass (*Stipa*) in the Eurasian grasslands extending from the Black Sea to eastern Mongolia. In both these temperate grasslands, however, and in contrast to savanna, trees or shrubs of any type are absent or so rare as to be negligible.

The development of the North American prairie is typical of the formation of temperate grasslands. After the last ice age, some 11,000 years ago, the grasses rapidly colonized ground left bare by the retreating glaciers. They have remained dominant ever since as a result of the combined effects of burning and grazing. On the flat plains high winds can develop, fanning and spreading fires which woody plants cannot survive. In addition grazing by

Giuseppe Mazza

Above: African savanna. Grasslands can be divided into two basic types—tropical *savanna* and temperate *prairie* or *steppe*. Unlike savanna, prairie and steppe are usually totally treeless.

Right: How grasses survive grazing. The meristem of a grass is at the base of the plant and is unharmed if the leaves are eaten. Nettles, on the other hand, have a meristem at every node. Repeated grazing kills them.

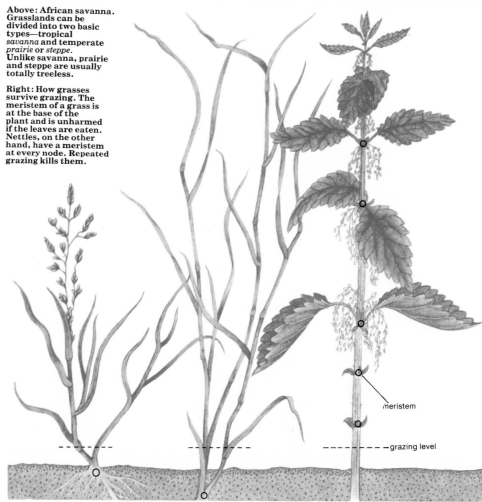

meristem

grazing level

Ann Ronan Picture Library

Left: An illustration dating from 1849 of a prairie fire. Without such fires there would be no prairie. Dry summers and flat open land, on which high winds can develop, are ideal conditions for extensive fires which destroy both woodland and grassland. Grass, however, can recolonize burnt areas far more easily than trees. Where settlers have prevented fires, woodland has gradually spread into the prairie.

Below left: The savanna dung beetle, *Scarabaeus*, collects dung into a ball on which it then lays its eggs.

Bottom left: The largest areas of savanna occur in Africa and South America but it also occurs in large areas of west and north Australia. The typical large herbivore of these grasslands is the kangaroo, *Macropus*. A large kangaroo can cover 9 m (30 ft) with a single leap and can travel at more than 60 kph (40 mph).

Below: Perhaps the most important family of grassland herbivores is the *Bovidae* which includes cattle, bison, buffaloes, giraffe, antelopes. sheep, goats, and the Mongolian yak, *Bos grunniens* (shown here). All of these animals are *ruminants*, containing a part of the stomach, called the *rumen*, in which the otherwise indigestible cellulose part of grass is broken down by bacteria. The food is then regurgitated and digested normally.

Frank Lane

bison, *Bison*, pronghorns, *Antilocapra*, and prairie dogs, *Cynomys*, have prevented the spread of woodland.

Tropical savanna is endowed with a greater variety of plants than temperate grasslands. It often includes drought-resistant woody plants, varying from low shrubs to tall trees. Nevertheless, savanna is always open and grass remains the dominant vegetation. It usually occurs where there is a marked seasonal drought but is occasionally found even where the humidity is high enough for forest growth, especially on plateaus.

Plateaus are usually formed when ground is geologically lifted, and the change in environment generally has an adverse effect on the soil. Iron-rich soils, in particular, are oxidized on exposure to the sun and acquire a hard crust, called *laterite*, often with an impervious layer, a *subsoil pan*, just below the surface. Rooting is restricted to the soil above this pan, so only shallow rooting plants, such as grasses, can grow. In addition the soil is usually water-logged in the wet season (water cannot percolate through the subsoil pan) and desiccated in the dry season. Few plants other than drought-resistant grasses and shrubs can survive in conditions like this.

Where deep soils do occur on plateaus, savanna may still be present because of nutrient deficiencies in the soil which prevent the development of woodland. Savannas formed because of soil defects (either nutrient deficiencies or the presence of laterite) are called *edaphic* savannas. Examples include the *cerrado* of South American plateaus, the mountain grasslands of West Africa, the *campo*

Frank Lane

John Massey Stewart/Bruce Coleman Ltd.

limpo of Brazil, and the *pampas* of the Argentine.

A second type of savanna owes its presence more to burning and the activity of man and other animals than to soil type. This is called *derived* or *secondary* savanna and has formed in a similar way to temperate grasslands. Land cleared by fire, caused either by man or by natural causes such as lightning, is rapidly colonized by savanna weeds, such as spear grass, *Imperia cylindrica*. These plants form a tough mat which prevents tree and shrub seedlings from germinating. Additionally, grazing by wild and domestic animals prevents the growth of herbaceous plants other than grasses.

Grassland animals

Open grassland can be a rich habitat but it is also a harsh one with wide fluctuations in temperature and humidity. The shortage of water, in particular, restricts the type of animals that can live there. All water loving animals, such as snails, wood lice and amphibians are rare. But animals which can exist with little water, especially reptiles and insects such as grasshoppers, *Acridiidae* and *Tettigoniidae*, and termites, *Isoptera*, thrive and can be very numerous. These animals obtain all the water they require from their food. Another problem of open grassland is the large difference between daytime and night time temperatures. In the Cameroon savanna, for example, a midday heat of 40°C (104°F) in the shade can be followed by a night temperature of 3°C (37°F).

Grasslands also lack shelter from winds and storms, and so grassland animals must provide their own shelter. To do this a great many burrow into the soil. Burrowing is more common among grassland animals than any others. Below a depth of half a metre (20 in), soil temperatures are remarkably static—close to the average annual air temperature for the region. The soil is cooler in summer and warmer in winter than the surface. Burrowing animals are thus able to obtain protection from large daily and annual temperature fluctuations. Furthermore, burrowing also gives a measure of protection from predators. There is little other cover where animals can hide.

Among invertebrate burrowers, ants, termites and earthworms are particularly important. In wetter grasslands earthworms, perhaps more than any other animals, are essential to the health of the grass sward. They help in the circulation of nutrients and decaying organic material, and their tunnels improve the drainage and aeration of the soil.

Larger vertebrate animals, too, burrow for protection. These include reptiles such as tortoises, *Testudo*, and skinks, *Scincidae*. But rodents are the most prolific vertebrate underground dwellers. A good example is the North American prairie dog, *Cynomys*, which forms large colonies, called 'towns', with intricate connecting tunnels.

Insects, such as grasshoppers, are important grassland consumers and can play a crucial role in affecting the quality of grassland vegetation. In areas of New York State, for example, insects were found to consume 94 kg of grass per square metre (19 lb per sq ft) during one summer season. These insects consumed roughly twice as much as cows on the same pasture. Nevertheless the main consumers of

Jacana

Zefa

Above: The largest land animal, the African elephant, *Loxodonta africana*, **is a grassland animal. It is one of the few large wild animals whose numbers are increasing in game reserves—it is often purposely culled.**

Right: Grasslands are rarely entirely natural and the most important grazing animals are normally domestic. These are some of the 50 million cattle in the Argentine.

Below: Birds need less water than other animals because they excrete solid *uric acid* rather than urine. They are also able to fly to water. These are red-billed weaver birds, *Quelea*, at a savanna waterhole in Kenya.

R.I.M. Campbell/Bruce Coleman Ltd.

Norman Myers/Bruce Coleman Ltd.

Above: Part of the cycle of life and death—vultures feeding on a corpse. Both American vultures, *Cathartidae*, and old world vultures, *Accipitridae*, have few or no feathers on their heads and necks. This allows them to feed on carrion without getting their feathers matted with blood.

Right: A cheetah, *Acinonyx*, surveying the world from a termite hill. Termite hills are very resistant to wind and rain because of secretions produced by the termites which bind the soil together.

Below: A typical savanna food cycle. Plant food eventually passes through the whole community.

Sassoon/Robert Harding Assoc.

SAVANNA FOOD CYCLE

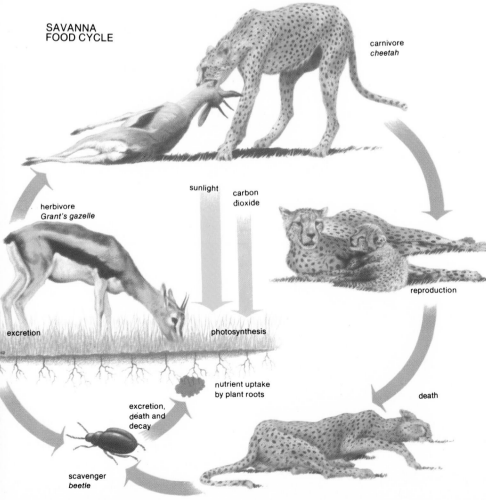

carnivore
cheetah

herbivore
Grant's gazelle

sunlight

carbon dioxide

excretion

photosynthesis

reproduction

nutrient uptake by plant roots

death

excretion, death and decay

scavenger
beetle

grassland (in the absence of interference by man) are normally large mammalian herbivores such as antelopes in Africa and the bison and pronghorn in North America. These herbivores have one noticeable adaptation to grassland life called the *cursorial habit*. Simply, they are adapted for speed of running. In grassland there is no danger of bumping into objects as would occur in forests. Moreover, there is no tall vegetation in which to hide from predators; hence good eyesight, keen sense of smell and, most important of all, speed are required to survive.

Many birds of open country are also adapted for speed of running. The ostrich, *Struthio camelus*, in Africa, the emu, *Dromaius novaehollandiae*, in Australia, and the rhea, *Rhea*, in the pampas of South America have all abandoned flight in favour of running. They have poorly developed wings, long powerful hind legs and feathers which do not lock together as they do in flying birds. They are among the fastest of land animals.

Another interesting protective adaptation is *herding*, exhibited by many grassland animals such as zebra, *Equus*, and gnu, *Connochaetes*. Being in a herd reduces the likelihood of any particular individual being taken by a predator. Additionally, a large group will be able to detect danger and warn each other more easily than individual animals which are widely dispersed. Herding also enables grazing animals to more efficiently exploit the grassland. A large herd covering a large area is able to detect useful food sites that an individual would miss. Once a good grazing area has been found all the attention of the herd can be concentrated on it.

Because large herbivores are so well adapted to protect themselves their predators must be equally well adapted to be able to catch them. In particular, they must be able to run as fast or faster than their prey. Animals which hunt alone, such as the cheetah, *Acinonyx*, can often reach very fast speeds—up to 110 kph (70 mph), though often only for short periods. Other, slower running carnivores, such as the cape hunting dog, *Lycaon*, increase the efficiency of their hunting by attacking in packs which can single out and trap prey from a large herd.

Cultivated grasslands

The biblical statement that 'all flesh is grass' is little short of the truth. The most important of all food plants, the cereals (including wheat, barley and rice), are grasses; and cereal fields therefore technically grasslands. The most productive agricultural areas of the world are often ploughed-up grasslands for this very reason. Those factors which benefit the growth of wild grasses also favour the closely related cereals.

Furthermore, many grasslands which are being used in a more 'natural' way—that is to support grazing animals such as cattle, *Bos*—are also entirely artificial. Without continuous attention from the farmer many of these fields would quickly revert to forest. The distinction between cultivated and natural grassland is certainly not well defined. Very few grasslands exist without some interference from man, even if this only takes the form of occasional burning. Most owe their continued existence, if not their origin, to man and to the domestic grazing animals that he keeps on them.

Coniferous Forests

The largest area of forest in the world grows in the cold temperate regions of the Northern Hemisphere. It extends in a band roughly 5,800 km (3,600 miles) long and 1,300 km (800 miles) wide across Europe and Asia to the Far East, between latitudes 55 and 70 degrees north. A smaller, but still considerable, area occurs in North America. Cold coniferous forest merges into treeless tundra to the north and into mixed deciduous woodland and meadowlands to the south. Because none of the southern continents extends sufficiently far south there is no comparable zone in the Southern Hemisphere.

Coniferous forests occur in areas where climatic conditions are too severe for deciduous woodland. Particularly important is the length of the growing season. Unlike most flowering trees, conifers can survive in areas where there are relatively few days in the year when temperatures are high enough for photosynthesis and plant growth.

The largest area of northern temperate or *boreal* forest occurs in central Asia, where it is known as *taiga*. In this region the winter is prolonged, with only three or four months of the year free of frost and January temperatures as low as —30°C (—22°F). Consequently the ground is permanently frozen below a depth of about 30 cm (1 ft) and only the surface thaws in the short summer, when the temperatures may average 10°C (50°F). The permanently frozen ground is called *permafrost*.

Surprisingly, as well as being cold, the taiga is also dry. Winds are dry and, although there is considerable precipitation (usually between 25 and 100 cm (10-40 in) per year), a great deal falls as snow. Especially during the winter months the frozen ground-water is unavailable to plant roots. The environment is said to be *physiologically dry*.

Conifers are well adapted to these adverse conditions. They have tough leathery evergreen needles ready to photosynthesize whenever conditions allow it, and the leaf surfaces are coated with a thick waxy cuticle which reduces water loss by evaporation. The leaves are highly resistant to freezing—even at temperatures well below the freezing point of water—and the narrow leaf shape may help by reducing the rate at which heat is lost by radiation at night. Conifers also have shallow root systems which take water from the thin layer of unfrozen soil. Furthermore, their narrow conical shape not only supports snow but also sheds it quickly when it starts to thaw.

Nevertheless, not all trees in the boreal forest are evergreen or even conifers. In the extreme north two deciduous trees are also common: the coniferous larch, *Larix*, and the most hardy of all flowering trees, the birch, *Betula*. Typically, however, the forest is dominated by evergreen conifers particularly the spruces, *Picea*, with the addition of firs, *Abies*, pines, *Pinus*, and cedars, *Cedrus*, in the southernmost areas

All of these trees form a dense canopy which, because there is no autumn leaf fall, produces deep shade throughout the year. For this reason there is no flush of

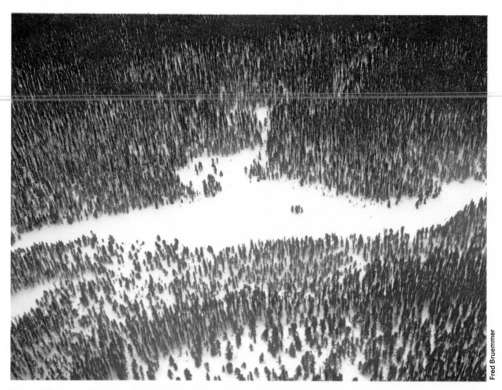

Above: The largest land habitat in the world is coniferous forest—it stretches in a band roughly 1,300 km (800 miles) wide around the north of the globe. It exists in areas that are too cold for deciduous woodland yet too warm for tundra, where cold-tolerant evergreen conifers can exploit weak sunlight throughout the year.

Right: The cold, waterlogged soils of the boreal forest are strongly acidic and because bacteria dislike acid conditions bacterial decay is negligible. Fungi are the most active decomposers together with small invertebrates likes mites, *Acarina*, and springtails, *Collembola*. This fungus is *Stropharia hornemannii*.

Below: Damp and cold also protect coniferous forests from fire. They are not invulnerable, however, as this photo of burned forest shows.

early spring flowers as there is in deciduous woodland. Few plants, in fact, grow on the coniferous forest floor which instead is often thickly carpeted with fallen needles.

Where there are gaps in the canopy, however, some shrubby plants such as juniper, *Juniperus communis*, and bilberry, *Vaccinium myrtilus*, flourish, along with occasional grasses and herbaceous plants such as the wintergreens, *Pyrola*, wild strawberry, *Fragaria vesca* and cloudberry, *Rubus chamaemorus*. In addition mosses are common on the ground and on the trunks of fallen trees; and vast areas of boggy forest, known as the *muskegs* in Canada and produced because the permafrost prevents drainage of the soil, are covered with carpets of sphagnum moss, *Sphagnum*. Other plants are epiphytes, living on the trees. These are almost entirely lichens, mainly *Usnea*, although some older conifer needles become covered with unicellular algae, *Pleurococcus*, and fungi.

130

Fred Bruemmer

Heather Angel

Bruce Coleman

The giant sequoia (*sequoia giganteum*), also called the Wellingtonia, is a species of evergreen found mainly in California and southern Oregon. Specimens have reached 267 feet (91.5m) in height, and 79 feet (24.3m) in girth.

Animals

Animal life in the taiga is greatly influenced by the short summer and severe winter. In the summer months insects are plentiful and mosquitoes and other flies, *Diptera*, briefly achieve very high populations. The conifers also provide habitats for bark boring beetles, *Scolytidae*, sawflies, *Symphyta*, and wood wasps, *Siricidae*, which all have wood-boring larvae which do a great deal of damage to trees in commercial forests.

These and other insects provide food for insectivorous birds, such as flycatchers, *Musicapa*, swallows, *Hirundo rustica*, warblers, *Sylviidae*, and wagtails, *Motacilla*; but since insects are only briefly plentiful, most taiga birds are not insectivorous. Instead most, such as the buntings, *Emberizidae*, finches, *Fringillidae*, and thrushes, *Turdus*, are seed-eaters. Apart from the conifers, taiga plants are commonly fleshy-fruited, probably because wind dispersal of seeds is impossible in the shelter of the forest. Seed and fruit are therefore available for much of the year. Birds are the main agents of seed dispersal.

The crossbills, *Loxia*, are a particularly interesting group of taiga finches. Their beaks have crossed tips and are specially adapted for removing the seeds from conifer cones, their sole source of food. Most taiga birds migrate to more favourable climates in winter. Exceptions are the insectivorous white-throated swift, *Aeronautes sexatilis*, and the poor-will, *Phalaenoptilus nuttallii*, which are among the few bird species known to hibernate.

Many smaller mammals also hibernate in order to survive the winter. During

Fabius Henrion/Jacana

Claude Pissavini/Jacana

hibernation complex physiological changes take place in which the animal becomes temporarily coldblooded. Respiration rates and the requirement for oxygen are reduced to a fraction of their normal level and the carbon dioxide content of the venous blood increases. Hibernation may be *complete*, as in the hedgehog, *Erinaceus europaeus*, and smaller rodents such as voles, *Microtus*, or *partial* as in the brown bear, *Ursus arctos*, and squirrels, *Sciurus*. Partial hibernators wake at intervals during the winter to feed; complete hibernators stay 'asleep'.

Many of the carnivores of coniferous forests are prized as game or hunted for their fur. In the past fur trading often provided the sole means of support for the inhabitants of the taiga who traded the skins for food and other supplies. Valu-

Above: Most coniferous forest birds feed on seeds as little other food, such as insects, is available. This is a male crossbill, *Loxia curvirostra*.

Right: The boreal forest contains the largest of all deer species, the elk or moose, *Alces alces*. The Alaskan moose (shown here) narrowly escaped extinction in the nineteenth century but has since recovered under protection. The European elk is also rare. It was once widespread throughout Europe—an exceptionally large form occured in Ireland—but has now disappeared from all but the northernmost part of its former range.

P. Morris

Stephen Dalton/NHPA

Bruce Coleman

Left: Many forest animals live in the trees. Well known are the squirrels, *Sciurus*.

Above: Monkey-puzzles, *Araucaria*, are conifers native to the Southern Hemisphere. Some grow in the tropical rain forest, but the most heavily exploited *Araucaria* forests are in Brazil and Paraguay.

There, stands of *Araucaria angustifolia* grow within the sub-tropical deciduous forest. This tree, however, is the Chile pine, *Araucaria araucana*, native to Chile and Argentina.

Below: A forest carnivore, the lynx, *Lynx lynx*, washing itself.

Above: The giant parasitic wood wasp, *Urocerus gigas*, boring through tree bark with its ovipositor in order to lay its eggs beneath the bark. The larvae which hatch from the eggs are not themselves immune from parasites however. Another wasp, the ichneumon *Rhyssa*, is able to locate the *Urocerus* larvae beneath the bark. It then lays its eggs on them. When the eggs hatch the developing *Rhyssa* larvae then feed upon the *Urocerus* larvae.

Left: A fox, *Vulpes*, caught in a steel trap set by Eskimo fur trappers in the boreal forest of northwest Canada. Many of the carnivores of the forest are hunted for their fur.

Frank Lane

able fur species include the sables, *Martes zibbelina* of northern Asia and *Martes americana* of North America, otters, *Lutra*, and the white winter form of the stoat, *Mustela erminea*, from which ermine is obtained. These animals all belong to the family *Mustelidae* which also includes polecats, *Mustela putorius* and skunks, *Mephitis* and *Spilogale*.

The mustelids are the most important coniferous forest carnivores but the large cats, *Felidae*, are certainly the most spectacular. They include the lynx, *Lynx lynx*, and the fierce European wildcat, *Felis silvestris*, of which there is a subspecies *Felis silvestris grampia* in the conifer forests of Scotland. Finally and surprisingly, because they are now thought of as animals of warmer climates, tigers probably evolved in the coniferous forest of central Asia. The Siberian tiger, *Panthera tigris*, is usually larger in size than the Indian and South-East Asian varieties, and is also paler in colour with less conspicuous stripes and longer hair.

Other coniferous forests

Although the taiga forms the largest area of coniferous forest in the world, conifers are by no means confined to cold temperate climates. They form smaller communities in the entire range of temperate, subtropical and tropical climates both in the northern and southern hemispheres. Indeed some single species grow throughout this range. The white pine, *Pinus strobus*, for example, is found from eastern Canada to the mountains of southern Mexico, although transplanted Mexican plants cannot survive frosts if they are replanted in Canada.

Perhaps the most famous area of tem-

perate coniferous forest, because of its enormous output of timber, is found along the west coast of North America in Washington, Oregon and British Columbia. Here long growing seasons, heavy rainfall and good soils encourage the development of dense stands of fast-growing trees. The most important species are Douglas fir, *Pseudotsuga menziesii*, which grows in pure stands or in mixtures with redwood, *Sequoia sempervirens*, pines, western hemlock, *Tsuga heterophylla*, and Sitka spruce, *Picea sitchensis*.

Further south in the coastal regions of northwest California and Oregon, where the climate is warm temperate, there are extensive forests of redwood. Redwoods require a moist environment, and although there is little summer rain in the region there are frequent sea fogs. Moisture from the fog is intercepted by the foliage and provides sufficient water, not only for the trees, but also for communities of the swordfern, *Polystichum munitum*, and redwood sorrel, *Oxalis oregana*, which grow at the base of the trees. When conditions are ideal redwood forests form the heaviest stands of timber in the world and an important timber industry is based on them.

Nevertheless, areas of temperate coniferous forest are greatly outweighed by the mass of deciduous woodland which is the dominant vegetation in most warm and wet areas. The reason there are relatively few conifers in temperate and tropical regions is not that they are unable to survive in hot and wet climates, but that they are unable to survive competition from the more highly evolved flowering trees.

Rainforest

The richest and most spectacular vegetation on earth is to be found in the rainforests. Broadleaved yet evergreen trees grow to at least 30 m (100 ft) and an extremely diverse collection of lianas, shrubs, epiphytes and ground flora produce a continuous, many-layered mass of vegetation from the ground to the top of the tree canopy. In it, too, a vast number of animal species have evolved, each filling a particular ecological niche. There are so many rainforest species that they have not all been found and collected, let alone identified and classified.

The climatic conditions which favour the development of rainforest are heavy rainfall—200 to 300 cm (80 to 120 in)—spread evenly throughout the year, and continuous warmth with little seasonal variation in either temperature or day length. Rainforests are therefore almost exclusively tropical, occurring in the Amazon basin of South America, coastal Central America, equatorial West Africa and the Congo basin, and much of tropical South-East Asia including Malaysia, Java, Sumatra, Borneo, New Guinea and the Philippines. Smaller areas occur in Madagascar, Queensland in Australia and the Pacific Islands.

Vegetation layers

Contrary to the popular image of tropical rainforest as a dense, impenetrable jungle, mature rainforest is fairly easy to walk through without resorting to machetes, since vegetation on the forest floor is relatively sparse. It is overhead that rainforest reaches its thickest development. The densest part of all is the *C layer* consisting of trees of heights from 5 to 20 m (16 to 66 ft). Because they are so close together these trees have tapering conical crowns much deeper than they are wide.

C-layer trees are not the dominant trees of the forest, however. Almost half

Heather Angel

Frith/Bruce Coleman Ltd

Left: This picture shows one of the fiercest forest predators, the mantis, *Tenodera*, with its catch, a gecko lizard, *Gekkonidae*.

Below: Epiphytic bromeliads, *Bromeliaceae*, form rosettes in which water collects—so much in some cases that they have been described as 'aerial marshes'. They provide ideal breeding places for tree frogs, *Amphodus* (shown here). Other animals, such as aquatic insects, leeches, *Hirudinea*, spiders, *Arachnida*, centipedes, *Myriapoda*, snails, *Gasteropoda*, and protozoa have also been found in them.

Oxford Scientific Films

Left: Luxuriant growth of palms, *Palmae*, screwpines, *Pandanaceae*, and ferns, *Filicinae*, in the bottom layers of sub-tropical rainforest in New Zealand. Rainforest only grows in warm wet climates, and mainly in the tropics, but small areas occur in sub-tropical areas like New Zealand.

Below: Unlike temperate forest, rainforests are many-layered with vegetation from the ground to the tree tops some 40 m (130 ft) or more high. Also unlike temperate forest, the densest growth is not the upper tree canopy, but the C layer of small and young trees between 5 and 20 m (16-66 ft) high.

Above: The iguana, *Iguana iguana*, is a common large lizard of the rainforests of Central and South America. It is a tree-dweller, eating leaves and fruit (though occasionally it will attack small birds and mammals) and has a camouflaged green skin broken by brown bands. The animal can grow up to 2 m (6 ft) long, including the tail, and its white meat is a delicacy enjoyed by South American Indians.

Left: Ants are probably the most numerous of all rainforest insects. There may be one and a half million in a single column of driver ants, *Eciton*—shown here crossing a living bridge between two tree trunks.

of them are young trees which eventually grow up to form an upper canopy of trees called the *A* and *B layers*. Apart from a few exceptionally tall trees which may grow up to 100 m (330 ft) high, and which are known as *emergents*, the tallest trees in the forest are the A-layer trees. They average about 40 m (130 ft) tall, are widely spaced, and have wide and shallow umbrella-shaped crowns. Beneath them the B-layer trees, reaching heights of 15 to 30 m (50 to 100 ft), form a more continuous canopy—although there are still some gaps—and their crowns are deeper than they are wide. Below these the C-layer trees form an almost continuous canopy.

Lower still the *D layer*, also known as the *shrub layer*, contains saplings, palms, tall herbs such as *Marantaceae*, woody shrubs and bamboos ranging from 2 to about 5 m (6 to 16 ft) in height. Finally, on the forest floor, the *E layer* contains tree seedlings and a few herbaceous flowering plants and clubmosses, *Selaginella*.

Forest plants
As well as containing more layers than temperate deciduous or coniferous woodland, rainforest also contains far more tree species. Temperate woods with more than 20 species per hectare are considered exceptionally rich but in the rainforest there are very often more than 100 species of tree per hectare, not counting many species of shrubs and woody creeper. Nevertheless, vigorous species can become dominant. For example, in Guyana and other areas of the Amazon basin, more than 50 per cent of all trunks more than 5 cm (2 in) in diameter, are wallaba trees, *Dicymbe*.

Despite its great diversity, to the casual observer the first impression of rainforest is often one of monotony. Because there is strong competition for light, trees grow as rapidly as possible to their full height and because of this their trunks are almost always straight, branching only near the top. Although there are many species they all look very much alike. The slender trunks are covered with a thin, smooth bark and even the leaves are surprisingly unvaried, almost all being a glossy dark green and lanceolate (long and narrow) with an undivided margin.

Rainforest trees are often buttressed with triangular sheets of wood, the edges of which may sometimes be as much as 6 m (20 ft) from the trunk, radiating from

135

Bruce Coleman Ltd

Explorer

Left: A South American tree boa, *Corallus caninus*, catching a parakeet. All boas kill their prey by crushing —the snake is sensitive to the minor vibrations produced by the beating heart of its prey and applies just enough pressure to stop the heart beating. *Corallus* can grow to about 1.3 m (4 ft) but

the larger *Boa constrictor* may reach lengths of 5.5 m (19 ft).

Above: The Amazon rainforest is the largest natural land habitat which has remained largely untouched by man. Nevertheless, it is steadily being reduced as forest is chopped down and burnt to clear

land for crops. It is to be hoped that the construction of the Trans Amazonian Highway (shown here) does not accelerate this process.

Below: African epauletted fruit bats live at the edges of the forest where they hang upside-down in trees during the day. This is *Epomorphorus gambiensis*.

J-P Hervy/Jacana

the trunk base. These buttresses can be thin enough to be used as boards and they ring when struck with a stick. Their function is not understood. They may give the trees support, and buttressed trees have been shown to have shallow root systems, but buttressed trees blow down just as often as those without buttresses. Also, if they are for support, it is surprising that they have developed in the rainforest, where strong winds are rare, while they are virtually unknown in temperate forests exposed to severe winds.

The flowers of rainforest trees, like those of most temperate tree species, are usually inconspicuous and greenish or whitish in colour. Unlike temperate trees, however, which always produce flowers on young shoots or on one-year-old growth, the flowers of rainforest trees often grow directly from the trunk or main branches, a phenomenon known as *cauliflory*. Two well-known examples are the cacao, *Theobroma cacao*, a C-layer tree of American origin from which cocoa is obtained, and *Diospyros* (family *Ebenaceae*) from which the hard black wood *ebony* is obtained.

Apart from trees, two other plant groups are particularly characteristic of rainforests. These are the epiphytes and the lianas. Epiphytes, plants which grow attached to, and entirely supported by other plants, occur in all wet forests from the tropics to the tundra, but achieve their greatest diversity in rainforest where they grow on almost every available plant stem, trunk, leaf surface, and even on telegraph lines, if any are present. Rainforest epiphytes include algae, lichens, mosses and liverworts, ferns and flowering herbaceous plants, particularly

bromeliads and orchids. All of these are small plants which have adopted the epiphytic habit to enable them to compete with trees for light.

Some specialized epiphytes send roots down to the ground, become self-supporting, and eventually kill the trees which originally supported them. These are known as *stranglers*, and the best-known are the strangling figs of the genus *Ficus* from Africa, Malaysia and Australia. Some of these become very large trees of the A and B layers.

The most important climbing plants of the rainforest are the lianas, which are woody plants rooted in the forest floor but which use trees for support while they climb to the upper layers of the canopy. Some are of great size, producing crowns comparable with those of the trees they use for support, and compete strongly with trees for space and light.

Rainforest animals

The habitat occupied and part played by any species in a living community is called its *ecological niche*. The difference between two niches may be extremely small, for instance how high up in the air, or at what time of day, two species of bird catch the same insect food; but provided there is some difference there is no direct competition between different species occupying different niches. In a stable community each niche is filled by just one species—the number of species depends on the number of niches.

In a rainforest the diversity of plant species and types produces a bewildering array of habitats and microhabitats each of which provides a niche for an animal species. The result is a vast number of

Left: An Amazonian heron (family *Ardeidae*), *Trigosoma lineatum*.

Above: Most rainforest mammals live in trees and have anatomical adaptations, like well developed hands and feet or a grasping (*prehensile*) tail, for climbing. In the primates these adaptations have taken different forms on different continents. New World monkeys, *Cebidae*, generally have prehensile tails while their counterparts in the Old World, *Cercopithecidae*, have long arms and grasping hands instead. The hands of monkeys also vary. The leaf eating langurs, *Presbytis*, of India and Malaysia have a functional thumb while the leaf-eating *Colobus* monkeys of Africa have a greatly reduced thumb. The monkeys shown here are squirrel monkeys, *Saimiri*, from the rainforests of Central and South America. Easily recognizable by their white faces, they feed on insects and fruit.

species, particularly invertebrates, of which a great many are still unnamed. Despite its high population, the rainforest fauna often appears sparse. There are several reasons for this. First, most of the vertebrates are nocturnal, spending the day in burrows or hidden among vegetation. Second, the main focus of animal activity is not at ground level but in the canopy where there is the greatest abundance of staple foods—leaves, fruits and insects (especially ants and termites). A third reason is that the butterflies and birds of the shaded lower reaches of the forest have dull colours while only those which live higher, like the parrots, *Psittacidae*, toucans, *Ramphastidae*, and the brilliant blue *Morpho* butterflies of South America, have dazzling colours in bold patterns.

The amount of dead organic material in the soil and litter layers is less in the tropical rainforest than in any other land ecosystem. Fallen leaves, trees, fruits and dead animals are rapidly consumed and returned to the nutrient cycle by decomposer organisms. Of these ants and termites are tremendously active and in terms of numbers are probably the most important animal group. Leaf cutting ants, particularly of the genus *Atta*, cut pieces from living and dead leaves and carry them back to the nest where they are processed in fungal gardens to provide a food source for the larvae. Termites are mainly tree-dwelling, although specialist species inhabit dead wood and are the main agents of its decomposition.

Rainforest mammals are mainly arboreal and have anatomical adaptations for climbing, such as well developed hands and feet, and prehensile tails. Probably the most uncompromisingly adapted group are the sloths, *Bradypodidae*, of Brazil. Sloths hang from branches, and have almost lost the capacity to walk on land. They spend most of their lives in sluggish movement or inactivity. Their hair is grooved or scaly and is colonized by algae which gives them a greenish colour of great value as camouflage.

Another characteristic family are the rainforest anteaters, *Myrmecophagidae*. These animals have a specialist diet of ants and termites. Anteaters are confined to the New World but in Africa their niche is occupied by the pangolins or scaly anteaters, *Pholidota*. Like myrmecophagids, pangolins have a prehensile tail and a long, sticky tongue adapted for catching insects.

Man and the forest

Man is by no means a newcomer to the forests. Native peoples have lived in rainforest regions for thousands of years. But modern agricultural man is greatly tempted to replace the forests' immense richness with equally rich crops, and great tracts of forest are felled and burned each year. Although the wood ash acts as a fertilizer, and supports vigorous crops in the first few years, the nutrients are rapidly leached from the soil which is left sterile. Since rainforests are exceedingly complex ecosystems they may take many decades to regenerate, so the current rate of clearance, of the Amazon forest in particular, is of great concern to biologists. Despite its immense size, if future exploitation is not more cautious and better planned its total destruction may become unavoidable.

137

Hedges, Pasture and Woodland

The dominant vegetation of temperate regions is deciduous woodland. It occurs wherever winters are relatively mild (although frosts may still occur), summers are warm, and rainfall is moderately heavy—75 to 150 cm (30 to 60 in) per year —without a pronounced wet or dry season. Such climates occur between latitudes 30 and 60 degrees north and extend across thousands of square kilometres of North America, Europe and Asia. Not all this area is deciduous forest. It is interrupted by the Rocky Mountains in the US—which restrict it to the Eastern states, by a large area of low rainfall and semi-desert in central Asia— which restricts it to the Far East and to Europe, and everywhere by the activity of man, who has continuously cleared woodland for towns and agriculture. In the Southern Hemisphere the continents only just extend far enough south to reach the temperate zone, and deciduous

Above right: Snowdrops, *Galanthus nivalis*, taking advantage of spring sunlight in a deciduous wood. Spring flowers are a feature of deciduous woodland because it is only during the winter and early spring that enough light reaches the forest floor for them to grow. For the rest of the year the floor is shaded by the dense canopy of tree leaves.

Right: Every autumn the forest floor becomes carpeted with fallen leaves. In this way many of the nutrients taken up by the trees during the year are returned to the ecosystem. Invertebrates, fungi and bacteria break down the leaves so returning the nutrients to the soil.

Far right: Just two layers are normally recognized in deciduous woodland—the tree canopy, and the forest floor and leaf litter. The soil can be considered as a third layer, however. Here one underground dweller, a mole, *Talpa*, feasts upon another, an earthworm.

woodland only occurs in New Zealand, Tasmania and the southern tips of Africa and South America.

Plants of deciduous woodland

In its best development, temperate deciduous woodland rivals tropical rainforest in height, with trees growing up to 30 or 40 m (100 to 130 ft) tall. But deciduous woodland has quite a different look to it. The trees typically produce a dense, closed canopy of leaves beneath which there is deep shade which inhibits the growth of smaller plants. Life is concentrated in only two layers: the tree crowns, and the soil surface and leaf litter. Only where the canopy is more open is there a ground layer of herbaceous plants.

The dominant trees are the oak, *Quercus*, beech, *Fagus*, maple, *Acer*, ash,

Fraxinus, and birch, *Betula*. All of these trees produce extensive forests, but only rarely are they found in mixed woodland, growing together. Normally only one or two species grow in any particular area. Which species is dominant, and hence the structure of the forest which develops, depends on a wide range of environmental factors. In particular the type of soil is important: acid clay soils, for example, favour oak woodland with few other tree species, while more alkaline clays support a more mixed woodland, richer in tree species and containing shrubs such as privet, *Ligustrum*, spindle, *Euonymus*, and buckthorn, *Prunus*.

Winter temperatures and levels of sunshine in temperate regions are sufficiently low that the amount of energy a broad-

leaved tree would consume in winter, if it kept its leaves, is greater than the amount of energy it could obtain by photosynthesis. Temperate broadleaved trees, therefore, save energy by losing their leaves in winter and becoming dormant. (That is, they are *deciduous*.) As a result, the environment of deciduous woodland changes dramatically with the seasons: only in winter and spring can light reach the ground. Herbaceous plants are greatly affected by this seasonal change and many species, such as the wood anemone, *Anemone nemorosa*, bluebell, *Endymion non-scriptus*, and wild strawberry, *Fragaria vesca*, synchronize their leaf production and flowering to take advantage of the light of early spring, before the tree buds burst and their leaves shade the ground.

The red deer, *cervus elaphus*, is found in deciduous forests all over Europe. It also has close relatives in Asia, North America and North Africa. In Britain, as forests disappear, it is becoming a moorland species, smaller and lighter than the forest deer.

Hans Reinhard/Bruce Coleman Ltd.

Other woodland plants have adapted to the deep shade by adopting a *saprophytic* way of life—deriving their nourishment from organic material in the soil, and thereby dispensing with the need for light. The most important saprophytes are the fungi. They are particularly important in the decomposition of leaf litter to release nutrients into the soil.

Woodland animals

Insects and other arthropods, especially mites, *Acarina*, and woodlice, *Isopoda* are also important in the decomposition of forest litter, breaking it down for fungi and bacteria. In turn they are an important food source for birds. A small insectivorous bird may eat up to 20 insects per minute during feeding periods. Insects also disperse fungal spores and pollinate trees. The most important pollinators are honeybees, *Apis*.

Most larger woodland animals are shy species, which live in the woodland for protection. However, the forest habitat has been altered to such an extent by man that many once-common animal species are now absent or rare in areas where man has lived for any length of time. This is particularly true of the larger mammals. For example the wild boar, *Sus scrofa*, and the grey timber wolf, *Canis lupus*, were once widespread throughout Europe but have been extinct in Britain since the 17th century and are uncommon elsewhere.

The disappearance of animals such as these can have far-reaching effects besides the loss of zoologically interesting species. In extreme cases it can lead to the long-term destruction of the forest itself. Smaller mammals, especially rodents such as mice, *Apodemus*, voles, *Microtus*, squirrels, *Sciurus*, and rabbits, *Oryctolagus*, eat the shoots, buds and roots of trees, often killing them. Deer also damage trees by browsing lower branches and by debarking them with their antlers. In an undisturbed forest such damage would be kept in check by predation by carnivores, but where the carnivores have been hunted to extinction the numbers of rodents and other browsing animals may become so large that the forest is prevented from regenerating after it has been damaged.

Cultivated grassland

Where deciduous woodland has been cleared for agriculture, the moist temperate climate favours the growth of grassland. In most countries of the world livestock is grazed on semi-natural unmanaged grassland known as *rough pasture*, but in Britain and Europe the most productive grasslands are cultivated. They are of two types: *temporary grassland* which is planted, grazed and ploughed all in a few years, and *permanent grassland* in which the turf is left undisturbed for much longer periods. Permanent grassland is also of two types: *pasture*, used for grazing animals, and *meadow*, grown for hay. Grazed pasture generally contains shorter and more palatable grasses, encouraged by the maintenance of a short sward, while hay meadows develop coarser, taller grasses which shade out the smaller plants.

The best pastures are mostly of perennial ryegrass, *Lolium perenne*, but leguminous plants, especially white clover, *Trifolium repens*, and lucerne, *Medicago sativa*, are also widely grown because

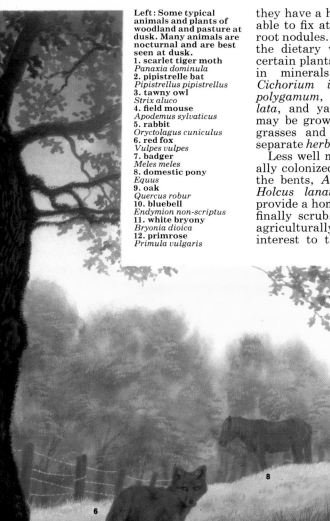

they have a high protein content and are able to fix atmospheric nitrogen in their root nodules. Good farmers also recognize the dietary value to their livestock of certain plants which are tasty or are rich in minerals. Among these chicory, *Cichorium intypus*, burnet, *Poterium polygamum*, plantain, *Plantago lanceolata*, and yarrow, *Achillea millefolium*, may be grown, either together with the grasses and legumes or sometimes in separate *herb strips*.

Less well managed grassland is gradually colonized by coarser grasses such as the bents, *Agrostis*, and Yorkshire fog, *Holcus lanatus*. Still poorer meadows provide a home for rushes and sedges and finally scrub. These areas may be poor agriculturally but they are of great interest to the naturalist because they tend to support more plant and animal species than planted pasture.

The typical larger animals of cultivated grassland are those that prefer open spaces to the dense cover of woodland. The skylark, *Alauda arvensis*, common partridge, *Perdix perdix*, and lapwing, *Vanellus vanellus*, are the commonest meadow birds, and they nest on the ground. In addition woodland and hedgerow birds, such as rooks, *Corvus frugilegus*, feed in meadows while kestrels, *Falco tinnunculus*, hunt for small mammals among the grass. Several species of mammals are to be found in meadows though few are truly confined to them. Nevertheless, hares, *Lepus*, and the long-tailed field mouse, *Apodemus sylvaticus*, prefer the open field to hedges or woodland. Other animals like moles, *Talpa*, and rabbits, which prefer cover, create their own by burrowing underground.

Hedges

Hedges form a habitat very similar to that of a woodland edge. A hedge consists of a line of shrubs or trees, often on an earth bank, planted close enough together to provide a barrier to wandering livestock. Often a hedge will follow the line of a drainage ditch in order to avoid breaking up a field more than necessary. Hedges are planted as an alternative to walls and fences, and have the advantage over them in that they are self-repairing. They are grown throughout the world, but reached their most extensive development in Europe, and particularly in Britain, when the Enclosure Acts, passed in the 1790s in the reign of George III, forced farmers to subdivide their fields.

Hedges are man-made and the dominant shrub species are therefore those put there by man. In Europe, hawthorn, *Crataegus monogyna*, is the most commonly planted species because of its rapid growth and because hawthorn hedges are stockproof. Ash, elm and oak are also planted. New hedges, because they are artificial, contain few species. Over the years, however, they are colonized by other hedge plants including trees and

Below far left: Because deciduous woodland occurs in the climatic zone most favourable to man it is the natural habitat which he has most destroyed or severely modified. The larger carnivores, in particular, have been hunted for sport and to protect livestock—though the greatest threat to their survival is the destruction of their habitat. Even in North America, where the forest was virtually untouched until comparatively recently, both the wolf, *Canis lupus*, and the brown bear, *Ursus arctos*, have been eliminated from most of their former ranges. In England one of the few remaining large carnivores, the fox, *Vulpes*, is still ceremoniously hunted.

Below left: Smaller animals are affected by man's activities as well. Forming a ball does not protect hedgehogs from cars, for example—though some (like the one here) have now learnt to run.

Below: A common meadow bird, the skylark, *Alauda arvensis.*

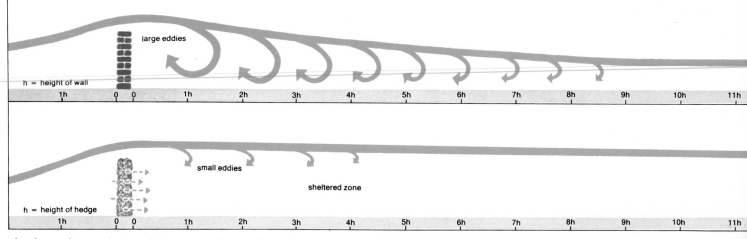

large eddies

h = height of wall

1h 0 0 1h 2h 3h 4h 5h 6h 7h 8h 9h 10h 11h

small eddies

sheltered zone

h = height of hedge

1h 0 0 1h 2h 3h 4h 5h 6h 7h 8h 9h 10h 11h

shrubs such as privet and dog rose, *Rosa canina*, which do not on their own form stockproof hedges.

Besides the hedge shrubs themselves, more than a thousand other plant species have been recorded in hedges. Only about a quarter of these, however, can be regarded as true hedgerow plants. Most are woodland species or are annual weeds, such as nettles, *Urticaceae*, of the type found on disturbed ground and wasteland. The true hedgerow plants are the climbers, like honeysuckle, *Lonicera periclymenum*, hop, *Humulus lupulus*, and old man's beard, *Clematis vitalba*, which must rely on other plants for support.

Hedgerow plants are extremely attractive to insects. Hawthorn, for example, is the food plant of more than 100 species of moths while the flowers of *Umbelliferae*, such as hogweed, *Heracleum sphondylium*, and sweet cicely, *Myrrhis odorata*, attract hordes of hoverflies, *Syrphidae*, longhorn beetles, *Saperda* and *Hylotrupes*, and soldier beetles, *Cantharidae*. Of the 20 butterflies which breed in hedges, the most typical is the brimstone, *Gonepteryx rhamni*, whose caterpillars feed on buckthorn.

Hedges also provide an ideal habitat for amphibia and reptiles—especially if they are planted alongside a ditch—since they possess the ideal combination of warm sunlit spots, cool shade and damp cover. If the ditch contains enough fresh, slow-

Above: A permeable hedge provides far better shelter against the wind than a solid brick wall through which the wind cannot pass. Both force the mass of air up over the barrier, but with a solid wall the creation of a partial vacuum immediately behind the wall causes eddies—whose speed is greater than that of the undisturbed wind in some cases—and a rapid return to ground level of the air stream. The air which filters through a hedge, however, prevents the formation of a vacuum so that the main air stream only slowly returns to ground level. Thin hedges with a permeability of about 40% are the best wind breaks. A thick hedge, or a block of woodland, acts like a solid barrier.

**Below: Two hedgerow and pasture animals, a fire bug, *Pyrrhocoris apterus*, and a rabbit, *Oryctolagus*. Rabbits were extremely common in Europe until 1953, when the introduction of the disease *myxomatosis*, which originated in South America, devastated their numbers. The disease is still endemic but the population has now returned close to its old level.

Oxford Scientific Films

Above: The large white (or cabbage) butterfly, *Pieris brassicae*, lays its eggs on species, both cultivated and wild, of the cabbage family, *Cruciferae*, and the caterpillars which develop cause serious damage to cabbage and other *Brassica* crops. The adult butterfly, however, feeds on nectar.

**Right: A long-tailed field mouse, *Apodemus sylvaticus*, eating a rose hip.

Jeff Goodman

Leslie Jackman

running water amphibia lay their eggs there, and their young provide food for snakes and birds.

Most hedgerow birds are woodland species which use hedges as a substitute for woods if the woodland population is high. Some species, however, will not nest in hedges because they offer insufficient cover (nightingale), or because they nest exclusively in mature trees (jackdaws, tits and woodpeckers). Those species which are most typical of hedgerows are the chaffinch, *Fringilla coelebs*, and blackbird, *Turdus merula*, which readily nest in all types of hedge. Robins, *Erithacus rubecula*, wrens, *Troglodytes troglodytes*, and hedgesparrows, *Prunella modularis*, only nest if the hedgebottom is dense enough to give protection from ground predators like stoats and weasels, *Mustela*.

Hedgerow mammals are rarer than birds but several rodent species in particular are common, including the long-tailed field mouse, voles, the brown rat, *Rattus norvegicus*, and shrews, *Sorex*. These smaller mammals are preyed on by stoats and weasels which, together with the brown rat, may also take the eggs and young of birds from their nests.

Deciduous woodlands occur in the climatic zone which is most favourable to man, so it is not surprising that man has greatly affected them, clearing and burning them to make way for agriculture, hunting forest animals for food and sport, and using the timber for fuel and building materials. Only about half of the former area of deciduous woodland now remains. Hedges, too, are now under increasing attack. This is partly because hedges can be a source of insect and fungal pests of crops. For example, a particularly damaging aphid, the black bean aphid, *Aphis fabae*, overwinters on spindle trees before moving on to the bean crop in the spring. Similarly, the fungus which causes the disease *wheat rust*, *Puccinia graminis*, overwinters on barberry leaves, *Berberis vulgaris*. Attempts have been made to eradicate both spindle and barberry from hedges but it is often easier to remove the whole hedge.

Hedges are also criticised for harbouring weeds, often unfairly since most weeds are annuals and the hedge flora is mostly perennial. However good the agricultural reasons for removing hedges, ecologically their loss is regrettable. Hedges contain a reservoir of harmless or beneficial species which can help to replace the populations killed in the fields by ploughing and the use of insecticides.

Below: Railway and roadside verges are often bordered by a hedge and by a strip or bank of flat ground which is equivalent to woodland flanking an uncultivated field margin. They therefore contain species characteristic of hedges, meadows and woodland edges. On roadsides in particular, however, a special set of environmental conditions also applies. Overgrown verges can be a threat to safety on the roads and road authorities, hard pressed for a cheap answer, sometimes remove the vegetation by spraying with herbicides. In the process the perennial plants are destroyed and annual weeds take over. Verges are also subjected to other pollutants from the vehicles themselves, especially lead compounds from the combustion of *tetraethyl lead*, the anti-knock additive in high octane petrol, and common salt, used to de-ice roads in winter. Lead compounds are poisonous to plants, but they may develop tolerance to it in time. Small mammals, however, eating the poisoned plants, concentrate the lead in their body fat and carnivores, such as kestrels, feeding on these animals, concentrate the lead still further. Lethal levels may be reached in this way, the kestrels dying of lead poisoning, although the smaller animals are unharmed.

Above: Where a hedge runs alongside a drainage ditch it provides an ideal habitat for amphibians and reptiles. Here a grass snake, *Natrix natrix*, is swallowing a frog.

Top right: A weasel, *Mustela nivalis*, caught in a spring trap. Weasels can be distinguished from stoats, *Mustela erminea*, by the absence of a black tip on the end of the tail and by their smaller size.

A wood of beech
trees in the Autumn
— the time of year
when trees change
so dramatically.

Index